GW00750448

Banking: In search of relevance
A new model for a new reality

Graham Flower, Phil Fawcett & Stuart Harle

Matador
9 Priory Business Park,
Wistow Road, Kibworth Beauchamp,
Leicestershire. LE8 0RX
Tel: (+44) 116 279 2299
Fax: (+44) 116 279 2277
Email: books@troubador.co.uk
Web: www.troubador.co.uk/matador

ISBN 978 1780883 113

British Library Cataloguing in Publication Data.
A catalogue record for this book is available from the British Library.

Typeset in 11pt Garamond Roman by Troubador Publishing Ltd, Leicester, UK

Matador is an imprint of Troubador Publishing Ltd

Printed and bound in the UK by TJ International, Padstow, Cornwall

"Simple, yet insightful and comprehensive, a manual for understanding what banks need to do to regain trust and indeed survive."

Richard Newland, Managing Director, Customer Expertise Limited

"This book provides a diagnostic of the key developments in retail banking over the last 20 years; it then builds to provide insights on the key success factors for banks in the future.

Simply it takes us from an industrial age in banking to a refined and personalised information age, where enduring relationships will be based on the banks ability to 'sense and respond' to their customers needs.

This book should resonate with bankers as it will surely with their customers!"
Huw Morgan, Head of Business Banking, HSBC Bank plc

"The authors' depth of knowledge and expertise in customer management and channel strategy brings an insight that few can offer. This is how bankers really manage the way they should interact with their key asset – the customer."
Dr Tony Gandy, Senior Faculty Member, ifs School of Finance

Table of Contents

In search of relevance

You work for a bank. How many times have friends or family mentioned that they received another irrelevant mail shot from your bank pushing a product that they didn't need, maybe asking them to fill in the enclosed blank application form and visit the branch to complete the paperwork? And, in the same breath, comment that they wished, with all the information that the bank had on them, that they did something that helped them manage their finances better…

INTRODUCTION

Relevance: it is one of the great topics for debate in the late 20th and 21st Centuries. Technology, changing economic situations and future uncertainties are causing people concerns about the 'meaning of life' and they are questioning the relevance of work, governments, economics and financial institutions in their lives.

It is evident that the relationship between banks and their customers is changing and the customer is, rightly, gaining more control of the relationship. The ongoing economic crisis has only further destroyed trust in banks and has accelerated this trend, creating a point of inflection. As a result, they are no longer grateful for what their bank gives them, they want more – something that benefits them individually, or helps them solve a problem. They are searching for the relevance of their bank in their lives. All this in an era when governments across the globe are withdrawing from all but the minimum pension and health provision; arguably there has never been greater latent demand for the products and services banks traditionally provided. A perfect storm.

In response, banks are searching for differentiation, something that distinguishes them from their competitors in a crowded market. Maybe it's the striking colour of their branding or a snappy brand-marketing message. But this misses the mark with many customers who have a totally different real-life experience of the brand.

A bank that is looking at these solutions to differentiate them in the market is not necessarily thinking about customers first and it is an example of 'bank-in' thinking. Banks should be thinking about their relevance to customers as their primary differentiator. This will unify the many disparate customer experiences and business process re-engineering initiatives into a common customer-centric and practical solution that differentiates them from the competition – and makes them valued by customers.

A bank's size and position in the market will not protect it from the changes now occurring. Some argue, and we wouldn't disagree entirely, that its size might work against it in the new reality.

So how did banks lose relevance with customers?

Open at 9.30, close at 3.30 weekdays only, and definitely not open on Bank Holidays!

Hard to believe but that was banking just 20 years ago. Arguably, it was a much simpler world where banking was delivered through one channel and almost all processing was done in each branch. Having a bank account was far from a given and more of a privilege, requiring two or more personal references.

Products were created to fit the organisation's needs and then 'pushed' at customers.

Getting your account balance involved driving to a branch in a street where parking is impossible, queuing at the enquiry counter, signing a form and a member of staff would disappear into a back room, check your signature, obtain your balance from the mainframe and scribble it on a piece of paper. Not something you would do every day.

The first-generation of channel strategy revolved, surprisingly, not around the customer but was focussed on reducing operational costs. Branch-based back offices were centralised, first in the local area and then to regional, national and often offshore centres. Call centres were created to take calls out of branches and provide 'efficient' handling. Strangely, few, if any, banks achieved the cost reductions; instead a new problem arose, driven by increased customer demand, as it became easier to contact the bank.

So was born the second-generation of channel strategy: as banks started to compete on convenience of access, new thinking such as the 24x7 bank First Direct came into existence. However, banks suddenly realised these multiple channels were not connected by data or culture. The experience became fragmented; service quality declined and the inadequacies of legacy 'silo' systems were exposed directly to the customer.

A world of banking based on product silos moved slowly towards channel silos, the customer often an unwelcome interruption. Relevance started to evaporate and was replaced by increasing disintermediation.

Now we live in a world where the market is saturated with banks (some of which are new non-traditional players), much of banking is becoming commoditised and choice of contact methods proliferates. Being relevant to your customers and having the capability to deliver the right experience will decide who will ultimately survive or fail.

How do banks regain relevance?

So we come to third-generation of thinking. This is in response to the real world where consumers, regulators and markets demand transparency, joined-up secure data, where customers are treated with evidenced fairness and, of course, intelligence!

Two main agents of change, the customer and technology, are starting to shape banks' established channels. In this new reality second-generation channel thinking will increasingly fail to meet customers' needs for relevancy.

This new reality requires a new model. In this book we chart how the banks implemented their multi-channel strategy in response to first- and second-generation thinking that eventually contributed to the loss of relevancy.

We introduce third-generation thinking – Intelligence, that is, driven by the customer, where the bank senses and responds to the customer in real-time and where all interactions with the customer are relevant, timely and personalised.

Fundamental to this new way of thinking is accepting that banks really cannot create customer demand; they need to focus on stimulating latent demand and building or sourcing products that meet this demand, transparently and effectively.

To emphasise what banks must do to become relevant again we discuss examples of new initiatives being implemented around the world, provide some insight into how banks can change their channel strategy to meet the changing needs of their customers and regain relevance. This includes: organising around customer (not products or channels); the sort of culture they should have and how they can build mutually beneficial relationships with their customers; how they can achieve the right mix of physical and virtual presence; how they manufacture, promote and manage their products and services; and how they incentivise the right behaviour from their employees.

Welcome to the new reality, enjoy!

Graham, Phil and Stuart – May 2012

Chapter 1 – Who is in control?

Do you control your channels …
or do your channels control you?

INTRODUCTION

Banking used to be very simple. Bankers decided what hours they would operate and which channels their customers would use. A golden age.

And, like most golden ages, it is a bit of a myth with a solid foundation of truth. Banks have always been willing to respond to the demands of their customers, especially if they have been able to cut costs or increase revenues in the process.

What is undeniably true is that bankers used to feel that they controlled which channels their customers would use. We call this 'bank in' thinking. The banks were willing to respond to customers, but did so in a manner and at a pace of their own choosing.

'Bank in' thinking is one example of an old world mindset that is threatened by increasing consumer power and the digital age. There are others: the branch-centric model; the presumption that information technology should be used for the automation of existing processes; the traditional approach to marketing, based on customer segmentation and outbound contact. We will critically examine all of these preconceptions in this text as they have a direct bearing on the loss of the relevancy of banks in consumers' lives.

We will call this old world mindset 'first-generation thinking'. Banks relying on first-generation thinking were prepared to develop new channels, but did so in response to factors within the organisation rather than real customer demand. The most important of these factors was cost.

THE AUTOMATED TELLER MACHINE

Consider the example of the Automated Teller Machine (ATM). This was developed and deployed in the 1960s and 1970s, at a time when banks were recruiting a large number of new customers. These customers had different needs from the banks' traditional customer base and wanted to be able to access their accounts outside normal banking hours. It would have been possible to meet this demand by extending opening hours, but this would have been very expensive. It was the need for a lower cost solution that led to the development of the ATM.[i]

This type of thinking has also been called the 'bring principle'.[ii] This suggests that banks bring an offering to their customers, which they choose whether or not to accept.

The first ATMs required customers to buy a pre-paid token, which the ATM retained, but this was soon replaced by magnetic strip technology and rapidly adopted by customers as it made getting cash at any time of the day easier than it had been.

The ATM replicated the processing that would have taken place at the branch counter. The only difference was that the customer presented a token or a card instead of a cheque. It did not attempt to expand the range of services available. This is a typical example of first-generation thinking although, in fairness, it must be noted that the technology available at the time limited what could be achieved. In spite of this, the introduction of the ATM was a great success.

The problem was, that it was expensive to buy and install ATMs. Therefore the banks started to share ATMs. In the United Kingdom, for example, three main networks (Four Banks, Mint and Link) developed. In the United States, there were more than two hundred networks at one point, although these were eventually consolidated into five main networks. Other countries took a more radical approach. In Portugal, all ATMs are owned and operated by Multibanco, whose shares are owned by the Portuguese banks.

All of these networks relied on interchange fees, which were charged when a customer of a bank withdrew funds from an ATM provided by a different bank – so-called 'disloyalty'. The Four Banks and Mint networks were alliances between the major High Street banks. There was an underlying assumption that the number of disloyal withdrawals between them would be similar, and the interchange fees would represent a small balancing charge.

The Link network was different. It included a number of quite small organizations, such as local building societies, which might expect many more disloyal withdrawals with a correspondingly high level of interchange fees. Therefore, unlike the other networks, it included a provision that allowed members to levy disloyalty fees on customers.

This was, perhaps, the moment when the golden age started to end.

There were two problems. The first was that it became possible for a bank to offer a cash withdrawal service using ATMs without itself owning any ATMs. The second was that it provided an opportunity for non-banks to enter a market traditionally closed to them, by providing ATMs and taking the disloyalty fees as revenue. Independent ATM operators, organisations that provide ATMs but do not issue cards, were allowed to join Link from 1999.

Allowing banks to offer cash withdrawals without owning any ATMs reduced the entry cost for new banks, because they no longer needed to invest in an ATM infrastructure.

The idea of entry cost is well known – it is the cost that a new entrant must pay in order to enter a market. Traditionally, the cost to enter the banking market had included the cost of building a branch network and, after the deployment of ATMs, the cost of building an ATM network. Now, new entrants no longer needed an ATM network. If only there were some way of avoiding a branch network…

Allowing non-banks to enter the market did not have any immediate impact. The cost of installing ATMs was too high and the return too uncertain, especially given that the major High Street banks had no plans to levy disloyalty fees. However, it marked the point at which the banks' vertically integrated operating model first came under challenge.

Retail banks were vertically integrated organisations. They owned all of the channels through which they interacted with customers, and operated all of the processes in the value chain. The introduction of disloyalty fees was the first point at which it became possible for a third party provider to become part of that value chain.

THE CALL CENTRE

The next major development was the call centre. This was another example of the first-generation mindset.

Banks had been allowing their customers to telephone their branches for many years. This caused a problem at busy times, where staff had to choose between answering the telephone and serving a customer in the branch. Call centres allowed the banks to provide a telephone-based service at a lower cost. Instead of employing staff to answer the telephone in every branch, they could employ a smaller number of people at a central site. This would cut costs.

Of course, it did not work out in quite the way that they anticipated! They found that the number of calls that the call centres received was much higher than they expected. This reduced the cost savings that they were able to make. There were two reasons for this.

The first reason was that the number of calls actually received in branches was higher than reported. Customers had not been able to get through, especially at busy times. Staff who were meant to be answering the telephone had been busy serving customers and had not been able to take the call. This is called strangled demand – the demand was there, but had been neither satisfied nor recorded.

The second problem was more fundamental. Call centres create their own demand. By providing a telephone-based channel that was convenient and that gave the customer certainty that the call would be answered in a reasonable time, the banks had created demand from customers who would only have considered telephoning their branches as a last resort.

This is called the 'M25 effect', after the motorway that encircles London. The demand for a peripheral motorway had been calculated based on existing roads. But this demand was far exceeded. Before the M25 was built, motorists would choose indirect routes instead of taking the congested 'circular' roads around the city. The M25 was so much better that motorists no longer needed to change their routes. This is sometimes expressed in the phrase: "Build it and they will come".

If disloyalty charges had been the end of the beginning (to use Winston Churchill's famous phrase) of the transition from the golden age, the call centre marked the beginning of the end.

New banks no longer needed branches. They could provide a service based on the telephone and shared ATM networks. This further reduced the entry cost to the banking market.

Problems with the call centre

The call centre posed a number of challenges to the banks. First, it posed the problem of how to identify customers. Second, it broke the link between the customer and the branch. It was this that started to erode relevance of the bank to the customer.

There is a long-standing presumption in British law that 'the banker knows the customer'. This was feasible in the branch environment of the 1950s and 1960s, where branch staff would have known the relatively small number of customers using the telephone. It became more difficult even in the branches with the expansion of the customer base in the 1970s, and was not possible in the call centre environment. Therefore the banks introduced identification and verification (ID&V) procedures to minimise the risk of fraud or the accidental disclosure of customer information.

Most banks perpetuated their existing, branch-centred model. Customers retained their relationship with their branch and the telephone banking service was merely an appendix to this. This is called the add-on business model.

An alternative was to set up a baby bank – a separate bank independent from the original. One reason for this was to extend geographical reach – to allow a regional bank to take its existing product range to new customers who could not get to its branches.[iii]

Call centres also further reduced the entry cost, as new banks no longer needed to develop a branch network. This allowed new entrants into the market for banking and financial services. Focusing on one channel in this way is called the monochannel model. Perhaps the most successful example in financial services is insurance company Directline.

The call centre was the point at which the bankers' mindset started to evolve towards second-generation thinking. Instead of the 'bank in' mindset – the banks will decide what channels to give to their customers – the industry started to ask them what they wanted. New entrants such as Directline and baby banks such as First Direct looked at what their target customer group wanted and tried to make themselves more relevant to these customers by designing their processes round this.

The case of First Direct is well documented.[iv] The add-on business model had been seen as a low-cost way of taking telephony out of branches. First Direct was aimed at upmarket (demographic segment ABC1) individuals who were not necessarily existing customers of the Midland Bank (now part of HSBC), First Direct's parent. The service offering was based on speed, convenience, value for money and quality of service – factors that had been identified by all bank customers as being relevant.

It is easy, with hindsight, to say that First Direct was certain to succeed. However, it is important to recognise that there were initial problems. The bank hedged its bets by developing an add-on telephone banking solution for its own customers. There were technical problems. First Direct remained dependent on its parent bank's branch network for moving paper, in particular for clearing cheques and credits.

But there is no doubt that First Direct did succeed in the end. It attracted customers from all of the High Street banks, has achieved very high customer satisfaction levels and maintains a low cost income ratio. Like Directline, First Direct proved the value of second-generation thinking. However, Directline and First Direct were the exceptions.

Writers on management draw a distinction between evolutionary (or incremental) and revolutionary (or discontinuous) change.[v] Evolutionary change involves small changes to existing processes. It can be thought of as doing things better. Revolutionary change involves a radical rethink of what the organization is attempting to achieve and may require the existing processes to be scrapped and replaced with something new. It can be thought of as doing better things.

The call centre is an agent of evolutionary change. It allows businesses to do things better, but not to do better things. It is significant that only one completely new service – bill payments – was developed for telephone banking.

INTERNET BANKING

It was the Internet, an agent of revolutionary change that ended the golden age.

Online banking was not new. Banks had been experimenting with online banking, using an old technology called videotex, since the 1980s. This was another example of first-generation thinking. The banks introduced it because the technology was available, not in response to genuine customer demand.

Videotex was not a commercial success. The take up of the service was not high enough to support an online banking service. The banks next turned to PC banking.

PC banking was a 'thick client' solution, in that the customer loaded software, provided by the bank, on a personal computer (PC). This included security software and allowed the customer to use the Internet safely to communicate with the bank.

The problem with a thick client solution such as PC banking is that the software needs to be installed before it can be used. Customers could not take any computer, anywhere, and manage their accounts. Convenience, which First Direct had already identified as a key customer demand, did not form part of the solution.

Banks had introduced PC banking, instead of a browser-based (thin client) solution, because they were worried that poor security on the Internet would lead to fraud. This was a real concern, but such was the commercial potential of the Internet that third party providers soon developed solutions.

This allowed new entrants to join the market, offering a browser-based Internet banking service and using the established ATM network to allow customers to draw cash. The pioneer was the Security First Network Bank (SFNB), although some commentators have suggested that SFNB was intended as a demonstration of a secure Internet banking system, rather than a bank in its own right.

Industry and academic commentators were enthusiastic about these new pure play Internet banks. Banking was a service industry, and their low costs were expected to give them an unbeatable advantage over the established banks.

But, again, it did not work out in quite the way that everyone had anticipated. The pure play Internet banks did not make the expected breakthrough. The established banks responded by introducing their own browser-based Internet banking services.

By September 2001, the Banking Journal of the American Bankers Association had concluded that the delivery channel revolution was over and the branch's crown was still in place.[vi] The call centre revolution had failed and the Internet banking revolution seemed to be failing.

The problem was: even though the tangible entry cost of building networks had gone, there was still an intangible entry cost. The established banks had the existing customer base, the existing information base and a level of credibility that the pure play Internet banks could not match.

But the golden age was over. The banks no longer controlled their channels. The threat of new entrants remained. And banks had become a little less relevant to customers.

The Internet is a disruptive technology. It combines low entry cost and great reach. This allows start-ups and individuals to reach a large number of people quickly and cheaply.

The lack of success (failure would be too strong a word) of the pure play Internet banks demonstrated that the intangible advantages of the established banks make it difficult for a start-up to compete across a wide range of banking services, but there is no reason why they should not be able to compete on a single product or a small range of products. This is called the monoline model.

There are a number of successful examples of monolines. Directline started as a monoline offering car insurance, although it now offers a much wider range of insurance products. Two other examples are E*Trade and PayPal. Both of these offer a very limited range of financial services through a single channel.

A different form of specialisation is the price comparison service. These web sites allow customers to compare prices and interest rates for different providers. They introduce new business, in return for a commission, but they also increase price transparency.

The other major development has been Web 2.0 and the rise of the social media. These have been defined as: "A group of Internet-based applications that build on the ideological and technological foundations of Web 2.0, which allows the creation and exchange of user-generated content."[vii]

The advantage of social media to banks is that they provide additional communication channels that are used by people who are difficult to reach through traditional media channels. The disadvantage is that they are impossible for the banks to control.

Both of these will be considered later in this text.

Chapter 2 – Second-generation thinking

The future isn't what it used to be

Paul Valery

FIRST- AND SECOND-GENERATION THINKING

So far, we have discussed first-generation thinking in some detail and introduced the idea of second-generation thinking.

Second-generation thinking is characterised by a desire to ask what customers want and respond to their demands. Second-generation behaviour includes business process reengineering, but the development and deployment of new channels is still driven by the provider rather than the customer.

Business process reengineering

Business process reengineering (BPR) seems to be rather unfashionable now, but it was a critical element of second-generation thinking because it put what the customer wants at the centre of process design.

Michael Hammer developed the idea of BPR, originally through an article in the Harvard Business Review[viii] and later in a book[ix] written with James Champy. In their book, Hammer and Champy define BPR as "the fundamental thinking, rethinking and radical redesign of business processes to achieve dramatic improvements in critical contemporary measures of performance, such as cost, quality, service and speed."

There are a number of different 'lifecycles' that describe the stages that BPR goes through. One of these[x] is:

- Identify the core business processes;
- Map and cost these core processes;
- Conduct detailed analysis of customer requirements to identify what the customer wants;
- Prioritise the core processes for BPR;
- Radically redesign the processes by simplifying and rationalising;
- Manage the change to ensure benefits are achieved;
- Establish ongoing measurement systems to ensure continuous improvement.

We will not be discussing BPR in any detail here, but it is important to notice the centrality of the customer requirements (stage 3). This is a key difference between BPR and other techniques to improve business processes, such as total quality management (TQM), which were much more focused on the process itself.

Customer management

Another feature of second-generation thinking, which remains an important component of third-generation thinking, is customer management. Three definitions that may prove useful are:

Customer management is the active use of customer research and data to build and deliver via Customer Relationship Management (CRM) value creating propositions for business and the customer.

Customer relationship management is: "The intelligent use of information and people to identify, predict and learn from customer behaviour and contact in order to initiate appropriate action to develop and maintain a relationship with the customer to achieve commercial benefit.[xi]"

Customer information management involves: "The collection, synthesis and secure delivery of the right information at the right time to the right person or delivery channel in order to optimise the return for both the business and the customer."[xii]

It is possible to think of customer management as what the bank is trying to achieve overall; customer relationship management as the means of realising this; and customer information management as the enabler that underpins the other two.

The limitations of second-generation thinking

Second-generation thinking was clearly an improvement on first-generation thinking and produced some notable successes. However, even second-generation thinking is insufficient.

The problem is that the established banks no longer control their channels. This requires a new type of thinking, which we will call third-generation thinking. This requires banks not merely to consult their customers but to collaborate with them.

The competitive environment

Before we describe the characteristics of third-generation thinking, we need to look at the competitive conditions in banking. The best model for this is Michael Porter's well-known diagram.

Figure 1 – The five forces model (Porter 1979) [xiii]

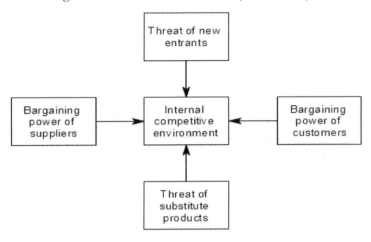

Source: Harvard Business Review

The strength of competition in an industry is determined by five factors:

- The threat of new entrants
- The threat of substitute products
- The bargaining power of suppliers
- The bargaining power of customers
- The internal competitive environment
- Most of these have changed, in a way that increases competition, during recent years.

The threat of new entrants depends on the attractiveness of the market and the barriers to entry. Banks continue to earn good operating profits, so the market remains attractive. Barriers to entry include regulatory barriers and entry cost. Regulatory barriers were reduced in the United States and the United Kingdom during the period of deregulation in the 1980s.

The barriers to 'full banking' (current accounts and a range of other products) should not be underestimated and many new entrants have focused on the credit card and personal loan markets where it was easy for firms to enter and exist.

The recent UK Independent Commission on Banking (ICB) reported on 12 September 2011 that since 2000 there had been very few entrants into the personal current account market: just five in the past decade, which between them had acquired less than 2% of the market from 2001 to 2010.

Independent Commission on Banking – New Entrants 2001 to 2010

	Personal current accounts	Mortgages	Savings Accounts	Personal loans	Credit cards
Total number of new entrants	5	16	19	23	34

Regulatory barriers, such as UK FSA authorisation and capital and liquidity requirements, pose the highest formal barriers to entry and those that take the longest to overcome, with other barriers, such as OFT consumer credit licences and access to payments systems, posing less of a problem.

However, some of the greatest barriers were customers themselves: this includes low levels of switching in the personal current account market. The ICB reported that brand loyalty and lack of familiarity with new brands are factors that probably explain the low number of entrants compared to other stand-alone product entrants. Finally, a significant barrier to personal current account entrants is the lack of a branch network. According to the ICB, "Alternative distribution channels remain complements not substitutes".

The ICB commented that in 2009 and 2010 switching rates for personal current accounts were low (7%) related to other markets such as energy providers (31%), telephone providers (26%) and insurance providers (22%).[xiv]

The report also provided a snapshot of the reasons why people chose their personal current account provider given by those who switched provider in 2010. Whilst almost 40% stated that 'product' was the reason for switching, 42% reported that 'branch/outlet' was the reason for switching. 'Charges and interest rates' was next highest at 24% with 'services on accounts' at 23%. 'Recommendation' and 'dissatisfaction with previous supplier' were at 18% and 17% respectively, whilst 'incentives' was stated at 9%.[xv]

Our take on this is that the branch network remains a powerful channel for attracting and retaining customers, but also as a competitive barrier to new entrants.

This is borne out by the terms of 'Project Verde', the Lloyds Banking Group (LBG) divestiture, required by 30 November 2013 as one of the conditions of its receipt of public money during the financial crisis. The proposal stipulates a personal current account market share of at least 4.6% and at least 600 branches (including their infrastructure, staff, customers, customer accounts and support infrastructure plus the Cheltenham & Gloucester mortgage and savings network, LloydsTSB Scotland branches and banking licence and Intelligent Finance). On 4 August 2011, LBG stated that the 'Project Verde' business consisted of 632 branches and approximately 5.5 million customers, with around £64 billion of assets (around £16 billion of risk-weighted assets) and £32 billion of liabilities.

We believe that, by stipulating a market share, minimum branch network size and product range, this is what it takes to enter the UK market as a sustainable long-term competitor to the 'big four'. There are doubts, however, whether 'Verde' can achieve that objective.

Brand equity, which we discuss in chapter 4, is important as an intangible barrier to entry. Banking relationships are of a fiduciary nature – they are based on trust. Customers will trust an established brand and are willing to pay a higher price for products and services bearing that brand. However, although the banks have invested heavily to maintain and increase the value of their brand equity, they have been less successful than some non-financial organizations. Brand equity makes it more difficult for completely new players to enter the banking market, but can make it easier for established brands to diversify into banking.

The structural changes within the industry have greatly reduced the entry cost to the banking market. We have already discussed two factors – shared ATMs and the development of direct channels such as the telephone and the Internet. But these are symptomatic of a wider change in the industry. Banks have increasingly become virtual organisations, handing over large areas of their operations to outsourcers and joint ventures. This includes what were traditionally core functions such as cheque processing, cash handling and foreign currency, as well as administrative functions such as information technology and facilities management.

The idea of the virtual organisation first appeared in the 1980s.[xvi] Virtual organisations have a relatively small core of strategic activities and use a variety of partnership arrangements to manufacture and deliver goods and services. Although this allows better focus, and reduces their exit cost if they choose to leave a particular market, it creates a group of third parties who can make their knowledge and skills available to new entrants. This reduces the entry cost.

The threat of substitute products depends on the characteristics of the product. All banking products are ultimately about money and money is fungible – money taken from one source can be used to fund debts owed to another party.

This does not mean that banking products can be substituted for each other. Other characteristics include currency, maturity, risk and security, and these limit substitution. The development of markets in these has allowed a greater degree of product substitution but as the credit crunch showed, these markets are not perfect.

One factor that affects the threat of substitute products is perceived product differentiation. This is the extent to which customers see a difference between products. This was greater when there were fewer banking products. As banks have attempted to secure competitive advantage by developing new and packaged products, this has reduced customers' perception of product differentiation.

The bargaining power of suppliers depends on the supplier's ability to control the market. Monopoly suppliers and suppliers controlling scarce resources have high bargaining power. In markets where there are many small suppliers, suppliers have low bargaining power.

Banking is unusual in that its customers are also its suppliers. Bank customers are both borrowers and depositors (lenders). Therefore the bargaining power of customers, which we consider below, also affects the competitive environment for suppliers.

Deregulation and the development of markets have had the effect of increasing the number of suppliers.

The bargaining power of customers depends on the customer's ability to control the market. Monopoly customers (monopsonies) and customers who are large in size relative to their suppliers (and therefore represent a large proportion of the supplier's business) have high bargaining power.

Corporate customers and multinational companies possess high bargaining power. The number of large corporate customers and multinational companies has increased and these companies now usually put their banking arrangements out to tender every few years to ensure that they are getting the best deal.

Switching costs are an important factor in bargaining power. Banks used to increase their bargaining power by locking customers in to their accounts. Consumer protection legislation has made this more difficult in many countries.

Another factor that increases the bargaining power of customers is price transparency. If customers know the prices charged by all suppliers in the market, they can shop around for the best price or they can bargain with their preferred supplier to get a lower price. The newspapers and the Internet have increased price transparency by allowing the publication of prices.

The internal competitive environment depends on the mechanisms that can be used to secure competitive advantage in the market. There is little inherent difference between banking products and competition is largely based on brand and price. Successful product innovations are easy to copy and difficult to protect.

Channels offer more scope for competition and banks such as First Direct have successfully differentiated themselves from their competitors. However, they have had to constantly reinvent themselves in order to achieve this.

Being the first organisation to introduce a new channel has traditionally been thought of as a source of competitive advantage – first mover advantage. First mover advantage has been said to: "arise from three primary sources: (1) technological leadership, (2) pre-emption of assets, and (3) buyer switching costs. Within each category there are a number of specific mechanisms."[xvii]

However, channels can be easily copied and first mover advantage seems to be of less benefit in banking than in some other markets. It is difficult to build up enough of a customer base to secure a lasting competitive advantage. The reason for this is that the take-up of a new channel (or a new product or service) follows a pattern that resembles the shape of an 'S' in that it starts slowly, accelerates later and finally levels out. The S-curve adoption model is discussed in chapter 11.

The banks rely on a mix of advertising, sponsorship, targeted marketing and propensity to sell products. Targeted marketing and propensity are discussed in more detail in chapter 19.

This analysis shows that competitive conditions in the banking market have changed to the disadvantage of the established banks and in favour of customers and new entrants. Therefore the old, 'bank in' thinking, is no longer an effective way to run a bank. Banks need a new way of thinking that accepts the deterioration in their competitive position. We will call this 'customer in' thinking.

BEYOND THE SECOND-GENERATION

Customer in thinking goes beyond the second-generation approach of asking what the customers want and deciding whether to provide it. Customer in thinking is about working with customers and third parties to develop solutions.

This idea is less radical than it might seem. We can identify two precursors: customisation and Web 2.0.

Customisation is a key component of the 1-to-1 marketing concept, developed by Don Peppers and others.[xviii] This was a four stage-process: identify, differentiate, contact, customise.

It is not the intention of this text to go into 1-to-1 marketing in any depth, although it will be considered in chapter 19. Customisation involves providing products that match the customer's own individual needs – "building the bank round the customer", to quote HSBC General Manager Irene Dorner. One example is Lloyds TSB, which allowed customers to design their own credit card by choosing which features they wanted.

Web 2.0 had been defined as: "An expression which was used for the first time in 2004 and referred to the second-generation of Internet. The main characteristics of new era in Internet is connected with its constant development and delivering services tailored to the needs of each user."[xix] Key features of Web 2.0 are collaboration between users and user-generated content.

THIRD-GENERATION THINKING

Customer in thinking is part of a broader mindset that we will call third-generation thinking. The other key components of this are: that the branch-centred model of first-generation thinking is replaced by an Internet-centred model, and that marketing based on propensity is replaced by marketing based on analytics. Analytics is discussed in more detail in chapter 19.

The Internet-centred model

Why has the move to an Internet-centred model come about? There are two reasons. The first is that the branch-centred model resulted in the development of an operational and information technology architecture that was inherently inflexible. The second is that the Internet-centred model has allowed the development of a build-once-deploy-everywhere architecture.

The branch-centred model dates back to the early days of banking. At that time, branches operated in much the same way as independent businesses. They kept their own records and did their own processing.

Record keeping and much processing were gradually centralised, but the rigidities of the branch-centred system remained. For example, many banks found it difficult to get a consolidated view for customers who had accounts at different branches, and artificial 'branches' had to be created for new, centralised services.

The banks addressed these problems by adding complexity. For example, the problem of consolidating customer information taken from different sources was addressed by adding a 'single customer view', overlaid on top of the existing information technology infrastructure. Keeping these systems up-to-date, and making sure that the information held in the various systems was and remained consistent, became a significant overhead for the banks.

The Internet-centred model started with two advantages over its branch-centred predecessor. First, it was designed to provide a centralised service to all of the bank's customers. Second, it was developed in an environment that was already multi-channel. The branch-centred model had treated new channels as appendices of the branch, whereas the Internet-centred model treated all channels equally.

Internet banking is a classic example of the Gartner hype cycle. This proposes that all new technologies go through five stages: Technology trigger, peak of inflated expectations, trough of disillusionment, slope of enlightenment, plateau of productivity.

The technology trigger for Internet banking was not so much the development of the Internet as the development of robust Internet security software in the 1990s.

The world's first Internet bank – the Security First Network Bank (SFNB) – was launched in the United States in 1995. SFNB closed soon after launch but the banking system on which it was based was successfully marketed through software house S1.

The peak of inflated expectations was perhaps reached with the famous comment (often, incorrectly, attributed to Bill Gates) to the effect that banking is necessary, banks are not. Many commentators confidently expected the transaction cost advantage of the new Internet banks to relegate the established banks to a minor role.

Although the Internet banks rapidly gained market share, this was from a very low base and none of the Internet banks broke through in the way that First Direct had done. Most customers seem to have regarded the Internet banks as secondary banks, useful because they offered better rates, while retaining their primary banking relationship with an established bank.

Although Internet banking is something of a special case, it was caught up in the broader hype cycle surrounding the use of the Internet for commercial purposes, often called the dot com bubble.

Many of the Internet firms that failed when the dot com bubble collapsed had completely unsustainable business models. This was not true of the Internet banks – no bank would be allowed to operate if it were not financially sound – but they were inevitably damaged by the collapse.

The trough of disillusionment was perhaps most clearly expressed by the article in the Banking Journal of the American Bankers' Association in September 2001 that was mentioned in chapter 1. This stated, unequivocally, that the channel revolution was over and that the branch retained its crown.

Internet banking

The problem with any disruptive technology – which the Internet clearly is – is that it is very difficult to determine the best way to exploit it. Most of the early Internet banks saw the Internet only as a low-cost delivery channel.

Much the same had happened when call centres were introduced. Most banks regarded them as a low-cost add-on to the branch-centred model. The exception – First Direct – was the only telephone bank that broke through into the mainstream banking market.

Internet banking entered the slope of enlightenment as both pure play Internet banks and established banks started to look at Internet banking from the customer's perspective. Customers are not interested in the Internet as a low-cost delivery channel, although they may be attracted to the better rates that result from this. The great benefit of Internet banking to customers is convenience.

Internet banking also facilitated the migration from the branch-centred model to the Internet-centred model. This has allowed the banks to develop truly multi-channel systems, unencumbered by the branch legacy and deploy these back into the call centre and branch network.

It is an open question whether the plateau of productivity has been reached. Internet banking now has three clear roles: as a low cost delivery channel; as a convenience channel for customers; as a platform for the development of a multi-channel service.

The lack of success (it would be too harsh to say failure) of many of the original pure play Internet banks does not invalidate the role of Internet banking as a low cost channel and many banks offer accounts to low value customers that rely on the low transaction costs associated with the use of the Internet. However, it currently seems unlikely that any banks taking this route will break through into the mainstream.

Customers' desire for convenience in banking has come to be encapsulated in the phrase Martini banking – banking any time, anyhow, anywhere. The telephone call centre was the first step on that path, the Internet was the second and the Internet-enabled mobile phone or tablet is the third. Industry and academic research shows that offering convenience to customers also benefits the banks. Customers who use Internet banking are less likely to defect and are generally more profitable than customers who do not.[xx]

Multi-channel services

We have discussed the role of Internet technology in facilitating the development of multi-channel services, by providing a build-once-deploy-everywhere architecture. But it has also directly fostered multi-channel services. We will consider two examples: multi-channel transactions and changes to the way call centres are used.

A multi-channel transaction will typically start with customers using the Internet to look for a solution to specific needs. For example, customers may look up interest rates or use a loan or mortgage calculator to find out about borrowing costs. Instead of completing their transactions the Internet, customers may use another channel such as a branch. We call these multi-channel transactions journeys. We will discuss the idea of journeys in chapter 15.

Telephone call centres were originally developed as appendices to branches, to allow a reduction in costs by taking staff out of the branches. A significant percentage of their work now comes from Internet banking, through Call Me and web chat services. This is a further refinement to the journey, customers can start with a general enquiry on the Internet, get more specific information from a call centre through call me or web chat, and visit a branch to complete the transaction.

Chapter 3 – The customer

Customer needs have an unsettling way of not staying satisfied for very long

Karl Albrecht

THE NATURE OF THE RELATIONSHIP

This chapter is about customers. A question that has been raised is: Do banks have customers or clients? www.dictionary.com provides the following definitions:[xxi]

Customer: A person who purchases goods or services from another.

Client: A person or organisation using the services of a lawyer or other professional person or company.

Clearly both of these definitions could apply to banking. The definition of a customer emphasises the purchase, which implies a transactional relationship. The definition of a client emphasises the service aspect. As we will see, the nature of the banking relationship remains an open issue.

Even though the banks see their relationship with their customers as more than transactional, the current thinking is that banks have customers except in specialist areas such as private banking and investment management, where the term client is widely used.

Characteristics of banking

Although the term customer implies a simple buyer-seller relationship, in practice customers expect more from their banks than they would from a typical High Street retailer. In order to understand this, it is useful to consider the characteristics of banking. These can be categorised as:

- Intangibility
- Simultaneity
- Heterogeneity
- Perishability
- Fiduciary relationship

The first four of these characteristics are common to all services.[xii] The fifth applies to financial services.

Intangibility means that services, including banking, do not produce a physical product. Banking produces physical goods, such as cheque-books and plastic cards, but these are tokens allowing customers to access the accounts that they represent rather than products in their own right.

Simultaneity means that services are produced and consumed at the same time. The act of a customer requesting a service causes it to be produced.

Heterogeneity means that the quality of the service is naturally variable. Most services have traditionally been delivered person-to-person, and the interaction between the customer and the person delivering the service creates this heterogeneity. This is not the case for automated channels, of course.

Perishability means that services cannot be built 'for stock' before they are requested by a customer. This is a consequence of simultaneity, of course.

The fiduciary relationship means that the relationship is based on trust. Customers must trust their banks and vice versa.

ZEITGEIST OF BANKING GENERATIONS

Zeitgeist is the general cultural, intellectual, ethical, spiritual, and/or political climate within a nation or even specific groups, along with the general ambiance, morals, socio-cultural direction, and mood associated with an era.[xxiii]

In the past channels were designed and implemented based upon the bank's cost saving strategy, not relevance to the customers' needs, their socio-demographic characteristics or the current Zeitgeist.

We'd argue that the current Zeitgeist concerning banks is much deeper than the public debate over bankers' bonuses. Customers' attitudes concerning how their personal data is being collected and used are changing rapidly (through the growth of social media, stories of identity fraud and recognition that it is valuable). Some banks are still stuck in the 'Permissive Era' of marketing from the 1980s (a topic we discuss in Chapter 24). Banks that continue to believe that freely available personal data belongs to them and neither seek their customers' permission to use it nor use it primarily for their customers' benefit may find that both customers and regulators penalise them.

The impact of generations

Authors William Strauss and Neil Howe have been very influential in defining American generations in their book 'Generations: The History of America's Future, 1584 to 2069' (1991)[xxiv]. Whilst there are some cultural variations, it is accepted that the information holds true for most developed countries.

You may have heard of their generations expressed as 'Baby Boomers' (born between 1943 and 1960), 'Gen X' (born between 1961 and 1981) and 'Gen Y' (born between 1982 and 2004). In addition, 'Gen Z' (born after 2005) has been added. Frequently, Gen Y is also called the 'Millennials'.

'Digital Natives' is a term coined by Marc Prensky to describe the learning styles of students born in 'Gen Y' who have only ever known a world connected by the Internet, and consequently appear to be at odds with the traditional learning delivery style.[xxv] The insight and characteristics have become widely used in a number of other areas such as technology, finance, commerce and employment to denote the conflict between Digital Natives and Digital Immigrants (for example Baby Boomers).

17

Much has been written about the impact of the Gen X and Gen Y on technology adoption and the corresponding impact on society. Many people mistakenly tend to focus on one or two aspects – such as 'technology adoption' and 'social networking' – and not on the wider influences and characteristics of the different demographic groups.

In most developed countries Baby Boomers and Gen Y make up a similar proportion of the population, which is frequently two to three times the size of Gen X. They adopt technology quickly, but for different reasons. In 2011, and for the next few years one thing is certain: Baby Boomers are in a position of power socially and financially, having enjoyed an unprecedented period of economic stability to build their wealth, generous employer benefits and pension schemes. Baby Boomers grew up in a period of dramatic social change, privilege and affluence and are the healthiest and wealthiest generation to date. However, a changing economic situation and socio-demographic shifts threaten Baby Boomers' future.

In 2011, Baby Boomers control over 80 per cent of personal financial assets and more than 50 per cent of discretionary spending power. They are responsible for more than half of all consumer spending, buy 77 per cent of all prescription drugs, 61 per cent of OTC medication and 80 per cent of all leisure travel.

Although they lived through previous recessions and oil crises as children and young adults, the Baby Boomers have been shattered by the recent financial crisis, according to the 2011 Associated Press and LifeGoesStrong.com surveys:[xxvi]

44 per cent are not confident that they'll have enough money to live comfortably in retirement;

57 per cent lost value in investments because of the economic crisis;

42 per cent of those affected are delaying retirement.

Baby Boomers had 40 years to build up their retirement savings portfolio in a reasonably benign economic period, backed by generous employer pension schemes and helped by their government. Gen X and Gen Y are best described as being on their own, heavily in debt and shadowed by career and financial insecurity. Due to the impact of the financial crisis they are estimated to have only 25 years to prepare for retirement, with little support from employers and their government.

Longer life expectancy is already having an impact on later Baby Boomers (and Gen X and Gen Y), many of whom will not receive the inheritance nest-egg that their parents received and are often forced into the unenviable position of providing some financial support to both parents who are living longer and adult children at the same time.

Gen X (sometimes called the MTV Generation) was shaped by recession, oil and energy crises, cable TV, MTV, AIDS, divorced parents, Thatcher/Reagan, urban decay and punk rock. They have been described[xxvii] as a group of young people seemingly without identity, which faces an uncertain, ill-defined (and perhaps hostile) future.

Gen Y is growing up with some of the same social influences as Gen X, but with an increased emphasis on new communications, media and digital technology. Generally speaking, they are more neo-liberal (a market-driven approach to economic and social policy) than Gen X or Baby Boomers, due to the greater freedom of information, financial and social changes that took place during their upbringing.

Both Gen X and Gen Y face different economic and social challenges from their Baby

Boomer parents. For example, the Gen X and Gen Y cohort are the most educated generations to date and as a consequence many are saddled with significant debt arising from the change in how tertiary education is funded.

It is often cited that Gen Y is not loyal to employers or brands in the same way as Baby Boomers. This is true to an extent. But, they define loyalty in different terms, being something that is mutual and continually needs re-inforcement.

Gen X and Gen Y are frequently cited as lacking short-to-medium financial planning skills, being heavily in debt (arising from student loans and changes in social attitudes towards personal spending and debt) and not focusing on longer-term goals such as retirement. This is not unusual as even Baby Boomers went through this phase; however, it should be seen as a cue for banks to help these generations succeed in a world that is very different from their parents'.

It is often cited that because of their environment the technology skills and usage of Gen X and Gen Y differ from Baby Boomers – Digital Natives versus Digital Immigrants, so to speak. One should be careful of making broad assumptions. Who invented the Digital Natives' technology? It started with Baby Boomers (like Tim Berners-Lee, Bill Gates, Jeff Bezos and Steve Jobs) and was taken up by the elder Gen Xers (Jonathan Ives, Jerry Yang, Larry Page, Sergey Brin, Jack Dorsey – all born before 1976). Mark Zuckerberg, born 1984, is the most notable Gen Y technocrat and influencer.

Baby Boomers often take longer to adopt new technology, but remember, as a social group they are significantly larger and wealthier than Gen Y. There is also evidence that Baby Boomers see and use technology as a gift and not as a given, and therefore use it in different ways from other generations.

So how does this relate to relevance and channel strategy?

Banks need to remember that 'one size doesn't fit all', and groups of customers with similar technology skills, but different attitudes and needs will use your channels. The key is to design and implement channels that are relevant to your customers.

We think that some possible strategies might include:

- Build customer satisfaction and loyalty by providing the financial management tools that Baby Boomers, Gen X and Gen Y need to see them through a rapidly changing environment. It is tempting for banks to focus on the prevalent (more wealthy) demographic and ignore the others who may have different drivers and needs. An example is online Wealth Management tools that seem to be skewed towards Baby Boomers, rather than Gen X and Gen Y who may have different needs (getting out of student debt before being able to seriously invest, but lacking innovative strategies and products that are tax efficient and allow them to progress up the financial ladder). A 'one-size-fits-all' approach won't work as each generation will use the tools in a different way, and of course, don't make assumptions. Baby Boomers may use Gen Y tools and vice versa – there's no 'norm' anymore;
- Reconsider segmentation, and therefore marketing campaign rules – a 30-year-old in 2011 may not have the same needs as a 30-year-old had in 2000. The financial

pressures and needs may be quite different;

- Educate Gen X and Gen Y in the new financial realities and help them succeed. Help Gen X and Gen Y budget, but don't forget that retired Baby Boomers need to budget too;
- 'Gamify' (using game design techniques such as achievement badges and progress bars) your channels and financial management tools to make them more fun and encourage people to use them regularly. This can apply to all generations, not just Digital Natives;
- Give something to get loyalty from Gen Y. They are likely to have different triggers from Baby Boomers;
- Worry about Gen Z now and engage them with your brand now (but not financially);
- Design channels for Gen X, Y and Z, as well as Baby Boomers.

Men and women are different

The information-seeking needs and decision-making processes of men and women differ. According to research[xxviii], women are the 'alpha consumer' and rapidly becoming the 'alpha decision-maker' in the home.

Men are more likely to be selective in processing data – choosing data that reinforces what they perceive to be the dominant message and often rejecting information that may conflict with what they believe. In contrast, women are thought to be more deliberate, detail orientated and comprehensive in their information search. Female consumers are more likely to review all marketing cues, looking for subtle information that may influence their choices.

For banks to remain relevant it may mean providing more information to, and responding to more questions from, female clients than their male counterparts. It may also mean working harder to engender confidence as the 'trusted' source of complete and comprehensive information in all aspects of the subject. Men may see retirement planning as simply financial performance objectives: women are more likely to be more holistic and focused on overall family well-being in addition to meeting the financial performance objectives.

A 2007 survey of 1,400 Canadians revealed that women were more interested in how financial success would have an impact on others in the home. Questions such as how investments improve their ability to finance a child's education, provide eldercare or manage the risk that they might become a burden on their family in later life.

First- and second-generation marketing and sales process thinking focuses on efficiency and speeding the sales process up; this may leave female customers feeling that your offer is not relevant. Third-generation thinking needs to apply intelligence to understand and empathise with the needs of different target customers.

Socio-demographics analysis also reveals changes to the basic family unit in developed countries such as the UK. A woman born in 1937 had, on average, 2.4 children, compared to a woman born in 1964 who had 1.9 children, with the average birth rate expected to continue to fall. The percentage of families with no children has changed rapidly: 12 per cent of women born in 1937 had no children; this had risen to 20 per cent of women born in 1964, and is likely to continue to rise. Since 1971 the proportion of all people living in 'traditional' family households of married couples with dependent children has fallen from 52 per cent to

37 per cent. Over the same period, the proportion of people living in couples with no children rose from 19 per cent to 25 per cent. Nearly a quarter of children lived with only one parent last year and lone mothers headed 9 out of 10 of those households.

Single parent families are increasing for a variety of reasons, but it is likely that proposition and segmentation models are based on 'traditional two parent' nuclear families, and not ones where women are making all of the financial decisions. There are fundamental impacts on the way that customers are segmented, products designed and promoted through channels.

To remain relevant banks need to consider the information-gathering and decision-making needs of different genders – approaching both genders with a rigid sales process may force customers to seek alternative providers who have a more flexible approach. Providing female customers with more opportunities, and even encouraging them, when online (through virtual call centre) to ask questions may help them build trust. Consider providing material that is more balanced to meet the needs of female customers – men may simply filter out what they don't need!

Customer decision making has changed

There are four types of customer direction (decision maker) persona used in segmentation models, all having different needs and information research characteristics. There is evidence to suggest that the financial crisis has changed some of their needs and behaviours.

	Description	Financial needs	Characteristics
Self-directed	Take financial decisions on their own; seek best products and prices	Information, value speed and control	Keen self-service users, less likely to speak to a branch advisor than a 'validator', likely to use multiple sources of information including competitor and price comparison websites
Validators	Interested in finances; seek advice on complex decisions	Information, value advice, reassurance and a trusted relationship	Branch visitor and likely to speak to and buy from an advisor, less likely to use Internet banking than 'self-directed'
Delegators	Bored with finance; want others to take decisions for them	Advice, good service and a trusted relationship	Branch visitor and likely to speak to and buy from an advisor, less likely to use Internet banking than 'self-directed'
Avoiders	Neglect their finances; distrust firms and advisors; risk adverse	Simplicity	Unlikely to speak to a branch advisor, less likely to use Internet banking than 'self-directed'

Forrester's Consumer Adoption Study, Q2, 2005

One emerging customer behavioural trend since the financial crisis is an increased volatility. Customers are more willing than in the past to buy products from multiple providers. 46 per cent of customers surveyed by Accenture[xxix] say that they are more volatile as a result of the crisis and are more open to independently-sourced products from different suppliers, 29 per cent say that their volatility hasn't changed and 25 per cent will stick to 'tried and true'.

Accenture, in a separate report,[xxx] also said that the newest generation of customers, aged between 18 to 24 years old were 50 per cent more likely to move to another bank, with nearly one in five (19%) saying that they planned to switch one or more products from their current bank within 12 months, compared to only 12 per cent of older respondents who planned to make a switch. These younger customers showed a different emphasis – placing more significance on value for money compared to their elder counterparts who valued the promise of speedy and efficient service.

Banking was renowned for its customers' switching inertia, due to a large degree to the complexity involved in achieving it, but the financial crisis and the increasing availability and influence of price comparison sites may have reduced some of the barriers to switching. Governments are now starting to encourage it to introduce further competition.

In the Accenture survey, 16 per cent of respondents said that they had recently switched one or more products from their bank, and 14 per cent said they planned to do so in the next 12 months.

As a result of the financial crisis and the impact of the recession on them, customers were approaching banking services in a different way with 63 per cent saying that they shopped around, 63 per cent saying that they were price sensitive, 59 per cent reporting that their loyalty had decreased and 53 per cent said that their trust in banking brands had decreased, according to the survey.

Rise of the self-directed customer

A fundamental shift in power from bank to the customer has occurred, and is likely to increase due to improved information and a richer choice of suppliers, products, services and channels due to new technologies. This is the rise of the self-directed customer.

Accenture research outlined in their research report, Customer 2012 Time for a new contract between banks and their customers?[xxxi], how a new group of empowered self-directed customers will increasingly dictate how banks design and deliver their propositions.

They summarised that a self-directed customer wants a bank that:

- Provides value for money;
- Offers the ability to choose independently amongst simple products;
- Is responsive and knows when to offer help and when not to and is proactive or absent accordingly;
- Is flawless in execution;
- Provides all of the access points;
- Stays abreast of technology in offering him new propositions;

- Is an institution that they can respect and trust.

In short, self-directed customers demand relevance, timeliness and personalisation from their bank.

HOW CUSTOMERS SEE BANKS

We thought we'd let some customers speak through the following quotes from the Future of Banking Commission[xxxii] report.

> Why does my bank only want to talk to me when it wants to sell something?
> Participant, Which? Big Banking Debate

> You cannot deal quickly with banks nowadays as their clerks are made to delay what you want while they sell you something.
> Consumer, which.co.uk/banking

Where do we start!

You just have to open any newspaper or click on any online news site, watch the news on television or walk through some of the world's major cities these days to get a pretty good view of what people think of banks.

The financial crisis; bank bailouts; Payment Protection Insurance (PPI) mis-selling; bankers' bonuses; lending rate increases; poor service quality; poor complaint handling; lack of transparent fees and interest. The list goes on.

Banks have never had such a low reputation or level of trust from the general public. A recent report published by Ernst & Young[xxxiii] reported that UK customer confidence in the banking industry was the most negatively affected out of the 23 mature and emerging markets it surveyed. 63 per cent reported that their trust in UK banks had fallen in the previous 12 months and 36 per cent are dissatisfied with their main bank.

Putting aside the some of the re-capitalisation implications of the wider financial crisis for one moment and looking at the issues that are relevant to this text – what are the main causes of this widespread dissatisfaction? The Ernst & Young report provided further insight:

1. Poor service quality – 42 per cent of UK customers who have changed banks cited service quality and 27 per cent cited a specific service failing as the cause. Only 15 per cent left due to price, compared to the European average of 44 per cent;
2. Lack of personalised service – 53 per cent of UK customers reported that they receive no or only occasional contact from their bank. 77 per cent are not willing to pay for independent advice and believe that it should be part of the regular service they receive.
3. Inconsistent multi-channel experience – 82 per cent of UK customers reported that they were satisfied with Internet banking; 80 per cent with branch banking – but only

29 per cent were satisfied with Mobile banking and 49 per cent with Telephone banking.

Which? (the UK product-testing and consumer campaigning organisation, also known as the Consumers' Association) launched its 'Which? Banking Manifesto' on 24 June 2010 and calls on banks to "put customers at the heart of their business and ensure that customer service comes before short-term profit."[xxxiv] The Manifesto's ten demands are an indication of the concerns and feelings of many customers and whilst we do not believe that they will all be implemented in their current form they offer an insight into the direction that consumers want banks to go.

We believe that banks' multi-channel strategy and their search for relevance will be impacted in several ways, that we will explore in more detail in this book:

Training and qualifications – the manifesto calls for customer facing staff to be suitably qualified, with all advice on investment products being provided by advisers who are qualified to at least Certified Financial Planner (CFP) level. Combined with the fact that there is considerable customer resistance to paying for investment advice this will seriously impact future viability of banks' RM propositions.

Greater transparency of charges and fees – this calls for all bank charges and fees to be fair, transparent and proportionate to the costs incurred in providing the service. This may mean that channel pricing is introduced to reflect different costs where customers use Internet banking or the branch to complete the transaction, giving the customer a choice. To comply it may also mean a significant redesign of all channel processes to be able to display potential charges in real time, as they are about to be incurred, so that the customer has a choice, and does not find out about the charge until after the event.

Reward, incentivisation and sales culture – the manifesto calls for sales incentives and commissions that incentivise mis-selling to be banned and calls for a switch to rewarding employees for providing high-quality service linked to overall levels of customer satisfaction, complaint levels and regulatory compliance (senior executives only). Many customers commented about a noticeable shift away from more personalised banking service to one driven by sales targets that led to one comment: "Why does my bank only want to talk to me when it wants to sell something?" Consumers also commented that banks are pushing products that they don't want or need. This calls for a radical rethink of how banks use all of their knowledge of the customer to give them access to the right expertise, at the right time, on the right channel.

Complaint handling – the manifesto calls for banks to handle complaints in a fair and timely manner and to be more transparent in their reporting to customers. This means that banks will need to fully integrate complaint handling into all channel processes and management information streams.

No penalty for using branches – this calls for banks not to penalise customers who want to transact via branches and must not exclude those customers who are unable or unwilling to conduct their banking online. This has implications for banks wishing to reduce their channel costs – the role of the branch must be re-evaluated, as customers will not totally abandon branches for online channels at any time soon.

The manifesto calls for banks to continue to provide and process cheques for all consumers until there are viable alternatives in place. We have already seen the Payments Council abandon their published timetable and banks will have to continue to provide an infrastructure for a diminishing service. This has an impact on the costs of maintaining a branch network to process cheques at a time when costs are rising and income (from cheque processing) is falling.

Customer service from non-branch alternatives, such as Internet banking and Telephone banking, needs to improve too. As one participant in the Which Banking Manifesto debate commented: "At least 50 per cent of my time I can't perform the transaction I've logged on to make, which leaves me waiting on the phone for 20 minutes while I wait to speak to a human… I plan to vote with my feet and transfer my banking business elsewhere next year". It is clear that from the Ernst & Young report above that the level of service in channels is inconsistent and needs to be redesigned to improve the customer experience.

Treating customers fairly – this covers several manifesto points. Firstly, it calls for banks to allow existing customers the same access to more favourable products as new customers and removes any pricing competitive advantage to attract new customers. It will certainly impact operating costs as most existing customers will be expected to respond to the offer of more favourable terms and banks will have to ensure that it can be completed efficiently in the channel of the customers' choice.

Secondly, it calls for banks to provide better support for customers who manage their finances poorly, by allowing customers to 'opt-in' to unauthorised overdrafts and a fair application of charges. This may require banks to implement innovative real-time communications that allow customers to opt in to an unauthorised overdraft or not (in full knowledge of the consequences).

In addition, the manifesto calls for banks to inform customers of the risk of having a savings balance that is close to, or above, the limit of the Financial Services Compensation Scheme (FSCS) limit. This requires a more customer-centric view and means that banks have to create and maintain a single customer view across all business units, channels and subsidiaries to be able to consolidate the information accurately.

Finally, the manifesto calls for banks to remove all barriers to switching financial products (a call that is supported by the Independent Commission on Banking). As we saw above, UK current account switching is driven by service failures and not price, putting banks with high levels of service failure or complaints at a disadvantage, and will drive further emphasis and investment in the need to be relevant and the customer experience across all channels.

Should the views of these consumers matter to banks? We think so. As one consumer put it:

"People can only take financial responsibility if they have financial knowledge. With more widespread financial knowledge, the banking industry will have to adapt and begin to be more transparent."

Participant, Which? Big Banking Debate

Due to the Internet, customers now have increased access to information about banks' brand values and ethics, their products, services and delivery channels; and have the power influence by expressing and sharing what they have experienced with an almost infinite number of people through the social media.

Welcome to the age of the customer.

WHAT CUSTOMERS WANT

What is the extra dimension, beyond the purely transactional, in the relationship between banks and their customers? Research carried out by HSBC[xxxv] into what customers want identified the following needs:

- Recognise my value to you
- Know me and treat me as an individual
- Provide expertise I can get at
- Be on my side (and reassure me that you are)
- Leave me in control
- Be my trusted advisor
- Notice what I need
- Be easily available

This is clearly much more than a buyer-seller relationship!

Another list of customer wants comes out of the 2007 United Kingdom Customer Satisfaction Index (UKCSI) survey, conducted by the Institute of Customer Service.[xxxvi] This identified the following needs:

- Overall quality of the product/service
- Being treated as a valued customer
- Speed of service of staff
- Friendliness of staff
- Helpfulness of staff
- Handling of problems and complaints
- Handling of enquiries
- Competence of staff
- Ease of doing business
- Being kept informed

Although these are not specific to banking, the overlap between the two lists is clear.

CUSTOMERS AND CHANNELS

This text focuses on how banks can improve their relevance to customers through the distribution channels that they use every day. What factors influence customers in their choice of channels? We will discuss the psychology of individual channels later, but there are a number of general factors that need to be considered. These include:

- Their attitude to the relationship
- The location at which they need access to banking services
- Their perception of complexity
- The risk associated with what they want to do
- Their attitude towards technology
- The way in which they take buying decisions
- Their experience of channels

Attitude and location

We can think about customers as being traditional or transactional. Traditional customers value their relationship with their local branch and regard other channels as appendices to the branch. Transactional customers use the most convenient channel for the transaction that they want to complete. One academic study[xxxvii] calls these b (for branch) and e (for electronic) customers.

We can also think about customers being fixed or mobile. Fixed customers carry out transactions in a fixed location such as a branch, or at their home or office. Mobile customers carry out transactions in a public location or on the move.

We can show how these factors affect customers' channel usage as a matrix:

Channel usage	Fixed	Mobile
Traditional	Branch, telephone, Internet	Mobile phone
Transactional	Internet, telephone, branch	Mobile phone, tablet

Industry and academic research shows that the proportion of customers who could be regarded as traditional, while in decline, remains significant. For example, research in the UK showed that 54% of customers used the branch as the only channel to manage their current accounts in 2006. This declined to 43% in 2009:

Figure 2 – Channels used to manage current accounts 2006 and 2009

2006

2009

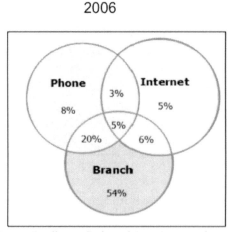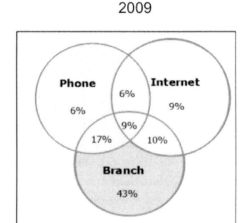

Source: Intelligence Delivered (Asia) Limited research

Perception and risk

The customers' decision about which channel they will use does not only depend on their overall attitude towards channels, whether they are traditional or transactional. It also depends on the transaction that they wish to undertake. The critical factors are perception and risk.

Customers perceive a transaction such as a balance enquiry as being quick and simple. Only the most traditional customers would be reluctant to use an automated channel for a balance enquiry. A mortgage application, on the other hand, is perceived as complicated. Customers are much less willing to use automated channels alone for a mortgage application – recent research suggests that only 20 per cent of customers are willing to use the Internet end-to-end, throughout the process of obtaining a mortgage, although this varies by country.

Figure 3 – Customer channel preferences for purchases of financial products (UK 2008)

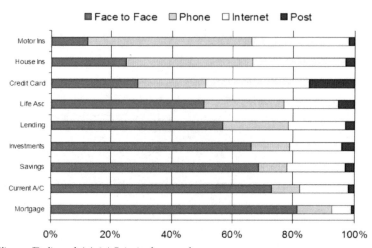

Source: Intelligence Delivered (Asia) Limited research

This chart also shows the extent to which customers perceive different financial products as commodities. Commodities are goods and services that are supplied without qualitative difference – i.e. they are the same irrespective of the supplier.

There are two reasons for this commoditisation. Some goods and services are inherently simple. A balance enquiry is a balance enquiry and, provided that it is accurate and up-to-date, it is impossible for a bank to differentiate itself from its competitors on the basis of the quality of its balance enquiries.

The other reason is familiarity. The more familiar customers are with a product, the more they are likely to regard it as a commodity. The insurance products are an example of this. Although insurance products are complex, customers renew or replace them every year. This makes them familiar and customers have no concerns about buying them over the telephone or through the Internet.

This could, perhaps, be summarised by saying that familiarity breeds commoditisation.

There is an important implication of this. As customers become familiar with more financial products, they will increasingly treat these as commodities. Therefore they will increasingly buy these through automated channels, in particular the Internet and mobile phone. This will further reduce footfall in the branches. We will consider this issue in a later chapter.

It is interesting to note that current accounts are second only to mortgages in the order of preference for face-to-face purchase. This is because opening a current account is the critical step in starting a relationship between customer and bank. Although the current account is a simple product, the relationship adds complexity.

The current account is also an example of a product where the bank incurs regulatory risk. Know your customer regulations, introduced to combat money laundering, require banks to establish the identity of their customers before opening a current account. This often requires face-to-face contact unless the customer is known from other sources.

Customer attitudes to technology

There has been a lot of academic research on customer attitudes towards the adoption of new technology. The most widely used model is the Technology Acceptance Model.[xxxviii]

This says that the most important factors for the adoption of new technology are perceived usefulness and perceived ease-of-use. Perceived usefulness is the extent to which customers believe that using the new technology will help them to achieve their objectives (for example, making enquiries or carrying out transactions). Perceived ease-of-use is the extent to which customers believe that the new technology will be easy to use.

For both of these factors, the word 'perceived' is of critical importance. Banks must communicate the usefulness and ease-of-use of new channels to their customers.

A related theory is the Lazy User Model of Solution Selection.[xxxix] If customers are in a position to choose between a number of different solutions, each of which will allow them to achieve their objectives, they will choose the solution that requires least effort. For the purposes of the model, the effort required takes account of monetary cost and time needed, as well as physical and mental effort.

Organisations sometimes make the mistake of assuming that customers will adopt a new technology, for example by using a new channel, because it is better than the technology that it is replacing. The Lazy User Model shows that this is a fallacy. If both technologies meet customers' needs, the technology decision will be based on effort rather than quality.

Research into customer attitudes towards the adoption of individual channels will be discussed in later chapters.

Customer buying behaviour

A customer's decision whether to use a particular channel is similar to the customer's decision whether to buy a particular product or service and can be understood using standard models of customers' buying behaviour. Sandra Vandermerwe's Customer Activity Cycle[xl] is widely used as a basis for this. This looks at buying behaviour in terms of pre-purchase, purchase and post-purchase activities. These stages are sometimes described as research, purchase and servicing.

Banks need to consider customers' pre-purchase and post-purchase activities, as well as the purchase itself. They need to consider how they can put capabilities in place that will help customers through these stages.

For example, the pre-purchase activities for taking out a mortgage include saving a deposit, comparing mortgage terms and rates, and looking for insurance. Banks can support customers through these by providing suitable savings products, mortgage calculators and buildings insurance.

The process of taking out a mortgage is, of course, often associated with buying property. Therefore the banks can use channels such as estate agents and the property pages of newspapers to bring these to customers' attention.

The banks have their own value chain:

Figure 4 – The banks' value chain

Time

Contact opportunity	Contact made	Quote	Appointment	Sale	Value creation	Ongoing servicing

Most of the activities within this form part of the customer's purchase activity. This makes it harder for the banks to focus on the customer's pre-purchase activities.

From the banks' point of view, customer post-purchase activities should not only include servicing but also renewal, replacement, cross-selling and up-selling.

The customer experience

The banks' support for the customer's pre-purchase, purchase and post-purchase activities contributes towards the customer experience. The customer experience is a measure of the customer's satisfaction with the transaction, which includes factors such as how well the purchase satisfies the customer's needs and the level of customer service received.

A good customer experience helps to promote customer loyalty. This is a valuable commodity for banks. H. Eugene Lockhart, President and Chief Executive Officer of MasterCard Europe, once said that he could double profits if he could extend the average time a cardholder stayed with the organization from five years to seven.

However, length of relationship may be a rather superficial interpretation of loyalty. Research by Citibank showed that about 20% of customers destroy value for banks – they cost more to service than they produce in revenue. Do the banks really want these customers to remain with them indefinitely?

We are seeing a shift in the concept of loyalty from tenure – how long a customer has been with the bank – to value.

MARTINI BANKING

In many societies, there has been an important change in consumer psychology over recent decades. This has been characterised by a move towards a 24x7 society – a society that operates twenty-four hours a day, seven days a week – and where consumers expect to be able to get anything they want immediately. This has manifested itself in banking through the idea of Martini banking.

Drinks company Martini & Rossi ran a famous series of adverts based on the slogan, 'any time, any place, anywhere'. This has been changed slightly – it now appears as 'any time, anyhow, anywhere' – and has been adopted as an expression of customers' desire to carry out banking transactions at any time of day, in any location, and using any convenient channel.

The first channel to make Martini banking a serious possibility was the telephone call centre. The main problem with the call centre is that there is a limit to the complexity of transactions that can be undertaken. Automated telephone banking services were even more limited. Another problem was that banks were still limited by their traditional processing cycles, which had been determined by branch opening hours. This made 24-hour operation difficult, although this has largely been overcome.

Early experiments with online banking did not use the Internet. The banks were limited by the technology, which was based either on home computers such as ATARI (which was used in Chemical Bank's Pronto system) or the videotex system, which used a television and a phone line (used in Nottingham Building Society's Homelink system). These were unsuccessful for a number of reasons including their technological limitations and high charges.

Indeed, a 1992 report by the Electronic Frontier Foundation said: "home banking has two basic drawbacks: it can't be used for cash transactions and most consumers don't do enough banking to justify the initial costs or recurring charges. Quite simply, it's not very useful and customers aren't demanding it."[xli]

It is often instructive to look at old predictions! The problems with home banking, as it was implemented in the 1980s, were cost and complexity, not utility and demand. However, the experience of the time shows the dangers of applying first-generation thinking to new channels.

Personal computer (PC) and Internet banking provided a more cost-effective and technically robust solution. In one way they were a step backwards from the telephone call centre, as customers needed a PC instead of being able to use a telephone from anywhere. PC banking was particularly restrictive because it required the customer to load software onto a PC and could only be used on that PC.

PC and Internet banking had compensating advantages, however. Customers could enter information, using forms, and see what they had entered. This made it possible to undertake more complex transactions. Information such as rate tables and terms & conditions could be published. Tools such as rate and mortgage calculators could be used. Customers could download information, making new services such as e-statements possible.

The mobile phone is the ultimate Martini device. Smartphones are completely mobile and offer access to the Internet. The only problem is the small screen size, but this is being overcome as screen sizes are increased and as mobile phone technology is incorporated in devices such as tablets. This is discussed in more detail in chapter 9.

As with online banking, the early experiments were not very successful. Many of these used Wireless Access Protocol (WAP) technology, which was not fast or robust enough to be used for mobile banking. I-mode technology, used in Japan, was more successful, but screen size remained a problem.

Third-generation (3G) mobile phones are based on more robust technologies. General Packet Radio Service (GPRS) is arguably 2.5G rather than 3G, but can be used for mobile banking. Newer technologies such as Wideband Code Division Multiple Access (WCDMA) are even better.

Chapter 4 – The brand

COMMODITIES AND COMPETITION

We introduced the idea of commodities in the last chapter, in which we said that commodities are goods and services that are supplied without qualitative difference – i.e. they are the same irrespective of the supplier.

This implies that commodities have another characteristic: they are fungible. A commodity from one supplier can be replaced by a commodity from a different supplier without making any difference. Financial products are concerned with money, which is the ultimate fungible commodity.

If there is no qualitative difference between goods and services, what is the basis of competition?

The usual basis of competition between firms dealing in commodities is price. But price competition creates very difficult market conditions. Therefore firms in the financial services industry try to avoid it.

Another traditional basis of competition in financial services has been risk. For example, customers have been able to choose between safe investments with low rates of return or riskier investments with higher rates of return. Customer loyalty towards the High Street banks in the UK owes much to the perception that they are safer than the smaller banks.

It is still true that economic problems lead to a 'flight to quality', with customers switching their deposits to the banks that they feel are safe. However, it has become much harder for banks to differentiate themselves on risk. There are a number of factors behind this.

Deregulation and convergence within financial services mean that customers are no longer able to choose to place their funds with ring-fenced 'safe' organizations. The Savings and Loan (Thrift) sector in the US gives a clear example of this. Until deregulation, the Thrifts were low risk, low return organizations. Deregulation allowed them to greatly expand their operations, but many of them did not have the management skills to operate in the new markets. A sector of the financial services industry that had once been totally safe became very high risk and many of the Thrifts either collapsed or had to be taken over. About 747 out of the 3,234 savings and loan associations in the United States failed during the 1980s and 1990s. 'As of December 31, 1995, RTC (the Resolution Trust Corporation) estimated that the total cost for resolving the 747 failed institutions was $87.9 billion.'[xlii]

Many financial products are so complex that it is impossible for customers to assess the level of risk. Other problems include: product values linked to market risk (rather than the risk of underlying physical assets), an increase in the number of unexpected events (sometimes called 'black swans'), and the difficulty of valuing the underlying assets. The collapse of the market for collateralised debt obligations (CDOs), which caused the recent worldwide credit crunch and recession, is an example of how even professional investors can fail to understand risk.

Most countries now operate deposit insurance schemes that protect customers (up to a limit) in the event that their bank fails. This means that all licensed banks are risk free for deposits within that limit.

If banks do not want to compete on price and find it difficult to compete on risk, what is the basis of competition? The banks have tried to compete by creating brands.

BRANDING

A brand is an identifier that is used to differentiate a product, product range or producer from its competitors. A brand is associated with a set of values, for example fairness and security. Buying that brand provides customers with an assurance that what they are buying has those values.

This, in turn, allows producers to charge a higher price. The products that they are selling are no longer commodities, competing on equal terms against the products of other producers, but are branded. The additional revenue that the producer earns by selling branded products rather than commodity products is the brand equity.

Brands can be created for individual products, product ranges or as umbrella brands that cover all core products from a producer. Banks have also branded distribution channels.

PROTECTING BRAND EQUITY

The banks have invested heavily to increase their brand equity. For example, Interbrand's[xliii] 2010 ranking of the top 100 global brands included nine banks: JP Morgan (29th), HSBC (32nd), Goldman Sachs (37th), Citigroup (40th), Morgan Stanley (42nd), Santander (68th), Barclays (74th), Credit Suisse (80th) and UBS (86th).

As we said in chapter 3, banking products are intangible. One consequence of this is that many of the brand values are derived from the customer experience. A poor customer experience can undermine the brand values and reduce brand equity. Therefore banks go to considerable lengths to protect their brand values. This will be a recurrent theme in this chapter.

BRANDING PRODUCTS AND PRODUCT RANGES

Some banks have attempted to brand individual products. For example, Midland Bank (now part of HSBC) introduced a branded account called the Orchard Account. However, it is difficult to brand banking products such as accounts. Their intangible nature makes it difficult to establish a clear brand identity.

Establishing a brand identity is easier if the brand name conveys a clear set of brand values. For example, Lloyds Bank offers the Classic Account. The word 'classic' carries a set of implied brand values (including quality and integrity) that can be expected to appeal to customers.

There is more scope for branding products such as credit cards. Their physical nature (customers view the credit card, rather than the account to which it allows access, as the product) allows card issuers to use design and advertising to build a brand identity. Examples include Goldfish (now part of Barclaycard) and HSBC's Welsh credit card. Goldfish used images of goldfish on its cards to reinforce the brand identity. The HSBC Welsh credit card used Welsh imagery (in particular the Welsh dragon) to define itself as a brand appealing to a patriotic market segment.

Other banking products are marketed under umbrella brands, which are often the corporate brand of the supplier or legacy brands. Both of these are discussed below.

One reason for branding individual products or product ranges is to protect the umbrella brand. Banks may create individual brand identities for products that do not relate to their core activities or for experimental products if there is a risk that they may fail and damage the bank's brand image.

Another reason for creating an individual brand is for products that are developed as joint ventures. Examples in the UK include credit cards (Access) and e-cash cards (Mondex).

CORPORATE BRANDING

Banks usually sell most of their mass market banking products under a brand that corresponds to their corporate identity, for example HSBC or Citi.

Other lines of business may be branded based on the corporate brand (for example, Barclays Capital Markets) or using a legacy brand (for example, Coutts).

LEGACY BRANDS

Most banks have grown through acquisition. During this period they have inherited existing brands, as well as customers and products. They must decide between keeping these brands and replacing them with their own brands. Lloyds Banking Group illustrates this.

Figure 5 – Lloyds Banking Group mergers and acquisitions 1971 to 2011

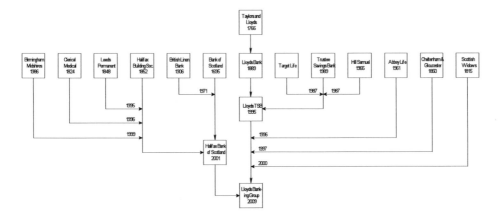

Note that this only includes major mergers and acquisitions – for example, it does not include Ambassador Life. Each of these organizations came with its own brand or portfolio of brands, although some of these (Abbey Life, for example) have subsequently been sold.

Legacy brands are discussed further under brand management below, but banks will generally continue to use them where the brand values for the legacy brand are stronger than those for the corporate brand in a particular market, for example Coutts in private banking.

BRANDING CHANNELS

Banks also brand channels. There are two reasons for this. The first, of course, is to protect the brand equity by making sure that any problems with a new channel do not damage the reputation of the corporate brand.

The second is to attract new customers to the bank. Although brand values contribute to the brand equity by reinforcing the relationship with existing customers, they can make it more difficult for the bank to recruit new customers. For example, bank brand values may seem old-fashioned to younger people. Introducing a new brand identity for channels may be attractive to this group.

Examples of branded channels include credit cards, ATMs, telephone banking and Internet banking. We have already discussed the branding of credit cards. Some banks branded their ATMs (the First National Bank of Atlanta branded its ATMs as 'Tillie the Teller') to overcome customer uncertainty about the technology.

Telephone call centres and the Internet allow banks to offer a much wider range of services and, in effect, to operate a parallel bank. This gives them a choice of operating models, one of which is to set up the new channel as a 'baby bank' apparently not connected with its parent.

For telephone banking, Midland Bank (now part of HSBC) is a good example. It set up two separate telephone banks. One of these was an add-on to its existing branch-based service; the other was a separate baby bank, First Direct. We will discuss First Direct later, in chapter 8, but separating the First Direct brand from the Midland Bank brand allowed it to recruit customers from the population as a whole, not just Midland Bank customers. First Direct was the first direct bank to develop a significant market presence.

Internet banking examples include Smile (set up by the Co-operative Bank) and Cahoot (set up by Abbey National, now part of Santander). Non-banks also diversified into banking by setting up baby banks, for example Egg (set up by the Prudential and later acquired by Citigroup – it is currently being dismantled: its mortgage book and savings accounts, and Egg name, have been sold to the Yorkshire Building Society and its card operations have become part of Barclays). All of these names were chosen partly to appeal to people outside the banks' traditional customer base.

BRAND STRATEGY

We have already considered why banks may have multiple brands and some of the advantages of this. To summarise:

- Brands may have been inherited (legacy brands) from precursor financial services organizations.

- New brands may have been introduced to allow recruitment from a demographic group with different brand values.
- New brands may have been introduced to protect the corporate umbrella brand.
- Legacy brands may be retained if the brand values for the legacy brand align with the brand values sought by that group of customers.

However, multiple brands also impose costs. There are two main problems.

First, each brand has costs associated with it. These include advertising, livery (letter headings etc.) and brand management costs. Although these are lower for intangible products than they would be for tangible products such as cars (the need to rationalise the number of different marques is a major issue in the motor industry) they are not insignificant. Also, money spent on advertising a product or channel brand cannot be spent on advertising the corporate brand.

Second, multiple brands can be confusing and undermine the corporate brand. For example, would a customer who, at the start of the millennium, had a TSB current account, a Cheltenham & Gloucester mortgage and a Scottish Widows investment portfolio realise that these were all brands owned by Lloyds Bank?

Even if the customer realised this, what would the customer experience be like? Each of the above brands maintains its own corporate image, websites, security etc. Also, since there is no single view of the customer, the customer could not be sure of getting consistent information. We will return to the need for a consistent experience and consistent information in chapter 13.

We have already seen how the Lloyds Banking Group has acquired brands over the last forty years. The table below shows which brands were part of the group as at 1st July 2011, and which products were marketed under these brands.

Lloyds Banking Group	Current account	Savings	Credit card	Loans	Mortgages	General Insurance	Life Insurance	Investments	Pensions
Lloyds TSB – England & Wales	✓	✓	✓	✓	✓	✓	✓	✓	✓
Halifax Retail Bank – England & Wales	✓	✓	✓	✓	✓	✓	✓	✓	✓
Cheltenham & Gloucester					✓				
Lloyds TSB – Scotland	✓	✓	✓	✓	✓	✓	✓	✓	✓
Bank of Scotland – Scotland	✓	✓	✓	✓	✓	✓	✓	✓	✓
Birmingham & Midshires – England & Wales		✓			✓				
Intelligent Finance – UK	✓	✓			✓				
Scottish Widows – UK					✓		✓	✓	✓

This table shows not only the number of separate brands that are part of Lloyds Banking Group, but also the amount of overlap between them.

Brand strategy needs to consider questions such as:

- Do existing brands have sufficient brand equity to justify the cost of maintaining them?
- Does each brand have a clearly defined purpose and market demographic?
- Do existing brands compete with each other?
- How does the existence of a range of brands impact on the corporate brand?

BRAND MANAGEMENT

Brand management was originally developed at consumer goods firm Proctor and Gamble in the 1930s. The guiding principle is that each brand should be run as if it were a separate company, with its own management, balance sheet and profit & loss account.

Brand management in banking could be the subject of a separate book, and we will not attempt to cover the subject in any depth. Brand managers focus on creating a unique identity and image for the brand. The values of the brand must align with the needs of, and be relevant to, the target market segment. This promotes brand loyalty and increases brand equity.

Changing a brand can be very difficult and very expensive. The re-brand of the Marathon confectionery bar as Snickers in the UK in 1990 was accompanied by a massive advertising campaign and a lot of public opposition. However, it was successful, unlike the attempts to re-brand the Post Office to Consignia, and PwC Consulting to Monday, both of which failed in 2002.[xliv]

Which leaves the problem of what to do with a legacy brand whose brand equity is no longer sufficient to justify the cost of brand management. In many cases, the bank closes the brand for new business and stops active brand management. The brand remains on the books, but is not actively promoted. The Target Life brand is an example of this. There are still Target Life policies in existence, but they are not dealt with by a dedicated Target Life brand manager.

Other brands require more active measures to tempt customers away. The process is similar to the dilapidation process that is used for obsolete channels and is discussed in chapter 12.

THE MULTI-CHANNEL CHALLENGE

Perhaps the greatest challenge facing banks is: How do they protect their brand in a multi-channel world? It has been said that banks are judged on their weakest channel. If customers have a bad experience with one channel, then the reputation of the bank as a whole will be damaged in their eyes.

Banks can get round this problem by individually branding new channels. But this increases costs and may damage the corporate brand.

Chapter 5 – Channels

WHAT ARE CHANNELS?

Channels are any means by which banks interact with their customers. They include traditional core channels, such as the branch, which are under the banks' control and through which the banks provide services. They also include the media, which the banks can influence but over which they have no control. And they include the social media, over which the banks have little influence and no control.

Figure 6 – Types of channel

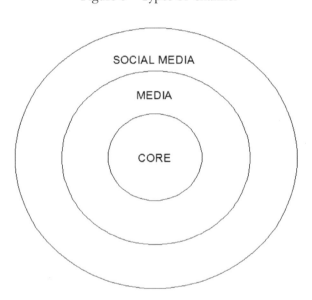

The core channels can be classified as:[xlv]

	Employee service	**Self-service**
Physical	Branch	ATM
Virtual	Telephone call centre	Internet

Each type of channel has its own advantages. To be simplistic:

- Physical channels offer customers the reassurance of a physical point of presence.
- Virtual channels offer customers greater convenience.
- Employee service channels offer customers a better customer experience and give

the bank the opportunity to collect information.

- Self-service channels offer the organization lower costs.

The challenge facing the organization is how to put the channels together into a coherent distribution strategy.

DISTRIBUTION STRATEGY

Purpose of the distribution strategy

The distribution strategy exists to answer a number of questions:

- Which channels will the organisation offer?
- Where will they be located?
- What products and services will be offered over each channel?
- To whom will the channel be made available?
- How will the channel operate?
- What, if any, interactions will there be between channels?

Which channels?

Most banks either operate a branch network, supported by a number of other channels, or restrict themselves to one or two channels, usually telephone call centres and/or the Internet. The second of these options is called the monochannel model. The distribution strategy defines which of these operating models they have adopted.

Banks must also decide how they are going to react to the development of new channels. They may choose to introduce these as they become available, or to wait until the channel has become established. Again, the distribution strategy defines this.

Where will they be located?

Banks need to consider physical location both for retail outlets and for processing centres. However, the distribution strategy will usually focus on the location of retail outlets.

Retail outlets, branches and ATMs, must be located where they are convenient for customers. Banks also need to consider the social impact of retail outlets and branches. Both of these are considered further in chapter 7.

The location of processing centres depends on logistics and risk. For example, mail processing centres (which are used to process and image incoming mail) need good road access and are usually located close to motorways. Banks also usually choose locations that are not at risk of flooding.

Banks also need to decide whether to locate processing centres and call centres in the same country as their customers or in another, lower cost, country. Locating these centres in another country is usually called offshoring, even when there is no sea border between the countries (for example, an American bank locating a processing centre or call centre in Mexico or Canada). Processing centres and call centres located in the same country as the bank's customers are described as onshore.

What products and services?

Banks do not offer all products and services over all channels. There are a number of reasons for this.

There may be physical limitations. For example, cash withdrawal is not possible by telephone or over the Internet. Customers have to visit physical outlets, such as branches and ATMs, or make withdrawals against credit or debit cards at third party outlets.

There may be security concerns. Virtual channels such as the telephone and the Internet rely on identification and verification (ID&V) procedures to establish the customer's identity. There may be a limit on the amount of money that can be transferred to a third party account through these channels as an additional safeguard in case anyone circumvents ID&V.

There may be legal restrictions. Some transactions can only be carried out if physical documents are exchanged. These may need to be signed or sealed, and may need to be witnessed. All of these present problems for virtual channels.

There may be regulatory risks. Know your customer (KYC) regulations were introduced to prevent money laundering and the funding of terrorist activities. These require the customer's identity to be established with a level of certainty that may be difficult for virtual channels to achieve. Governments are increasingly providing central databases that allow banks and other organisations to establish applicants' identities with a reasonable level of certainty, but there remains a level of risk.

The product or service may be too complex to deliver over the channel. Many countries regulate investment products and it may be too difficult to complete all of the necessary procedures through virtual channels.

Therefore financial services providers must choose which products and services to offer over each channel, and include this information in the distribution strategy.

To whom?

Banks may choose to segment their channels, either by only offering some channels to specific groups of customers or, more usually, offering the same channel but operating it in a different way.

The way in which banks segment their customer base varies, but for personal customers there will typically be segments corresponding to basic customers, mass market customers, premium customers and private banking customers. They usually also have separate segments for special customer groups such as students.

A common example of channel segmentation occurs when banks set aside a number of branches for the exclusive use of private banking customers. Premium customers may have access to their own exclusive branches or, more usually, to their own exclusive areas in branches.

How will they operate?

Banks can choose to provide products and services in a number of different ways. Each can provide different levels of service and different costs.

Telephone banking is a good example of this. The options range from a fully automated service (low cost but limited service), through an offshore call centre and an onshore call centre, to a named relationship manager. These options are discussed in more detail in chapter 8.

What interactions?

Channels do not operate in isolation. Multi-channel transactions are transactions initiated by the customer using one channel (often the Internet) and completed using a different channel (for example, face-to-face in a branch).

The distribution strategy must say which interactions are possible. Allowing more interactions between channels increases costs, as information must be passed between the channels. Not allowing interactions gives the impression that one part of the bank does not know what another part is doing, which can undermine the bank's brand image and the customer's experience.

Representing the distribution strategy

One way of visualising the distribution strategy is as a three-dimensional spreadsheet, or cube. The three dimensions are:

1. What channels and how (top to bottom)? This is a list of what channels the bank will offer and how it will operate them. For example, there may be two entries for the telephone channel, one for a fully automated telephone service and the other for person-to-person telephone service.

2. What products and services (left to right)? This is a list of the products and services that the bank offers.

3. Which customer segments (front to back)? This is a list of customer segments used by the bank.

Figure 7 – Distribution strategy

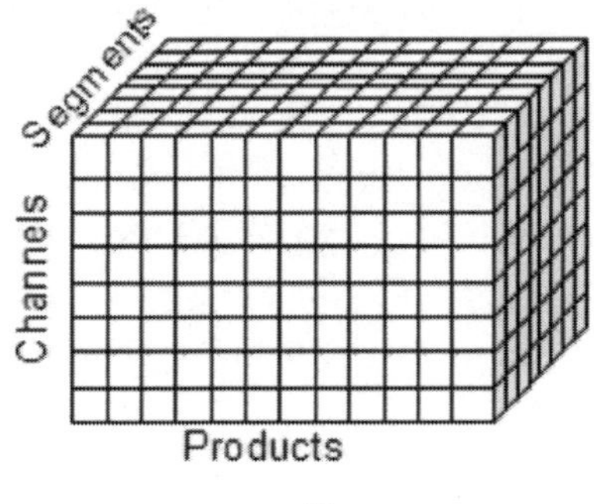

This gives a three dimensional spreadsheet, each cell in which represents a specific combination of channel, service and customer segment. The final stage is to populate the cube by putting (for example) 'yes' or 'no' in each cell to define the organization's distribution strategy.

Banks must keep their distribution strategies up-to-date, which means that they must not only match current customer behaviour for purchases and for service, but must also evolve over time as customer behaviour changes.

JOURNEYS

Journeys are the routes that individual customers can take between channels. They are not restricted to the channels in the distribution strategy because customers may start their journey using a channel that is outside the bank's control, for example the financial pages of a daily newspaper or a price comparison service.

The most important factor in determining whether customers will embark on a journey is the nature of the product or service. Customers will undertake a lengthy journey for a complex product such as a mortgage, but expect to buy a product that they perceive as simple, such as a credit card, in a single interaction with their financial services provider. This is related to the idea of commoditisation, which we discussed in chapter 3.

We will return to journeys later in this text.

THE PSYCHOLOGY OF CHANNEL USAGE

We have already discussed some of the psychological factors that affect customers' attitude towards channels in chapter 3. In this chapter, we will look at individual channels.

There has been a lot of academic research into the factors that affect customers' willingness to adopt Internet and mobile banking.[xlvi] Common factors seem to be trust, ease of use, usefulness and convenience.

Trust, in this context, means trust in the bank. Does the customer have confidence in the bank providing the service?

Ease of use means how easy the service is to use. As will be discussed later, this seems to have been a problem with many of the early online banking systems.

Usefulness means how useful the service is to the customer – what the service will allow the customer to do.

Convenience means the extent to which the service is available where and when the customer requires.

The factors that determine traditional customers' continued preference for branches are less clear. Branches have been described as "an awkward stop on the way to the shop, in a street where parking is impossible."[xlvii] It has been shown[xlviii] that customers telephone the branch in preference to using a call centre, even though the branches are not very good at delivering a telephone-based service (the reasons for this statement – which some might consider provocative – are discussed later in this text).

We believe that the attachment to the branch is emotional rather than practical, and is based on trust and on engagement.

Branches provide a physical point of presence. This reassures customers that their money is safe. Indeed, it was once common practice to design branches as impressive (if impractical!) buildings to emphasise this. Branches also have a role in time of crisis. The call centre and the website may be overloaded, but customers can always queue outside the branch to withdraw their money.

There is some suggestion that customers look to engage with their bank on an emotional level. This, of course, is the antithesis of first-generation thinking, in which the bank manager was a gatekeeper restricting customer access to financial services. The advantage of a branch is that it allows customers to put faces and names to the bank. It is much more difficult to engage emotionally with a voice on the telephone, and it may be impossible to engage emotionally with an automated telephone response system or a website.

CHANNEL COMPETITION AND COORDINATION

All channels compete against each other to a greater or lesser extent. As we will see in chapter 12, one of the main reasons for a bank to introduce a new channel is in order to reduce costs. To achieve this, the bank must persuade customers to switch from the existing channels to the new channel. Therefore, the new channel is competing with the existing channels for the same customers and transactions.

It has been suggested[xlix] that there are three underlying models: coordination, free competition and managed competition.

Under the coordination model, all channels are fully coordinated. This guarantees that the customer will receive a consistent experience across all channels.

Under the free competition model, channels are free to compete with each other. The experience that the customer receives depends on the treatment strategy applied by each channel.

The managed competition model balances these extreme approaches. Channels are free to compete, but must operate within a set of ground rules that protect the brand and ensure a consistent customer experience.

The article referenced suggests that the managed competition is the most appropriate model for retail banks. However, there is evidence[l] that customers place great value on consistency, which suggests a preference for the coordination model.

We believe that the coordination model is the most appropriate model for a bank's established channels. Any form of competition, even managed competition, risks undermining the brand by sending mixed messages to the customer.

New channels are different. Research into the introduction of Internet banking[li] indicated four models: add-on, e-banking, baby e-banking and pure play new entrant. We will discuss these in more detail in chapter 6, but we will look at the add-on and baby e-bank models in the context of competition between channels.

The add-on model treats Internet banking as an additional service offered to customers. This ensures a high level of coordination with the existing channels but does not exploit the potential of the channel for recruitment or address the inefficiency inherent in the traditional branch-centred model.

The baby e-bank model introduces a new bank, with a separate brand, for Internet banking. This is an example of the free competition model. It is brand-neutral. It does not enhance the brand – but any problems at the baby e-bank do not affect the bank's reputation.

New channels are an area where the managed competition model may be appropriate. It is impossible to predict how successful a new channel will be (the example of interactive digital television being a salutary warning) and the managed competition model gives channel managers the freedom that they need. At the same time, the model protects the brand.

A number of banks chose to adopt the baby e-bank model when they introduced Internet banking. We would suggest that there were two reasons for this. The first is that the banks had very real concerns about Internet security and believed that any security problems would have a particularly damaging effect on their reputations. The second is that the banks were trying to target a new demographic segment and believed that a brighter image (the baby e-banks adopted names such as Smile and Cahoot) would be advantageous.

What role, if any, should the free competition model play? It must be remembered that the banks also operate services that have little impact on the vast majority of their customers. Most of these are aimed at business customers and can include activities as diverse as share registration and auction sites. There is no reason why these should not operate under the free competition model as there are no brand implications.

Therefore we believe that a mixed model – coordination for the established channels, managed competition for new channels aimed at mainstream customers and free competition for peripheral activities – is the most appropriate approach.

ROLE AND IMPORTANCE OF CHANNELS

The move from first-generation 'control world' thinking to third-generation 'networked world' thinking has had a profound effect on the role and relative importance of the main channels. To summarise this:

Channel	Control world	Networked world
Branch	Central to relationship	Point of presence
Telephone call centre	Appendix to branch	Appendix to Internet
Internet	Low cost add on	Central to infrastructure
Mobile phone	Unimportant add on	Martini device
AND		
Customer	Passive recipient	Active collaborator

We will discuss the individual channels in greater detail in chapters 6 to 10.

This is the world in which the banks are now operating. It is outside their comfort zone for many, but they must adapt or die.

Chapter 6 – The Internet

On the Internet, nobody knows you're a dog

Steiner's Law[lii]

THE ROLE OF THE INTERNET

As we have already discussed, the Internet is a disruptive technology and the impact of introducing such a technology is very difficult to assess in advance.

In addition, the role of the Internet is complex and the Internet cannot be described as fulfilling a single role in the banks' distribution strategy. One role is to use banking systems developed for the Internet as a technological platform for the development of new channels and for the redevelopment of existing channels. We introduced this idea in chapter 2. We will consider three more roles that reflect how banks use the Internet: Customer convenience, low cost delivery and communication.

Internet banking offers customers convenience in a number of ways. Customers can access the Internet at a time, in a place and in a manner of their choosing (Martini banking). Customers can enter relatively complex transactions in a way that gives them control. Customers can receive confirmations and information sent to their own personal computers.

Many banks introduced Internet banking as a low-cost delivery channel, as an alternative to telephone banking. It proved difficult to obtain sustainable competitive advantage through this, but the Internet remains an essential component of 'basic' offerings, low-cost accounts made available to low-value customers. The Internet also diverts demand for transactions such as balance enquiries away from higher cost channels such as the telephone call centre and the branch.

The Internet is an ideal communication channel. The cost of publishing information on the Internet is very low and organizations can monitor whether or not the information that they publish is opened (they cannot, of course, be certain whether it is actually read). The main problem is security.

Channel segmentation

Many channels are segmented. Some branches are set aside for high-value customers and are not available to mass-market or low-value customers. High-value, mass-market and low-value customers will usually have different telephone banking services and may be served by call centres located in different countries and by a different mix of person-to-person and automated agents. This is not usually the case for Internet banking, except in as far as personal and business customers may have their own websites.

There are two reasons for this. It is much easier for Internet banking to apply individual treatment strategies through a single website. If a customer is entitled to apply for particular products they will appear as options, if the customer is not entitled to apply for them then they won't. In addition, providing a single set of Internet banking transactions is much cheaper and less risky than providing multiple sets, that have to be maintained separately.

This means that a single Internet banking system can be deployed across the entire customer base.

INTERNET BANKING

An Internet banking system will typically provide:

- Transaction processing
- Account opening
- Account maintenance
- Statements and recent transactions
- Information, calculators and simulators
- Secure email, web chat and call me

Transaction processing includes transfers between accounts and payments to third party accounts.

Account opening includes sale of savings products and may include loan applications, subject to credit scoring. Customers can also apply to upgrade to a different type of account.

Account maintenance includes making changes to customer and account information, for example telephone numbers. There may be restrictions on changing information such as addresses because of the risk of fraud.

Statements and recent transactions includes viewing recent transactions and viewing and downloading statements.

Information and calculators includes branch locators, terms & conditions, loan calculators and mortgage calculators. Calculators and simulators are also used for wealth management.

Secure email, web chat and call me are different ways that the bank can communicate with its customers and vice versa. Secure email – web-based email inside the bank's secure website – was introduced because of well-founded concerns about the security of the public email system. However, there is evidence[liii] that customers do not pay much attention to it. 45 per cent of European banks currently offer secure email, with an additional 15 per cent planning to offer it within a one-year time period and 17 per cent planning to offer it within a one- to three-year period.[liv]

Web chat is a secure version of instant messaging (IM) and call me allows customers to ask for a call from an agent. Web chat and call me, in particular, have extended the scope of the Internet to allow person-to-person interaction. 38 per cent of European banks offer or plan to offer web chat.[lv]

Limitations of Internet banking

One limitation of the Internet is the extent to which it can be used for the sale of complex products. The sale of complex products has been very profitable for the banks. Not only are the margins on them higher than the margins on simple products, but they also tend to lock customers in to the bank because the switching costs are higher.

There are three problems with using the Internet for the sale of complex products. The complexity of the sales process may deter customers from using the Internet, and leads to a risk that customers will make mistakes. There is a regulatory risk, in that mistakes by the customer could lead to a risk of mis-selling. Customers generally prefer to use face-to-face channels to buy complex products.

It should be noted that face-to-face selling of complex products also incurs regulatory risk. The risk of mis-selling is greater through face-to-face channels than through the Internet. Proposed changes in the UK, the Financial Services Authority's Retail Distribution Review, require increased transparency about fees and commissions on the part of the banks and make face-to-face channels, with their greater costs, less attractive.

One approach, which has been adopted by investment management firm Hargreaves Lansdown, is to use the Internet as a filter and a way into the sales process. Their web site provides information and tools to support customers' pre-purchase research and customers can use web chat to get further information and clarification. Customers who want to proceed with a purchase can then contact a qualified advisor.

This is an example of a journey. We introduced the idea of journeys in chapter 3. This particular journey starts with Hargreaves Lansdown's website and concludes with telephone contact with an advisor.

Portals and multi-channel transactions

This is also an example of using the Internet as a point of entry for access to financial services. This could, perhaps, be considered as a fifth role for the Internet in the banks' distribution strategy.

Banks may be less advanced than other retailers in this. Many retailers' websites have an 'order online and collect in store' capability that has no equivalent in most banks' web sites. Aside from the branch locator, the Internet provides little support for the branch network. It is usually possible to order copy statements through the Internet, but it is not always possible to order new cheque-books and paying in books. Web chat and cards are relatively recent additions to bank websites.

The banks went through a stage at which they tried to position their websites as portals. A portal is a point of entry to the web – Internet users choose a portal and set it as their home page. One method used to attempt this was for some banks to set themselves up as Internet Service Providers (ISPs).

This was quite short-lived. It is possible to suggest a number of reasons why it was not successful. Putting a lot of other information on the bank's web site reduces the impact of its own message. Operating a website as a portal diverts a lot of management time and effort into a non-core activity. Problems with other websites could cause damage to the bank's reputation.

Banks have also tried to position themselves as financial portals – portals for financial information and services. They have included links to third party providers, in particular investment managers, through a marketplace. This seems to be have become less common as banks have expanded their own offerings.

Another example of using the Internet as a point of entry into a financial transaction is the multi-channel transaction. This is a transaction that uses a number of different channels, typically starting on the Internet with the transaction being completed in a face-to-face environment.

A mortgage is a good example of a multi-channel transaction. Customers can research the mortgage products available on the Internet, using the website to look for offers applicable to them and mortgage calculators to estimate their repayments. They may use the telephone call centre to clarify their eligibility for offers. They will usually visit the branch to complete the purchase.

JOURNEYS

It is important to recognise that the multi-channel transaction represents only a part of the journey. Customers will carry out a range of pre-purchase activities even before they start to investigate their mortgage options. These will include looking for properties and saving money for a deposit and for furniture.

Some of these activities are outside the oversight of the banks. For example, customers may choose a property based on the traditional media, such as newspapers, or websites to which the banks have no access. They may also use estate agents. As we discussed in chapter 3, these are pre-purchase activities in the customer activity cycle and the banks should support them.

At one stage, banks operated their own chains of estate agencies. This created a vertically integrated model for property purchase. However, as with operating as an ISP, it is a non-core activity. Estate agent profitability fluctuates widely depending on the state of the property market, which could affect the bank's share price. There is a potential conflict of interest between estate agency (which aims to maximise sales) and mortgage lending (which aims to manage risk). There is also some risk of reputational damage.

Estate agents can be used to place advertising and to introduce customers to the bank. This is a hands-off relationship that will not affect the bank's reputation.

Banks can also support savers by providing suitable savings products. Customers' use of these products can also be a factor suggesting that the customer is contemplating a major purchase such as a property. Banks can use this as an indicator of future customer behaviour.

There are also post-purchase activities. These include insuring the property and its contents, servicing the mortgage, furnishing the property, carrying out maintenance and improvements, and eventually either downsizing or trading up.

Banks can support these activities through a mix of insurance products, payment products, consumer finance products, loans, second mortgages and mortgage products. They can also provide equity release schemes.

ADVICE AGENTS

We have discussed the limitations of the Internet as a channel for the purchase of complex products. We have also said that one way of getting round this is to treat the purchase as a multi-channel transaction. The Internet is used to allow the customer to research the products available and for the initial fact find, which collects information about the customer's financial position. The purchase can then be completed face-to-face, with an advisor.

The Internet allows this to be extended. The information collected during the fact find can be analysed to identify solutions appropriate to the customer's financial position and needs. This has led to the development of advice agents.

Advice agents vary from simple filters and search agents through to sophisticated systems that use animation (avatars) and natural language programming to simulate a face-to-face interaction. It is perhaps worth remembering that the 'Turing Test' of machine intelligence is the ability to conduct a conversation with a computer without being able to distinguish it from a human.

Although these are commonly described as advice agents, the extent to which they can give advice is debatable. In many countries, investment and pensions are regulated products and advice can only be given by qualified advisors Automated advice agents can give customers a narrower range of choices but need either to operate on an 'execution only' basis (which must include an explicit statement that no advice has been given) or to allow the final purchase decision to be made with the assistance of a human advisor.

Expert systems and artificial intelligence

Expert systems are computer systems that are designed to duplicate the reasoning of a human expert. Artificial intelligence (AI) systems go beyond expert systems in that they are capable of self-learning.

There are four commonly used technologies associated with expert systems and AI: Rules-based systems, neural networks, genetic algorithms and case-based reasoning.

Rules-based systems capture rules from a human expert. For example, an investment advisor might sit down with an analyst and explain the process used to reach an investment decision. The analyst will then translate this into rules, which may take the form of a decision tree or may simply exist as a set of rules that the computer will apply one-by-one. Rules-based systems are expert systems but they are usually not AI because they do not incorporate a self-learning capability.

Neural networks are arrays of processors. They, like humans, learn by example. A large number of examples are processed through the neural network. When they come up with an outcome that is correct, that path is reinforced. When a similar example comes up, it is more likely to go down that path. They can self-learn, by incorporating new examples as they are presented.

Genetic algorithms use software to carry out a similar process. A number of algorithms are developed and tested using examples. The least successful algorithms are discarded and the most successful are mutated. More examples are used to test these new algorithms until a satisfactory success rate is achieved. They are not self-learning.

Case-based reasoning has a library of examples from the past. This also indicates the correct decision. The case-based reasoning software compares new examples with those in the library, and takes the decision from the historic example that most closely resembles the new example. Case-based reasoning can self-learn if new examples are incorporated in the library.

The great advantage of rules-based systems is that they can provide an explanation of how the decision was reached, by saying exactly which rules were triggered. Another advantage of rules-based systems is that they do not self-learn, which means that their decisions do not vary over time.

Are automated advice agents an example of expert systems? Are they an example of AI?

The answer to the first is probably yes, at least for the more sophisticated agents, and the answer to the second is probably no, although they may contain elements associated with AI such as natural language processing.

INTERNET SECURITY

The greatest single problem with the Internet is security. The Internet is an open network that can be accessed by anyone. This means that it is open to attack. In addition, the packets of data that are sent over the Internet pass through public servers. These are also open to attack.

There are two main types of attack: attacks designed to obtain information and attacks designed to halt the service. Banks are concerned about both types, although attacks designed to obtain information are perhaps the main focus as this information can subsequently be used to defraud the bank or its customers.

There are a number of technological security measures that can be taken, but these are outside the scope of this book. Instead, we will focus on the identification and verification (ID&V) procedures that protect customer information from hackers.

When Internet banking was originally introduced, ID&V relied on a user ID and a password. This was a very simple system and was much the same as the system used internally in most offices, including banks.

However, hackers were able to use various tricks, such as key loggers, to obtain this information. A key logger is a computer virus that runs on a customer's personal computer (PC) and records the key strokes. Sophisticated key loggers can also take an image of the screen.

The next stage was to use secondary verification information, such as mother's maiden name. This was not really much better although, by asking for different pieces of secondary verification information, it made it slightly harder for hackers to access customers' accounts.

The next stage, two-factor authentication, relies on three pieces of information: a user ID, a password and a piece of memorable information. Instead of being asked to enter these in full, the customer is asked for selected characters from either the password or the memorable information. This has the great advantage that key loggers only capture part of the security information.

An alternative approach is to use a one-time password generator. These are devices of varying levels of complexity. Some simply require the customer to press a button to generate a password. Others require a token, usually a debit card, and a password. Both types generate a different password each time they are used.

This is used in conjunction with the user ID and a piece of memorable information to access the system. The advantage is that these are immune to key loggers because the password changes every time. However, they represent an additional cost to the bank and customers may find them inconvenient. They are battery-powered and the battery can run out at an inconvenient moment, and they are yet another device (along with the mobile phone and MP3 player) to be carried around.

In spite of these disadvantages, one-time password generators are becoming more common as banks become more concerned about the risks of Internet banking fraud.

Biometrics has been used. The most common approach is to use a thumbprint reader, either built in to a special mouse or attached through a USB port. Other biometric technologies, such as iris recognition, could also be used.

BUSINESS MODELS

We identified the four business models, and discussed the add-on and baby e-bank models, in chapter 5. The other two models are the pure play new entrant model and the e-banking model.

The pure play new entrant model introduces Internet banking as a completely stand alone service, operating without branches and (in its purest form) without a call centre. The pure play new entrant model is an example of the monochannel model.

The monochannel model first became feasible when telephone call centre technology became available and banks were able to operate without a branch network. The rationale behind the model is that the bank has much lower operating costs. Cash withdrawal, the most important banking service that cannot be provided over the Internet, can be made available using shared ATM networks.

Another reason for adopting this model was the idea of first mover advantage, which we discussed in chapter 2. First mover advantage claims that the first firm to enter a market, especially on the Internet, gains a huge competitive advantage by building market share and setting de facto standards that competitors are forced to follow.

There are examples of firms successfully achieving first mover advantage on the Internet, such as Amazon. But there are also examples of firms locking themselves into particular technologies and processes, only to be overtaken by competitors who have learned from their mistakes.

There is a more fundamental problem, however. Is the monochannel model viable for banking? There are three disadvantages: Recruitment, customer quality and complex sales.

The established banks' branch networks are a significant source of new customers. As we will see in the next chapter, branch location is a major factor in the choice of bank and the physical presence of the branches, with their prominent logos, helps to keep their names in customers' minds. Banks without branch networks are forced to rely on advertising and word of mouth.

Customer quality may be a problem for the pure play new entrants. New customers may only join in order to take advantage of better interest rates or more accommodating credit standards. It can be difficult to make a profit out of these customers because any cut in rates for savers will lead to customer defections, and levels of bad and doubtful debts may be higher. There is some suggestion that intensive advertising over a long period, a feature of the monochannel model, can reduce customer quality as more and more marginal customers decide to apply.

Complex sales are also more difficult. There is evidence that customers prefer to purchase complex products face-to-face. There is a correlation between the cost of a sale and the value added, and this has been ascribed to the human element.[lvi]

Social media

The Internet hosts the social media. Social media have been defined as: "a group of Internet-based applications that build on the ideological and technological foundations of Web 2.0, which allows the creation and exchange of user-generated content."[lvii] Social media are now the number one activity on the Internet.[lviii]

Why do people use social media? Psychologists have been exploring this question since the mid-2000s and seem to be divided over the reasons. We will not examine the reasons in detail as the purpose of this text is to examine how social media are changing financial services channel strategy, not to consider the full range of psychological aspects.

One reason is clear. Human beings have been organised socially for thousands of years, whether in family units, communities such as villages, or at work. During this time people have always placed a great deal of trust in the views of their friends, peers and family when decision-making. In recent times trust in corporations, especially banks, has declined and consumers are now placing even greater trust in the views of their social network – whether it is online or not.

It is no wonder that social media have grown the way they have since the Internet was able to facilitate this basic human need. All businesses, including banks that have a presence on the Internet, are now part of this social media eco-structure and their customers expect that they will engage with it to be relevant to them.

As a result banks are starting to invest in social media as a marketing tool in the belief that these new channels can overcome distrust, and falling response rates, in traditional marketing tools such as direct mail. One problem with this approach is that it is difficult for banks accurately to assess the real return on investment of social media initiatives compared with traditional marketing approaches. In addition, there are several conflicting theories and methods on measuring social media return on investment, some of which appear to be based more upon wishful thinking than solid data or statistical analysis.

A lot is said about social media – especially on social media channels! There is no doubt that social media channels such as Facebook, Twitter and YouTube are having a massive and irreversible impact on customer experience, marketing and communications. The impact of social media on culture, commerce, politics and even revolutions is staggering (we hesitate to provide numbers of users, tweets per day, video uploads or views per day as they're immediately out of date!). It simply cannot be ignored as part of a customer-centric multi-channel mix. But within only a few years of its inception it's becoming mainstream – as ubiquitous as traditional channels and the norm for many businesses. It has become ubiquitous so quickly that any potential competitive advantage by early movers may not have been realised.

As we discussed in chapter 1, the social media present the banks with something of a problem. On the one hand, they offer a new channel of communication, one that can be particularly effective in reaching younger people who may be difficult to reach through traditional channels. On the other hand, the social media are difficult to control. There are a number of examples of the use of social media by the banks.

Virtual worlds

Virtual worlds are computer-based simulated environments that allow users to interact with each other. These are often used for massively multiplayer online role-playing games. They offer opportunities for product and brand placement.

It could be argued that virtual worlds are not, strictly speaking, social media because most or all of their content is created by a designer rather than by the users. However, they are outside the control of the banks and they have a considerable amount of user content.

The best documented example of banks securing a presence in a virtual world is in Second Life. Banks such as ABN AMRO, BNP Paribas, ING and Saxo Bank have opened branches in Second Life.

The advantages are cost and engagement. Buying an island in Second Life cost about $2,000, whereas developing a website would typically cost $100,000. Customers also engage emotionally with virtual worlds and could develop an emotional attachment – which is very unlikely to happen with a website.[lix]

There are disadvantages. Banks cannot predict the success of virtual worlds, nor can they influence the direction in which they develop. Not all virtual worlds are suitable for banks. The most popular virtual world at present is probably World of Warcraft, which is set in a fantasy environment and may not be suitable for banks.

Banks are not currently investing heavily in a presence in virtual worlds.

Games are similar to virtual worlds in that they offer opportunities for product and brand placement. Again, banks are not investing heavily in these. Possible reasons might include doubts about the suitability of the most popular games and the relatively short life of games (which are updated or replaced quickly), which would undermine the value of the investment.

Communities and fan clubs

Communities are groups with common interests who use the social media to share information and experiences. British banks HSBC and NatWest have set up communities for small businesses.

Fan clubs use social media to celebrate their ownership of products. There are fan clubs for various makes and models of car, for example. These are less useful for banks because of the intangible nature of banking products.

As we have said, banks have no control over the social media. Therefore, disgruntled customers can use the social media, as well as traditional websites, to criticise them.

Responding to such criticism is a major challenge for the banks. HSBC faced this problem when it attempted to make changes to its graduate package. It received a lot of criticism, even though the changes would not have affected current students, and withdrew them. This is discussed in more detail below.

Paid advertising and opinion pieces

Banks can use the Internet in much the same way as they use the traditional media, for paid advertising. This can include opinion pieces written by apparently impartial commentators. This type of concealed advertising would not be possible in the traditional media, but the Internet has fewer restrictions.

Viral marketing is a form of advertising in which short videos (usually) are placed on the Internet, usually on video-sharing websites such as YouTube. These are designed to appeal to young people and may feature celebrities and sports stars. Viral marketing relies on the customers themselves to spread the message by recommending the video to their friends. Brands such as Nike are noted for making effective use of viral marketing, but banks (ING for example) have also used this technique.

YouTube

Isn't just for old bank adverts. Some banks, such as Barclays and First Direct, are using the channel to communicate to customers.

Barclays uses videos to provide guidance covering topics such as on-line security, setting-up and managing investment accounts, and general investment advice.

First Direct uses YouTube for information and marketing (for example, the 'First Direct Buddy' series highlighting customer service and promoting their iPhone app).

42 per cent of European banks have a presence on YouTube and a further 22 per cent plan to.[lx]

Blogs, Facebook and Twitter

Banks can operate their own web logs (blogs) and pages on social media sites such as Facebook and Twitter. Banco Sabadell is an example; Banco Sabadell also has its own YouTube channel.

32 per cent of European banks have their own blogs and a further 32 per cent plan to. 46 per cent have a presence on Facebook and a further 34 per cent plan to. 41 per cent have a presence on Twitter and a further 30 per cent plan to.[lxi]

The UK experience

All banks say that they want to engage more with their customers, but the following table shows that UK banks are passive in their approach to these new media:

Status of UK banks July 2011	Facebook page	Twitter account	YouTube channel
Barclays	No	Not active	Yes
Cooperative Bank and Smile	Yes	No	Media is 3 years old
First Direct	Yes	Media only	Yes
Halifax	No	No	No
HSBC	Yes	No	No
LloydsTSB	Yes	Yes	No
Metro Bank	No	Yes	Yes
NatWest	No	No	No
Santander and Cahoot	No	No	No

Source: Intelligence Delivered (Asia) Limited 2011 [conducted by searching for official sites]

Why have the banks been so cautious about social media? We would suggest that there are four problems: mindset, control, regulation and confidentiality.

Mindset problems

Exploiting the social media requires a third-generation mindset that most bankers, at the present time, do not possess.

Commentator and author Brett King described the five stages of social media grief for banks in his blog, 'Banking4Tomorrow'. These stages are:

- **Total ignorance.** During this stage, banks show no awareness of social media and do not believe that they are of any relevance to banking.
- **It's just a fad.** During this stage, banks recognise the existence of social media but do not believe that they are anything more than a passing fad.
- **I still don't get it, where's the money?** During this stage, banks start to realise that social media could be important. Unable to see how to make any money out of social media, they take their lead from what their competitors are doing.

It is a symptom of first- and second-generation thinking that the banks pay more attention to their competitors than they do to their customers! A sign that a bank has reached this stage is that it has a Facebook page – but no-one is managing it.

- **The sonic boom.** During this stage, banks finally realise that they have to do something. This is the stage that most banks are reaching today.
- **The mad scramble.** During this stage, banks realise that they should have been investing in social media for the past three or four years. This is the stage when massive, and often misconceived, initiatives take place.

The fifth stage may be brought on by a major public relations disaster. One example is Ann Minch's 'Debtor's Revolt'. She documented her refusal to pay off the balance on her Bank of America credit card through a video on YouTube.[lxii] More than half a million people have viewed this (July 2011) and she was successful in getting Bank of America to reduce her rate.[lxiii] The 'Fabulis debacle', in which Citibank closed the business account of social networking site Fabulis (now re-branded as Fab) for alleged 'objectionable content',[lxiv] is another example.

Brett King concludes by asking: "So how do you stop the grief cycle within your organization? The first thing bankers need to do is rethink their organisational structure around the customer. Social media are a tool for reaching customers, for engaging customers. It is as important as investing in branches, it is just as critical as having a telephone number for customers to call, but more than that, it can help you transform your business internally too."[lxv]

Control problems

We said in chapter 1 that the banks are unable to control the social media in the same way that they control their own channels. We have already discussed Ann Minch's Debtor's Revolt and the Fabulis debacle.

As we have said, HSBC offers another example.[lxvi] In 2007 the National Union of Students mobilised protests against HSBC using Facebook instead of protesting outside of the bank's headquarters in London. Thousands of recent graduates who found the bank had suddenly started charging them for overdrafts made their anger known by joining a Stop the Great HSBC Graduate Rip-Off! group on the website,[lxvii] started by NUS vice-president Wes Streeting. It attracted more than 4,000 members.

A spokesman for HSBC acknowledged the role of Facebook. "We are a service-oriented organisation and we have to listen to our customers – that is a priority for us. It's a good example of where a medium like Facebook has enabled customers to tell us something they feel strongly about," he added.

Mr Streeting said: "There can be no doubt that using Facebook made the world of difference to our campaign. By setting up a group on a site that is incredibly popular with students, it enabled us to contact our members during the summer vacation far more easily than would otherwise have been possible. It also meant that we could involve our former members – the graduates who were going to be most affected by this policy."

Regulation problems

Amongst other functions, the Financial Services Authority (FSA) (to be renamed the Financial Conduct Authority, which will focus on consumer protection and market regulation from April 2012) is currently responsible for governing the promotion of financial products and services in the UK.

Many firms appear to assume that a communication made using new media is an 'image advertisement' and exempt from the financial promotion rules. An image advertisement only consists of the following: the name of the firm, a logo or other image associated with the firm, a contact point and a reference to the types of regulated activities provided by the firm or to its fees or commissions. When a communication goes beyond the definition of image advertising in any way, it will need to comply with all of the relevant financial promotions rules.

New media channels include social networking websites (Twitter and Facebook), forums, blogs and smart phone apps (applications).

In February 2010 the FSA conducted a review of approximately 30 Twitter and Facebook pages using different search terms within the financial sector. They looked at the pages containing a wide range of promotions, including those from small and larger firms that offered a wide range of products, such as financial advice and investments.

They reported that the review had identified good and poor practice among firms who had adopted the use of new media to communicate financial promotions.

Some promotions lacked risk warnings. Other promotions, while not very specific about products or services, nevertheless went beyond the definition of image advertising. Firms may not have considered these factors to meet the definition of a financial promotion and therefore have not applied the relevant communication rules.

It is important to consider whether social media channels are a suitable method for the type of communication. For example, Twitter limits the number of characters that can be used, which may be insufficient to provide balanced and sufficient information.

It is also important to consider whether it is possible for risk information to be displayed prominently and clearly, in compliance with the financial promotion regime, using social media channels.

Confidentiality

One reason for banks' lack of presence, dialogue and engagement through social media may be their concern over how to ensure confidentiality while engaging with customers through highly public channels. Authenticating the identity of the customer from the information available on a Tweet, for example, is extremely difficult.

There is an implied term of the contract between customers and their banks and building societies that these firms will keep their customers' information confidential. This confidentiality is not just confined to account transactions – it extends to all the information that the bank has about the customer.

In the UK, this requirement is enshrined in case law (Tournier v National Provincial and

Union Bank of England 1924), industry rules (the Banking Code) and statute (the Data Protection Act 1998).[lxviii]

This does not prevent banks from using social media channels as a 'listening post' and engaging customers through these channels, provided that they follow the agreed ID&V procedures. These ensure that both parties can be confident about confidentiality, while ensuring that the channels remain highly effective.

'#Fail' – dealing with customer complaints

Twitter and Facebook have rapidly become powerful media for consumers to vent their dissatisfaction with suppliers, and many organizations have responded to the challenge and strengthened their reputations.

Financial services are more highly regulated than most other commercial activities. But the regulators themselves may not have fully grasped the relevance of social media in consumers' minds.

In its advice to consumers about complaining to their bank, the UK Financial Ombudsman Service encourages them to complain in writing or by telephone. No advice is given to consumers concerning social media.

The Handbook of the UK Financial Services Authority (FSA) says that the "definition of a complaint includes 'any oral or written expression of dissatisfaction, whether justified or not … about the provision of, or failure to provide, a financial service' where the complainant 'has suffered (or may suffer) financial loss, material distress or material inconvenience'. Firms' complaint-handling procedures should allow complaints to be made by any reasonable means. Firms should not attempt to limit the way customers can complain, for example, by requiring customers to make their complaint in writing (when other options are available). For example, allowing complaints to be made via all customer communication channels used by the firm (in branch, by letter, by email, by fax, by telephone etc.)." No mention of social media.

Some banks respond to complaint tweets by 'following' the tweeter and sending them a non-public 'Message' (formerly known as a Direct Message) to acknowledge the complaint and start the formal complaint process using another channel of the customer's choice. The challenge for banks is to be certain that they are dealing with a genuine customer from their Twitter or Facebook name – these don't always match the customer information that they hold (they are generally unregulated by social media sites). By listening to the customer, and responding quickly with helpful information about complaining, the bank may be able to manage customer expectations.

It is hard to imagine that most complaints could be expressed and satisfactorily resolved through 140-character messages (banks also need to store details of the complaint to comply with the regulator). In reality most complaints received via social media will require the customer to use another channel.

But this calls for a clear social media strategy and clear guidance to customers on how the bank will engage them through social media. Unfortunately, research by Intelligence Delivered (Asia) appears to reveal a deafening silence from banks and the universal lack of guidance on their public web sites.

Social media and risk management

"What happens in Vegas, stays in Vegas" was used to promote the city of Las Vegas by R&R Partners in 1998 and found its way into popular culture. It is probably truer now to say, "What happens in Vegas stays on Facebook/Twitter/Flickr/YouTube…"

Social media are a two-way communications street.

Once a bank starts to consider its social media strategy it is inevitable that it will ask itself this question: "How might we use social media to manage risk?"

They might ask themselves how might they use social media to manage their credit risk more effectively, in lending money, managing delinquent customers and collecting overdue money. It has been done and there is already litigation as a result of overzealous debt collectors using social media to locate and contact delinquent customers.[lxix]

In an effort to combat insurance fraud, one can imagine how insurance companies might be interested in considering an insurance claim based upon the person's status or location at the time of the reported loss.

Developing a social media strategy

Until banks are able to overcome these problems their presence on social media will be as limited observers rather than as active players. At present, whilst some banks have an official presence on these new channels, they are generally not actively promoting the brand and their sites are outweighed by unofficial or pressure groups who, deliberately or not, undermine the bank's brand.

Intelligence Delivered (Asia) suggests that banks need to consider the following topics:

- Are social media a marketing tool or more? Do banks have a social media strategy? Does that include marketing as well as complaint handling and risk management? Without a clear strategy banks will continue to miss out on the positive engagement benefits and may end up in trouble if they don't comply with their own guidance.
- Can a bank get its marketing message over in 140 characters or less? And how do FSA regulations impact or restrict what a bank can display? Many banks have failed to recognise that social media are not different from traditional media when it comes to advertising and promotion.
- Recognise that social media are where people now talk about your brand. Traditional wisdom states that the average number of people you tell after a bad customer experience is 11. What happens in a world where the average number of Facebook friends is 130? As a minimum, banks can use social media as a listening post or early warning system to detect changing customer needs and sentiment or growing dissatisfaction or problems.

An effective social media strategy requires the banks to do the following:

- Change their mindset. Social media use is unlike their current business and organisational model where customers are largely captive in their channels. Customers see channels very differently from banks, which have largely failed to recognise the change in customer behaviour and attitudes. As a result, some banks have tried to control social media or failed to appreciate their power. Banks have many fears about losing control of the conversation with the customer, especially from a compliance point of view.

- Understand and articulate how the organisation will use social media. Will it use Facebook, Twitter and YouTube to market to customers? If so, how will it make its marketing relevant to that social media user? Or for consumer advocacy? Will it open up Twitter and Facebook as a complaints listening post, and how will it handle what it hears? Will it use YouTube to market products or help customers understand how to manage their finances better – without pushing products down their throat? Or will they use it to promote how customers can join banks in non-financial social issues, such as climate change or financial social inclusion?

- Recruit people who understand customer behaviour in social networks. Most people in banks use social media in a personal capacity, but few understand how to communicate and build reputation in this new environment. Most senior executives are dismissive or fearful of social media (there are well publicised failures and examples of misuse that prove the point). But, social media use is a fact that won't go away, will only get more powerful and intertwined in everyday life. Senior executives will only overcome their fear by engaging with social media themselves, with guidance of experts.

- Set aside resources and budget to do it properly. Once you start you'll be expected to maintain your presence in the conversation and will need to keep it relevant. How do you get people to come to your social media sites and engage with you (when 'build it and they will come' may not work)? Experiment and learn, engaging customers in the evolution process to find what suits them and your brand best.

- Explain to customers and social media users how the bank uses social media, such as Facebook and Twitter, and how it can help them communicate better, ensuring that customers are aware of the risks of using public environments to communicate about financial matters. Customers are learning about social media too.

- Provide clear policy guidance on social media to employees and third parties who deliver services on behalf of the bank. Rigorously enforce the policy internally.

- Banks think that social media will make them money like other channels, but social media use isn't about selling, it is about communicating and building reputation in the 21st Century. Forget the return on investment (ROI) for social media. It's not about the ROI. If you're not there, you don't know who's talking about you!

- Social media are a tool for reaching customers and prospective customers, before a competitor does.

Finally, a cautionary note

Banks can get paranoid about social media. This can backfire. This was demonstrated in an article by Ewin Hannan, Industrial editor, The Australian on 5 February 2011.[lxx]

The Australian reported that The Commonwealth Bank of Australia threatened its employees with disciplinary action, including dismissal, if they did not report criticism of the bank made by others on social media channels, including Facebook. The story spread rapidly … through the social media.

The policy has since been reviewed, but it is ironic that the report was first published in a newspaper, republished in the on-line version and then widely disseminated via the very social media channels it sought to control! Any social media policy must be fair and reasonable if it is not to lead to reputational damage.

Banks also need to avoid setting unreasonable objectives for their social media strategy. According to the Aite Group: "Social media objectives are unrealistic. By 2012, two-thirds of financial institutions will look to social media to increase customer retention, and nearly half will expect to generate revenue from their social media efforts. These objectives are wishful thinking on the part of financial services marketers, and consistent with past delusions of marketing success. Marketers have expected increases in retention and cross-selling as a result of adoption in online banking, online bill pay and – more recently – e-bills and personal financial management."[lxxi]

Chapter 7 – The branch network

For most people, banks are an awkward stop on the way to the shop,
in a street where parking is impossible

HSBC presentation

THE ROLE OF THE BRANCH

Most books on channels start by considering the branch. This is the oldest channel and the traditional channel by which banks have serviced their customers.

However, the role of the branch has undergone great change over the last half century. The original customer service role was replaced by a general sales role and, most recently, by a high-value sales role.

Evolution of the branch

It is not the intention of this book to deal with industrial archaeology, but we will outline some of the critical factors in this evolution.

Branches were developed before the modern communications infrastructure and were the only way in which banks could service their customers at the time. The development of modern communications technology, and later information technology, allowed the banks to centralise the customer servicing function.

This reached its height in the 1980s, when the banks took advantage of new technology to centralise most customer service functions into processing centres. Until this time, the vast majority of branch space (some figures say 80 per cent) had been devoted to 'back office' customer service activities. The introduction of processing centres greatly reduced both the space and the number of staff required in branches.

This is an issue that presents a constant challenge for the banks. It has been said that all overhead costs are fixed in the short term. This is particularly true of branch costs. Space cannot be released overnight, and reducing staff costs and numbers is also a lengthy process. This was even truer in the 1980s, where many branches were held freehold or on long leases and a paternalistic management style made banks reluctant to make staff redundant on a compulsory basis.

The removal of customer servicing into processing centres led to the idea of converting 'tellers to sellers'. The role of front-line branch staff was changed from customer service to sales.

This gave rise to a number of problems. Some staff who had been recruited for a customer service role faced motivational problems. They were given training, but some of them lacked sales skills. A more fundamental problem was that the banks did not have the information to target sales. This led to a shotgun approach, in which customers may have been offered products that they did not want or that were inappropriate to their needs.

The distribution strategy

As we discussed in chapter 1, another feature of earlier distribution models was that they were branch-centric. Customer relationships were owned by a branch and all information technology systems and other channels were peripheral to the branch operation.

The modern view of the branch is more sophisticated. It forms part of an integrated distribution strategy and it fulfils a number of roles.

The main economic function and primary role of the branch is, as it has been since the 1980s, sales. However, the emphasis now is on supporting high-value sales.

Branches host a number of services relating to high-value customers and the sale of high-value products. They provide a base from which relationship managers and the specialist sales forces, such as mortgage advisers and financial planners, can operate. They provide a location at which the sale of complex products can be closed.

They also provide a physical point of presence. Branch location is still an important factor when customers decide to open an account. Customers are believed to find the existence of branches reassuring, which is why traditional branches were designed to emphasise solidity.

Branches are also important during crises. The call centres and Internet sites may be overloaded, but customers can still queue at the branch to get their money.

Branches have an important role in the recruitment of new customers. We have already said that branch location is an important factor in people's choice of bank, and branches act as a memory jogger to remind people of the bank's existence. People also tend to see all banks as offering a very similar level of service, so branch location is as a good a differentiator as any.

Branches provide an opportunity for banks to gather information about their customers. This comes from the face-to-face nature of the branch interaction. This information can then be used to generate marketing leads.

Branches provide a human face for the bank. This allows customers to develop an emotional engagement with the branch that cannot be achieved through other channels.

Branches still have an important customer service role, but they increasingly fulfil this by hosting a range of self-service and virtual channels such as automated teller machines (ATMs), paying in machines, enquiry terminals, and links to virtual services such as telephone banking and Internet banking.

BRANCH PROFITABILITY

The branch channel has high fixed costs and low variable costs. Fixed costs are costs that must be paid irrespective of the volume of business. Variable costs are costs that vary depending on the amount of business. Staff costs in a branch are fixed in the short term because staff have to be paid even if no-one uses the branch. The cost of agents in call centres is much easier to vary because call centres are able to use shift patterns to make sure that they only have the number of agents they need. Staff costs in call centres are not completely variable – the staff still have to be paid – but are much closer to being variable than the cost of branch staff.

This cost structure means that branch profitability is strongly affected by transaction volume. High volumes allow the banks to spread the fixed costs over a larger number of transactions, reducing average costs and increasing branch profitability.

Therefore the banks face a challenge. A high proportion of branch footfall – the number of customers visiting the branch – is made up of people carrying out routine transactions such as withdrawing cash and paying in cheques or cash. But the use of cash and (particularly) cheques is in decline. The number of cheques issued each day in the UK in 2009 was 3.5 million, down from 11 million in 1990, and is expected to fall further to 1.6 million by 2018.[lxxii] How can the banks continue to ensure sufficient transaction volume to meet fixed branch costs in the face of declining volumes of the bread and butter payment instruments, cash and cheques?

A number of different approaches have been tried, and the key is to be relevant to your customers. One Swedish bank has opened branches in small, rural, farming communities. This is the type of location that many banks would avoid, but they have the important characteristic that they operate cash-based economies. A small, local branch focused on cash-based services offers a low-cost method for meeting local needs.

Some American banks have set aside space for local community activities.[lxxiii] This increases footfall, increases engagement with the local community and makes use of space released by the centralisation of processing.

BRANCH LOCATION

Branch location is critical in generating footfall. Many banks traditionally located branches in High Street sites. They generated high footfall, at a time when the High Street was the main shopping street, and their prominent locations in high rent areas emphasised the banks' financial strength.

But people do not shop in High Streets as much as they used to. Few High Streets offer much in the way of parking, and shoppers need to be able to use their cars. Most shopping now takes place in supermarkets or retail parks, which have their own dedicated parking areas. This has reduced footfall near to the traditional High Street branches.

The problem is that there does not seem to be a natural replacement location for the High Street branch. The obvious solution – putting full service branches in retail parks and shopping malls – has not been very successful in practice.

Putting branches in supermarkets raises a number of issues. In-store branches, which do not offer the same range of products and services as full service branches, have been quite successful in the United States, less so in Europe. Some European supermarkets, especially in the UK and in countries such as France, have their own banks, but even these rarely operate in-store branches. Supermarket banking is discussed in more detail in chapter 10. In-store branches are discussed further below.

The critical issues for choosing a location for a branch are catchment area, footfall and site availability. Banks also need to consider the social impact of branch location.

Catchment area

The catchment area for the branch is the area from which it can draw customers. Distance is a factor, but other considerations include street access and public transport. Banks can use sophisticated mapping software and Geographic Information Systems (GISs) to identify appropriate locations for their branches.

The ideal catchment area for a full service branch will include a large number of customers having high-value products and will be an area in which levels of personal disposable income are high. This combination allows the branch to fulfil its customer service and customer recruitment roles.

Branch services may also be tailored according to the demographic of the catchment area. For example, a branch with a catchment area with a high proportion of migrants may place a greater emphasis on services such as remittances.

Footfall

Footfall is a measure of the number of people passing the branch. Ideally, branches should be located where there is high footfall both for the convenience of existing customers and to maximise the opportunities for customer recruitment.

If a branch does not have much footfall, it becomes a destination branch. In other words, customers and potential customers need to make a special journey to get to the branch.

Site availability

The availability of a suitable site is an obvious requirement. The location and the property must be appropriate to the bank – usually on a main road and in well-maintained premises.

Floor space is important. The removal of processing from the branches puts a premium on floor space that can be directly accessed by the customer, especially space on the ground floor. The site must be large enough, but not too large.

Security is another issue. This includes both the physical security of the branch and the safety of customers and staff entering or leaving it.

Many banks used to buy branches on a freehold or long lease basis. This meant that they were locked into premises that became unsuitable as customer shopping habits and the functions carried out by branches changed. Short-term leases have become more common in the UK, with major sites often being developed by the bank and financed on a sale and leaseback basis.

Banks in other countries may continue to buy freehold or long lease properties, especially if there are tax advantages to doing so. For example, some countries may allow property values to be written down to a nominal value in the first few years, allowing banks to create useful hidden reserves.

Social impact

The drivers that force banks to take account of the social impact of their decisions on branch location are governments and the media.

Government pressure on the Mexican banks to provide easier access to accounts and services led to innovative, low-cost solutions including delivering banking services through retailers such as 7 to Eleven stores.

Media pressure on British banks led to a 'last branch in town' convention by which they were very reluctant to close a branch if it was the last bank branch in a town. Royal Bank of Scotland included this in their customer charter, although they have been accused of breaking this pledge.[lxxiv] Royal Bank of Scotland is not the only British bank to be accused of disregarding the convention.[lxxv]

Types of location

It is possible to classify branches as: City centre, High Street, edge of town, and out of town.[lxxvi] City centre branches are destination branches. They usually offer the full range of banking services to both personal and business customers.

High Street branches are a legacy from the time when customers used the High Street for most of their shopping. They usually offer the full range of banking services, predominantly for retail customers. Villages also have High Streets, and High Street branches located in villages may offer a more restricted range of services. Mergers led to many banks having more than one branch in the same High Street. These additional branches have usually been closed.

Edge of town branches may be so located because rents are lower, to service a particular group of customers or to take advantage of a particular demographic. They will often offer a more limited range of services than the High Street branches.

Out of town branches are usually so located to take advantage of the high footfall in out of town shopping centres, retail parks or business parks. As has been discussed, these have not been particularly successful and may offer a limited range of services as a result.

BRANCH LAYOUT

Branches are traditionally divided into a customer-facing area, the front office, and a processing area, the back office. The back office was the largest part until the removal of processing in the 1980s.

Until this happened, the front office had little space available. Most of this was occupied by the counter operation, with some space for self-service channels (ATMs and paying in machines) and an interview room.

The removal of the back office has allowed the banks to take advantage of the experience of retailers. The front office is typically zoned into areas for: Reception, self-service channels, virtual channels, marketing displays, interview space and counter operations.

The self-service channels and (sometimes) the virtual channels can be made accessible 24 hours a day by placing them in a lobby (lobby banking) partitioned from the rest of the branch. ATMs and (sometimes) paying in machines can also be located on the outside wall of the bank, and ATMs can also be located at other sites such as supermarkets, shopping centres and railway stations.

Branches may have a reception area. This allows branch staff to assist customers with the use of the self-service channels and virtual channels. Other functions of the reception staff include answering general queries and steering customers away from the counter at busy times.

Self-service channels are discussed below.

Virtual channels may include Internet connections and telephones that can only be used for Internet banking and telephone banking. Internet banking and telephone banking are discussed elsewhere in this text.

Marketing displays include product information and application forms. Marketing displays are sometimes placed in the queuing area for the counter.

Interview space is increasingly open plan, although branches may have at least one closed interview room for confidential matters. Even in the open plan interview areas, care must be taken to make sure that sensitive information is not visible to people outside the interview area, for example by placing computer screens so that they face the wall.

The counter operation allows customers to transact business. There may be separate windows for business customers and *bureau de change* activities, and terminals at other counter positions may not be able to carry out some of these operations. Although business and foreign exchange customers have priority for using these windows, other customers may be allowed to use them at busy times.

Note that branches still have back offices. Much of their work is concerned with the preparation of work for submission to the central processing centres. They also have responsibility for administration, risk and compliance.

SERVICES

Of all the channels available, branches can offer the widest range of service. These can be categorised as: Transaction processing, sales, relationship management, and servicing.

Transaction processing includes paying in, encashment and currency exchange. Customers can use the counter for all of these, and self-service channels allow paying in and encashment.

Sales can be classified into the sale of simple products and of complex products.

Simple products include products such as credit cards that can be sold by unqualified staff with minimal training. The bank incurs little regulatory risk on the sale of simple products. However, profit margins are quite low. Sales of simple products may occur through counter positions or using virtual channels. Self-service channels can also be used. For example, ATMs are the main channel for loan applications in Mexico.

Complex products include products such as mortgages and investments. Staff selling these products must be trained and, for some complex products in some countries, must be qualified. The bank incurs a high level of regulatory risk as a result. Profit margins are quite high and customers may stay with the same provider for many years, further increasing the profitability of these products. The process of buying a complex product often involves several stages using multiple channels. The regulatory risk element of the sale means that it is usually closed face-to-face, either in one of the interview areas in the branch or at the customer's home or place of work.

Relationship management includes opening current accounts, sanctioning lending, analysing customer needs and managing the relationship. Some of these activities, for example sanctioning lending, may actually take place at a central site. Relationship management activities involve face-to-face contact, often in one of the interview areas or at the customer's home or place of work, and back office activities.

Regulatory risk and the requirement for increased price transparency imposed by the Financial Services Authority's Retail Distribution Review have made banks in the UK much less willing to provide advice in branches, undermining the 'trusted adviser' role mentioned in chapter 3. HSBC have recently[lxxvii] followed Barclays in reducing the number of financial adviser posts. HSBC plans to offer a free, but very basic, advice service for mass-market customers and a paid-for service for affluent (premier and private banking) customers.

Servicing includes keeping account and customer information up-to-date, managing regular payments (standing orders and direct debits), statements and customer enquiries. Customers can use virtual channels, self-service channels or the counter for these activities. Many of them also involve the back office.

Types of branch

Not all branches offer all of these services. We can distinguish between: full service branches, tailored service branches and virtual branches.

Full service branches, as the name indicates, offer the full range of the bank's services. Depending on their location, they may only offer these services to retail customers, or they may offer them to the bank's entire customer base.

Tailored service branches offer a subset of services, tailored to the needs of their customers. They will usually offer transaction processing, servicing and the sale of simple products. Their offerings in the sale of complex products and relationship management may be more limited and may use self-service channels such as kiosks.

In-store branches are an example of a tailored service branch. They are common in the United States, less so in Europe. In store branches have lower costs than traditional branches and earn more from the sale of simple products (one might speculate that they benefit from higher footfall). However, they earn less than traditional branches from the sale of the more valuable complex products.[lxxviii] A number of American banks have recently closed their in-store branch networks.[lxxix]

Virtual branches are unmanned branches that rely entirely on self-service channels and virtual channels. They can provide a surprisingly wide range of services, including transaction processing, sales and servicing. Lobby banking allows full service and tailored service branches to provide a 24x7 (24 hours a day, 7 days a week) service by acting as virtual branches outside of normal opening hours.

Self-service channels

The main self-service channels are paying-in machines, ATMs and kiosks. Some banks also deploy specialist machines such as statement printers.

There has always been a need for customers, especially business customers, to pay in money outside banking hours. This was originally met by the night safe. This did not have any processing capability and simply provided a secure place for businesses to deposit their day's takings – branch staff carried out all processing the following day.

This changed in the 1960s when the first automated paying-in machine was introduced in the United States. However, it was withdrawn after six months due to poor customer acceptance.

Paying-in machines were re-introduced and are now a widely used self-service channels. Most of the old night safes have been replaced by paying-in machines dedicated to the use of business customers. These allow bulk cash to be paid in and are separate from the paying-in machines used by personal customers. There may be separate machines for paying-in cash (banknotes) and cheques.

Some paying-in machines can image the documents fed in, which allows the bank to provide the customer with proof of deposit.

ATMs were also developed during the 1960s, in Japan, Sweden, the UK and the United States, as devices for withdrawing cash. The early machines used a token that had to be purchased in advance, but the introduction of magnetic strip technology allowed customers to draw funds directly from their accounts. The magnetic strip also held security information.

The functions available through ATMs have expanded greatly and can now include balance enquiries, mini-statements, inter-account transfers and mobile phone top up. We have already mentioned that they can be used to request loans in Mexico.

Kiosks, or assisted Internet terminals, can be used to provide product information and to facilitate the sale of complex products. For example, a customer can use a kiosk to apply for an insurance policy by entering information into the terminal. The kiosk can then print an application form, which also gives policy details, which the customer can take away to study. Customers who are happy with the policy will sign it and return it to the bank. Kiosks may also have video conferencing capabilities, allowing customers to contact staff to discuss problems or to get information.

Journeys

Face-to-face contact within a branch is often the final point of a journey, the point at which the sale is closed. This is also the most expensive part of the journey for the bank and, therefore, the banks try to maximise closures. To do this, they must ensure that customers receive as much information as possible at the earlier stages to ensure that the face-to-face meeting goes as smoothly as possible.

Consider investments. The traditional approach was for the customer to meet with a financial planner for the initial fact find. The financial planner would produce a list of recommendations for the customer's consideration at a follow up meeting. The sales funnel involved three stages (fact find, follow up meeting, closure) and the conversion rate was typically about 14% (i.e. seven fact finds produced three follow up meetings and only one sale). This is not a very good conversion rate and Barclays and HSBC recently announced that they would no longer be offering this type of financial planning service.

An alternative approach, used by Hargreaves Lansdown, makes use of a wider range of channels. The Hargreaves Lansdown website provides customers with full information and answers to the majority of questions. It also gives customers the opportunity to speak to an agent if they are unable to get answers from the website. The Internet and the agent act as filters, ensuring that Hargreaves Lansdown's advisors are only contacted when absolutely necessary.

Chapter 8 – The contact centre

THE EVOLUTION OF TELEPHONE BANKING

The banks' use of the telephone as a delivery channel has gone through a number of different phases, which we can categorise as: branch-based, call centre and contact centre.

One way of using the telephone as a channel is to give customers the branch telephone number, and this was the approach initially adopted. There are a number of ways of doing this. The number could be given to selected customers, for example business customers or customers with large balances. The number could be included on branch letterheads, ensuring that it is available to anyone to whom the bank writes. The number could be published through a telephone directory.

This was not telephone banking, in the sense that we now understand the term. Instead, it was a new method by which customers could use the branch channel.

One problem with all telephone-based delivery methods is that of establishing the caller's identity. This is the problem of identification and verification (ID&V) that we discussed in respect of the Internet in chapter 6. If branch telephone numbers were only made available to a small number of customers, it is likely that staff would have been able to recognise their voices. However, this was not possible when branch telephone numbers were published and available to all customers. Therefore staff wishing to establish a customer's identity had to do so by asking questions about the customer's account.

A problem with branch delivery is that branches are not designed to deliver a telephone-based service, and are not very good at it. There are a number of reasons for this. Customers who are in the branch are usually given priority over customers on the telephone. Answering the telephone is only a part-time activity, so managers may assign less experienced staff to the role. Branches do not have access to the same technology as call centres. As a result, many calls to branches went unanswered at busy times.

The next phase was to migrate the branch-based telephone service into centralised call centres. This was the result of a number of technological innovations, of which the most important were the Powerdialler and the predictive dialler for outbound call centres, and the Automated Call Distributor (ACD) and Computer Telephony Integration (CTI) for inbound call centres.

Outbound call centres are mainly used for sales, and inbound call centres are most important in the context of telephone banking. The majority of banks treated the new telephone service as an extension of the branch channel, following the add-on business model.

There are legitimate reasons for this. Research has showed that customers are reluctant to migrate from a branch-based telephone service to a call centre telephone service.[lxxx] One reason given was that customers were concerned about the need for transfers if the call centre agent was unable to deal with the query.

This desire to imitate the branch had the unfortunate effect of limiting banks' attempts to exploit the new channel. Only one new service, that of bill payments, was introduced when telephone banking migrated to the call centre.

There was one exception. Midland Bank, now part of HSBC, introduced an add-on telephone bank, aimed at its own customers. It also developed a baby bank, First Direct. First Direct was deliberately kept separate from its parent and was designed as a branchless, telephone-only bank aimed at wealthier customers (demographic group ABC1). First Direct successfully attracted customers from all of the High Street banks.

Banks were slower to deploy outbound call centres, as they were more interested in using the telephone channel for customer service than for telemarketing. However, they do use outbound call centres in areas such as the recovery of overdue or over-limit loans (collections).

The next major innovation was the introduction of automated agent technology. This used methods such as Interactive Voice Response (IVR) and speech recognition to replace human operators with a computer.

The final phase has seen the transformation of the call centre into a contact centre. Instead of being an appendix to the branch, or a dedicated telephone banking service, the contact centre is also responsible for supporting Internet banking by offering the web chat and call me services.

The role of the contact centre

There was a time when the call centre was seen as an intermediate technology. It offered neither the emotional engagement of the branch nor the very low cost of the Internet, and there was a belief that it would gradually disappear as Internet penetration increased towards 100 per cent.

This has been replaced by a view that sees the contact centre as playing a pivotal role in supporting the branch and Internet channels. This is illustrated by a slide from a Finalta presentation that illustrates how the role of the contact centre has evolved:

Figure 8 – Evolution of the contact centre

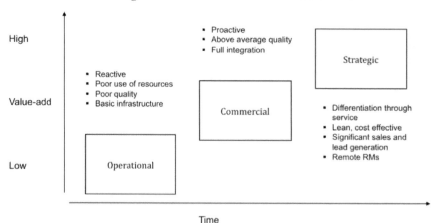

Source: Finalta Limited research

SERVICES

Telephone banking can be used for transaction processing, sales and servicing.

Transaction processing is restricted to non-cash transactions such as inter-account transfers. As mentioned above, bill payments is a new service that was introduced with telephone banking.

There is little scope for sales through fully automated telephone banking systems. Sales through telephone banking systems using human agents are usually restricted to the sale of simple products, although specialist contact centres (for example, mortgage helplines) have a greater capacity to sell complex products.

Contact relevance is an important issue. Outbound call centres place calls to potential customers. These interrupt what the customer is doing and, unless they are of high relevance to the customer's needs, are unlikely to result in a sale. Therefore outbound call centres should use Customer Relationship Management (CRM) systems to ensure that they are targeting customers who are likely to be interested in the product.

There used to be a view that inbound contact centres should not be used as a sales channel. There are differences in both skills and incentives between inbound and outbound centres. A better understanding of the issue of contact relevance is leading to a relaxation of this view. The CRM system can be used to provide leads to products that are of high relevance to the customer even in an inbound contact centre.

Servicing includes maintaining customer and account information, managing regular payments and customer enquiries. Fully automated systems may have limited capabilities because of the restrictions imposed by the telephone keypad.

TECHNOLOGY

Contact centres rely on technology.

The Automated Call Distributor (ACD) accepts telephone calls and routes them to agents. Different telephone numbers can be routed in to the same ACD that, for example, allows banks to give different numbers for general telephone banking and for mortgage advice. The ACD is aware of the number dialled and can route the call to an agent with the appropriate training. The ACD also collects information and statistics about calls, for example waiting times and call duration.

Computer Telephony Integration (CTI) allows telephone calls and computer information to move together. CTI is used when an agent transfers a call, to ensure that the customer does not need to repeat information. CTI used to be very important for the ID&V process, where 'blind transfers' were used to allow customers to change their passwords anonymously. Automated agents are now used for this, and CTI is less important than it used to be for transfers between human agents. However, it is still important for transfers between automated agents and human agents.

Automated agents are computer programs that can be used to answer calls. The ACD can route calls to automated agents in exactly the same way as it can route calls to human agents. Automated agents do not necessarily need to be able to take information from the caller (for example, they can be used for general information), but they usually do. Two technologies can be used: IVR and speech recognition.

IVR recognises the tones emitted by the telephone keypad. IVR is often used for menus, allowing the customer to choose an enquiry or transaction. IVR is also used for ID&V. IVR is a very robust technology, but is limited by the amount of information that can be entered using the telephone keypad. The term 'voice mail jail' has been used to describe the apparently endless series of menus that seems to be a feature of some IVR systems.

IVR automated agent technology is often used in conjunction with a human agent. The caller is initially connected to the automated agent. This is used for the ID&V procedures and to present the caller with a menu of choices. Some of these, for example a balance enquiry or a change of security information, are dealt with by the automated agent. If the caller needs to be connected to a human agent, CTI is used to transfer both the call and the associated computer records.

Speech recognition systems recognise human speech. The older Automated Speech Recognition systems required the speaker to pause between words. These have been largely replaced by Intelligent Speech Recognition, which can recognise continuous speech. Speech recognition technology has a wide range of applications, especially in 'hands free' environments. The limitations of speech recognition systems include a limited vocabulary and having problems with regional accents, but this is a technology that is improving all the time.

Responders are computer systems that interpret and respond to text. This may be email, text messages from mobile phones or messages sent through the bank's website. Responders use artificial intelligence methods to interpret what the message is about and send a standard reply, which may be in the form of a Frequently Asked Questions (FAQ) sheet. The response will usually also tell customers how to contact the bank if the reply does not meet their needs.

Scripting acts a bit like an Autocue, prompting human agents with what they need to say to the caller. Scripting is important for two reasons. Callers dialling different telephone numbers may be routed to the same agent, and scripting allows the agent to respond differently depending on the number dialled. More important, scripting makes sure that the agent includes any statements that are required for legal reasons. For example, the sale of shares through a call centre in the UK must be on an execution only basis (i.e. no advice is given) unless the agent is qualified. Scripting ensures that the agent will say that the sale is on an execution only basis.

Voice over IP (VoIP) uses the Internet to carry telephone voice messages. This allows telephone calls to be made at a lower cost. The banks use VoIP in their Call Me services.

Powerdiallers are used in outbound call centres. They take a computer file of names and telephone numbers and place calls to them. If the call is answered, the Powerdialler routes it to an agent if one is free. If no agent is free, the Powerdialler may terminate the call (this is called a silent call) or may ask the person answering the call to hold. Some countries may fine organizations that make too many silent calls, as these may be classified as nuisance calls.

Predictive diallers work in much the same way as Powerdiallers. The difference is that predictive diallers only place a call when they expect that an agent will be free when the call is answered. This reduces the number of silent calls.

Hunt groups are an older technology that is used in offices rather than call centres. If a telephone is not answered in a certain number of rings, often three, the call is automatically transferred to the next telephone in the hunt group (and may go to a contact centre). Hunt groups are widely used in environments such as business banking and premier banking, where customers are given a personal telephone number for their relationship manager.

Virtual call centres use agents who are not physically located in the call centre. They may even work from home.[lxxxi] Virtual call centres are feasible because the ACD can route calls anywhere. They are not widely used in the financial services industry, perhaps because of security concerns.

SECURITY

The telephone, like the Internet, relies on two-factor authentication for ID&V. The caller needs to give three pieces of information, one of which establishes the caller's identity and the other two verify and authenticate it. An important restriction with the telephone is that ID&V procedures are usually limited by the use of the telephone keypad.

The caller is usually first asked to enter either a credit card number or a sort code and account number. This identifies the caller. The caller may then be asked to enter a memorable date, such as a birthday, and two digits from a Personal Identification Number (PIN). Dates are often used because they are numbers and can be easily entered using the keypad.

Speech recognition can be used as an alternative to the keypad. The process is the same, although a password may be used instead of a PIN.

Voice recognition, which should not be confused with speech recognition, can also be used. Everybody's voice has a unique voiceprint that can be used to identify him or her. The main problem with using voice recognition over the telephone is that it is dependent on the quality of the microphone. However, it can be used.

Email is usually sent from within the bank's own website (secure email) and the ID&V process is that used for Internet banking. Public email is not secure. Instructions received through the public email system should not be accepted and it should never be used to send confidential information.

Web chat is sent from the bank's own website. However, it is not always necessary for the customer to complete the Internet banking ID&V to use web chat. Confidential information should only be sent if ID&V has been completed.

The identity of the sender of a text message sent from a mobile phone using the Short Message Service (SMS) cannot be authenticated. The channel is widely used for alerts and balances, but banks need to be aware that they cannot guarantee that the customer receives these messages. Therefore they need to ensure that the quantity of confidential information is kept to a minimum and that the terms and conditions for the use of the service provide the bank with adequate protection.

OPERATIONAL MODELS

There are a number of different ways to operate a telephone banking service. We will draw a distinction between four of these: automated agent, offshore contact centre, onshore contact centre and named contact. As has already been indicated, automated agent systems are often used as an entry point to a human agent in a contact centre.

Automated agent

A telephone banking service can be fully automated using automated agent (usually IVR) technology. It works through a series of menus, which usually limits it to a range of simple services such as balance enquiries and inter-account transfers. Speech recognition technology allows a slightly wider range of services to be offered.

Purely automated telephone banking services, with no option to speak to an agent, are usually only offered to basic customers. They are a very low cost way of providing a service, but they do not offer a good customer experience and they provide few opportunities for the bank to cross sell or up-sell.

Offshore contact centre

Offshore, in this context, means located outside the bank's country of operation and outside the country in which most of its customers live. Offshore contact centres are usually located in countries such as India and China, where large numbers of well-educated agents are available at a lower cost than in the United States and Europe.

There are two disadvantages to offshore centres. Some countries impose legal restrictions on the transfer of personal data to other countries. There has been a lot of customer resistance to offshore call centres.

European Union (EU) directive 95/46/EC restricts the transfer of personal data from EU countries to countries outside the European Economic Area unless the country to which the data is being transferred has equivalent data protection legislation or has taken other data protection measures. In practice, countries such as India and China have used contract law to provide this protection.

Customer resistance has proved a more intractable problem and some organizations that transferred their contact centres offshore have subsequently repatriated them. A recent example in the UK is Santander, which announced that it would be repatriating its call centres in July 2011.[lxxxii] Most UK banks now have onshore contact centres.

A number of different reasons have been given. It has been suggested that some customers have difficulty in understanding the accent of agents in other countries. It has also been suggested that customers have a shared cultural experience with agents from their own country, for example as a result of watching the same television programs. This makes them more comfortable with agents from their own country.

Following the global financial crisis, banks are also attempting to rebuild their customers' trust and using British workers gives customers the impression that the bank is more accountable and committed to them.

The nature of the call centre is changing. With many customers now satisfying their simple enquiries on-line, the call centre is dealing with more complex calls that require more skill and empathy.

Finally, the economic justification for offshore call centres is no longer clear. We will discuss this in the next section.

Offshore contact centres were often used for mass market customers.

Onshore contact centre

From the definition of offshore contact centres, it follows that onshore contact centres are located in the country where the majority of the bank's customers live.

Onshore contact centres are usually more expensive than offshore contact centres. Contact centre agents can move job very easily and are able to command premium rates as a consequence. Although this applies both onshore and offshore, the very large number of people available in countries such as India and China has allowed better control of labour costs in offshore centres until recently.

However, there have been signs of cost increases in recent years. Another company that has recently repatriated its call centres from India, New Call Telecom, gave reasons including higher staff turnover (which increases recruitment and training costs), and increases in salaries, property costs and accommodation costs.[lxxxiii] Accenture estimate that UK employees might have been five times more expensive than offshore employees ten years ago. Today it has reduced to something like two-and-a-half times.

An important decision is: how much training to give? Providing more training allows agents to perform more transactions but increases costs. Banks need to analyse how customers use the telephone banking service to determine which transactions customers are most likely to request, and therefore the level of training required. Pareto's Law, which is usually simplified into a form such as, '80 per cent of calls will be for 20 per cent of the available activities' can be used to prioritise training needs.

Specialist contact centres may be set up for events such as handling the affairs of deceased customers. These require specialist knowledge and a high level of training. Specialist contact centres and contact centres used for premier customers were usually located onshore, even when the banks' mass market contact centres were located offshore. The higher cost was justified by the higher customer lifetime value.

Named contact

The customers of the greatest value to the bank may be given telephone numbers for a named contact. These may direct the caller to an individual or a team. For some customers, for example private banking and corporate banking customers, this may include out-of-hours contact numbers.

Banks usually try to operate relationship management teams. This avoids the situation where the relationship is too dependent on an individual, with the associated risk that the customer may follow the relationship manager should the manager leave the bank.

MANAGING CONTACT CENTRE AGENTS

Contact centres are organised on industrial lines, and agents are set targets that must be achieved. The ACD or Powerdialler/predictive dialler collects the necessary statistics.

Inbound call centres are targeted on abandonment rates and how quickly calls are answered. The abandonment rate is the percentage of calls where the caller hangs up before the call is answered. The target for how quickly the call is answered is usually expressed in a format such as 90PCA20, which means that 90 per cent of calls must be answered in 20 seconds.

Agents in inbound call centres are targeted on measures such as availability, call duration and wrap up time. Availability is the amount of time that the agent is available to accept calls. Call duration is the length of the call. Wrap up time is the length of time between the agent completing the call and becoming available to accept another call – this wrap up time is usually needed to update records. Agents may also be measured on the use of courtesy words (such as 'please' and 'thank you'). Computer software can be used to analyse calls, or supervisors can listen in on a certain percentage of calls.

Agents in outbound call centres are usually targeted on results – for example sales. They may also be targeted on measures similar to those used for agents in inbound call centres.

Capacity planning

Capacity planning is a critical success factor for inbound contact centres. They must ensure that they have enough agents available to handle the volume of calls that they expect to receive within agreed service levels. However, they do not want to have too many agents available because of the cost.

The ACD provides information about the number of calls received, and this can be used to predict future call volumes. Contact centres may have complex shift patterns, calculated to time periods as short as thirty minutes, to ensure that they have the right number of agents at all times.

CHANNEL SEGMENTATION

Telephone banking is particularly well suited for channel segmentation. Different groups of customers can be given different telephone numbers. These can go to the same inbound contact centre, or different contact centres can be used, with the ACD routing the call to suitably qualified agents and with scripting being used to ensure that customers receive the response they expect.

Many different types of segmentation can be used. These include personal and business; by customer value; by customer product usage; and by life event. Banks can use any of these, or any combination of them, but need to be aware that the more types of segmentation they use the greater the complexity.

RISK

One problem with inbound contact centres is that they can represent a single point of failure. In other words, a failure affecting a contact centre can close the telephone banking service completely.

Therefore contact centres are usually very secure buildings, well protected from both natural disasters (such as floods) and criminal or terrorist activity. They have comprehensive disaster recovery plans.

Most large banks have at least two inbound contact centres, with arrangements to switch calls between them if one experiences problems. Smaller banks may have arrangements that allow them to use a specialist disaster recovery site.

Chapter 9 – Mobile devices

THE ROLE OF MOBILE BANKING

Mobile devices have provided the banks with another channel for delivering banking services.

Mobile devices include mobile phones and tablets, and present the banks with an opportunity – and a challenge – that is even greater than that presented by the Internet. It could even be said that the future of banking will, to a significant extent, depend on how the banks respond.

The opportunity is the result of four factors: the size of the market, the ability to provide a service to specific target groups, their role as Martini devices and the low cost of delivering services through the channel.

There are two main challenges. One is, as always, security. The other is the threat posed by third parties entering the financial services market.

There are more than five billion mobile phone connections worldwide,[lxxxiv] which creates a huge market for Mobile banking.

Specific targets for Mobile banking include mobile customers and telephone banking customers.

We discussed the idea of customers being fixed or mobile in chapter 3. Mobile customers carry out their transactions in a public place or on the move. They have limited space and little privacy. The mobile phone is an ideal device for allowing them to carry out their banking transactions under these conditions.

We have used the term telephone banking customers to describe customers who do not use Internet banking but who are prepared to use virtual and self-service channels. They currently use call centres, and switching even a small percentage of their transactions to Mobile banking would produce considerable cost savings for the banks. One obstacle to this is the banks themselves, many of which require customers to register for Mobile banking through the Internet.[lxxxv]

The mobile phone is increasingly looking like the ultimate Martini (any time, anyhow, anywhere) banking device as banks and the mobile phone industry include more and more features that can be used to deliver a banking service. 46 per cent of respondents to a recent survey saw the ability to receive messages anytime, anywhere as a benefit of mobile banking.[lxxxvi] It has been pointed out that consumers are more interested than ever in managing their finances actively, and need instant access to financial information to achieve this.[lxxxvii]

Financial services can be delivered through mobile devices at very low cost, with some studies suggesting that the cost of mobile delivery is less than half of the cost of Internet delivery (we will return to this in chapter 11). Mobile phone ownership among the unbanked and underbanked is also reasonably high. This means that Mobile banking may offer banks a solution to the challenge, set by many governments, for social inclusion without investing in branch infrastructures or diluting the service experience of their more valuable customers.

Security must always be a concern with any virtual channel. A particular problem with mobile devices may be the continued addition of new ways of communicating with them – including short-range communications methods such as Bluetooth and Near Field Communication (NFC) – each of which presents its own security problems.

The threat from third parties has existed since the development of the call centre, of course. However, there are two important differences with mobile devices. The first is that the entry costs to the banking market are much lower, as we discussed in chapter 2. The second is that the telecommunications providers – the Telcos – are taking a more active role in trying to enter this market than they did with earlier channel innovations.

As a result, the Mobile channel is becoming an increasingly important component of the banks' distribution strategy. This has been driven by customers and third party providers more than the banks themselves, and as such is an excellent example of third-generation thinking.

THE MOBILE PHONE

What makes the mobile phone such an important channel? It can be used as a telephone to access telephone banking (obviously). 3G smart phones can also be used to access Internet banking.

But mobile phones have a number of other capabilities that can be used to support mobile banking. These include: Short Message Service (SMS), Multimedia Messaging Service (MMS), Near Field Communication (NFC), Global Positioning System (GPS) and Applications (Apps).

SMS is a well-established technology that is used for sending text messages. It is the most widely used data application in the world, and about three quarters of mobile phone subscribers use SMS. It can also be used for sending bar codes, and this has been used by airlines to issue electronic boarding passes.

MMS is used to send multimedia content, particularly pictures, to and from mobile phones.

NFC is a standard that allows devices such as mobile phones to exchange data over a distance of up to about 10 centimetres. NFC is the emerging standard for contactless payment devices and is being built in to mobile phones produced by manufacturers such as Nokia and Samsung.

GPS uses satellites to establish where the mobile phone is. Mobile phones equipped with GPS are said to be 'location aware' and this can be used to alert subscribers to places in their vicinity.

Apps can be loaded on to mobile phones and devices such as tablets, and activated by tapping them. Apple's iOS operating system (used on the iPhone and iPad), Google's Android operating system and the Blackberry operating system can run apps. They have proved very popular with mobile phone users.

Two older technologies, which preceded 3G, were i-mode and Wireless Application Protocol (WAP). These were developed at a time when mobile phone networks did not have enough bandwidth to support a good Internet connection. They provided Internet access, but in a very limited form.

I-mode, which was developed by NTT DoCoMo in Japan, was and continues to be quite successful. WAP was less successful and has been largely replaced by 3G.

MOBILE BANKING

What is Mobile banking? Excluding services accessed by using the mobile phone as a telephone or through the Internet browser, we can identify the following: alerts, balances, apps, personal financial management and payments.

According to a recent survey, the most widely used m-banking services were:

Service	Used by
Check bank account balances	46 per cent
Contact customer service	37 per cent
Locate a nearby ATM or bank branch	30 per cent
Check credit card balances	30 per cent
Transfer money between bank accounts	24 per cent
Receive or pay bills	16 per cent

Source: Syniverse mobile banking survey[lxxxviii]

It is interesting to note that the four most widely used services are queries, rather than transactions.

Customers may be able to request that warning messages – alerts – are sent to them when certain situations arise. Examples might include an account balance falling below an agreed amount or an overseas credit card transaction. These are sent using SMS.

Customers may also be able to request that account balances are sent to them on a regular basis. Again, these are sent using SMS.

Apps

Many banks have developed mobile banking apps since the introduction of iOS and Android powered mobile phones in 2007. Apps have the advantage of being both more familiar and more convenient for customers. These are more user-centric in their design and mimic the apps that users access on a day-to-day basis. However, they must be custom written for each mobile phone operating system.

The advantages of apps include:

- They are designed for a smaller (typically 3") screen and input using a finger. Security is designed to be simple and easily input using the device's virtual keyboard and is usually more intuitive (automatically switching the keyboard to numeric input when the user is expected to enter numbers rather than requiring the user to switch manually).

- Access to services is designed around touch-sensitive icons for use with fingers rather than a mouse, leading to a simpler customer journey and improved customer experience.
- Screens are usually less cluttered than Internet banking sites. Lack of space has led to a rethink, focusing on what customers need rather than what the bank wants them to look at.
- Services are more focused on the needs of mobile customers and on making banking convenient: staying in control of their finances, paying bills and friends (especially when we forget!), finding the nearest ATMs/branches when they need cash.
- Some banks apps allow customers to review their portfolios, review the current state of the market and buy and sell shares. This is particularly common in Hong Kong, where most people build their wealth by investing on the stock exchange.
- Location aware services (using GPS and integrated with the device's own mapping app) allow customers to locate the nearest ATM or branch.
- Location aware services also allow banks to offer their customers deals on dining or other retail opportunities that the bank has negotiated. This builds loyalty, as the discount will only be enjoyed if the customer pays using their bank credit card.
- Some banks allow customers to open simple products, such as single trip travel insurance and time deposits, and to apply for personal instalment loans and mortgages. One Hong Kong bank also allows customers to trade gold on their iPhone.
- It is even possible to call the telephone banking service from an in-app list of services.

What can you do on a mobile phone?

This very much depends on your local market and the following table provides and overview of four mature banking markets: Australia, UK, US and Hong Kong, to provide a flavour of what is possible:

	Australia	UK	US	Hong Kong
Managing my money	✓	✓	✓	✓
Making payments	✓	✓	✓	✓
Foreign currency exchange				✓
Market information				✓
Managing my portfolio				✓
Financial calculators	✓			✓
Open products				✓
ATM/branch locator	✓		✓	✓
Offers				✓

Source: Intelligence Delivered (Asia) Limited research

Managing my money – checking balances and transactions, transferring money between accounts in the same bank.

Making payments – paying bills and making one-off payments to friends and family – for example, sending money for someone's birthday (at the last minute!) or settling half of the bill when 'going dutch'.

Foreign currency exchange – buying and selling foreign currency between different accounts in the same bank, using real-time currency exchange rates.

Market information – local stock exchange indices and news.

Managing my portfolio – buying and selling shares through an investment account.

Financial calculators – personal instalment loan and mortgage repayment calculators, or market-linked foreign currency exchange calculators.

Open products – open simple insurance and savings products and start the application process for more complex products such as personal instalment loans or mortgages.

ATM/Branch locator – location-based (GPS) locator. A simple solution to a common problem.

Offers – location-based (GPS) loyalty-based offers, such as dining or retail rewards if close to a participating retailer, providing the customer uses the bank's credit card.

At first sight it might seem that the capabilities of mobile banking are a step backwards from Internet banking. But the Internet is well developed compared to mobile. Consider:

- Many of the bank apps are in their first release (v1.0) and further functionality is promised in the near future.
- Local regulatory restrictions may limit what customers can do.
- Banks are only now developing an understanding of what customers want from their mobile phone, and how banks might meet their needs.

Another question might be why Hong Kong generally seems to offer more advanced services than the other countries? Part of the explanation is that the Hong Kong market is more orientated towards wealth management and customers are more likely to hold multiple currencies. For example, it is not uncommon for a Hong Kong resident to hold accounts denominated in Hong Kong Dollars, Chinese Renminbi and US Dollars. Additional services have been made available to accommodate this.

MOBILE COMMERCE

Mobile commerce is the use of a mobile phone to purchase goods and services. This can be charged to the mobile phone subscriber's bill, or it can be used in the same way as a prepaid card.

Coca Cola was one of the first companies to introduce this. It developed a drinks dispenser that was activated by a phone call. The cost of the drink was added to the phone bill.

Vendtxt Vending developed vending machines that could be activated by a code. The subscriber would send a text and receive an SMS message in reply that included a four-digit code. This would activate the machine and the cost would appear on the subscriber's phone bill.

Verizon's BilltoMobile system is used to make purchases over the Internet. Subscribers text their mobile phone number and zip code. They receive an SMS message in reply that contains a passcode, which they enter on the retailer's website. The item appears on the subscriber's phone bill. There is a monthly limit, which is currently $25.

ThinkLink's Facecash is one approach that can be used to buy goods in a shop. The subscriber's mobile phone shows a photograph of the subscriber (for security) and a bar code, which the retailer scans. Subscribers have to maintain an account with Facecash and cannot spend more than the balance of their account, which makes it more like PayPal or a prepaid card than the other approaches discussed so far.

Mobile phones can also act as contactless devices. Contactless devices can be used for making small payments by bringing the device close to a reader. Currently the most common contactless device is card-based, either a credit or debit card or a special card. The Octopus card, which was introduced in Hong Kong in 1997, was reported to be handling more than 11 million transactions each day in 2010.[lxxxix] This is made up of a mix of travel transactions (Octopus is primarily used for travel) and small payments. Contactless technology can be included in small devices and, unlike magnetic strip cards, does not have to fit into a reader, so it has also been incorporated into fobs that can fit on a key ring.

The emerging standard for contactless devices appears to be NFC. NFC is now being incorporated into mobile phone handsets (Sony Ericsson has recently announced that it will be incorporating NFC into its phones, joining other manufacturers such as LG, Nokia and Samsung). Therefore using mobile phones as a contactless device is a natural development. Orange and Barclaycard launched the first such service in the UK in May 2011.[xc]

This is an area of business in which the banks' dominance is under threat. In Germany, mobile operators Deutsche Telekom, Vodafone D2 and Telefónica (O2) Germany plan to launch a trial of their own mobile phone payment brand. They will get round the current lack of mobile phones with NFC by allowing customers to attach radio frequency identification (RFID) stickers to their phones.

Note also that customer demand for this type of technology remains unclear. One recent survey showed that only 21 per cent of consumers wanted to be able to pay in a shop using their mobile phones.[xci] An earlier survey showed that only 27 per cent of respondents in Germany, Italy, Spain and the United Kingdom were interested in this.[xcii]

As this is very much an evolving transaction channel, that has an impact on other channels such as branches, ATMs and Mobile banking we discuss it in more depth in chapters 18 to 20.

MOBILE PERSON-TO-PERSON PAYMENTS

If mobile phones can be used to pay for goods and services, why not use them to make other transfers? This is the idea behind Mobile person-to-person payments. Again, this is an area where the banks' dominance is being challenged. Of the examples given below, ING Direct is a bank but PayPal Mobile, M-Pesa and Obopay are not.

ING Direct

ING Direct has recently introduced an app in the US for Android phones that allows account holders to transfer money by bumping their mobile phones together.[xciii]

PayPal Mobile

PayPal Mobile has apps for the iPhone, Android phones and the Blackberry. These allow money to be transferred by bumping mobile phones and include other useful money management features such as calculating tips and splitting the bill.[xciv] Subscribers in the US can also top up their PayPal accounts by imaging a cheque – it is cleared on the image.[xcv]

M-Pesa

M-Pesa is a mobile phone-based money transmission system used in Kenya, Tanzania and Afghanistan. It has recently been launched in South Africa and there are believed to be plans to expand it to India and Egypt. It is currently a purely domestic payment system (i.e. it can only be used within the country), but there are believed to be plans to introduce an international money transmission service for Kenya.

The service allows its users to deposit and withdraw money; transfer money to others; pay bills; and buy airtime. M-Paisa, the version of the service that runs in Afghanistan, is also used for salary payments; some merchant payments; and loan disbursements and payments.

M-Pesa is operated by the telecommunications companies (Telcos), including the local Vodafone subsidiaries Safaricom (in Kenya) and Vodacom (in Tanzania). In Afghanistan it is operated by a joint venture between Vodafone and local Telco Roshan. Users do not need a bank account.[xcvi]

Other Telco-managed payment systems include GCash and Smart Money. Both of these operate in the Philippines and are provided by the local Telcos Globe and Smart.[xcvii]

Obopay

Obopay is another mobile phone-based money transmission system. Obopay is based in the United States and is used in the United States and India. It is neither a bank nor a Telco, but it operates in partnership with a number of Indian banks. It can be used to transfer money to another mobile phone holder.[xcviii]

Nokia has used the Obopay platform as the basis for its Nokia Money service, which it is piloting in India.[xcix] This allows mobile phone holders to transfer money to others; pay utility bills and top up SIM cards. Nokia are planning to allow this to be used to pay for goods and services in the future.

SECURITY

Security is an obvious area of concern with the use of the mobile phone to provide banking services. There are a number of issues.

Can mobile phone data transmissions be hacked? Mobile phones used for Mobile banking must use encryption and firewalls in the same way as PCs and laptop computers.

Can the mobile phone itself be hacked? Subscribers assume that their mobile phones are secure. This is not necessarily the case. The Internet suggests that mobile phones can be hacked using Bluetooth (there are even a couple of 'how to' videos on YouTube). Using the mobile phone as a contactless device requires encryption, as radio frequency devices can be read even from a distance.[c]

What happens if the mobile phone is lost or stolen? This can be a major problem for subscribers, equivalent to losing their wallets (loss of m-commerce and m-payment capabilities), boarding passes (some airlines can issue boarding passes as bar codes to mobile phones) and hotel room keys (there are experiments underway to use NFC to allow plastic room keys to be replaced with mobile phones), as well as losing their access to telephone banking, Internet banking and m-banking. Putting more and more functionality on mobile phones risks making them a single point of failure for consumers. And mobile phones, unlike laptops, have little in the way of back-up capabilities.

If the mobile phone is lost or stolen, can sensitive information be retrieved from it? Mobile phones can be protected using Personal Identification Numbers (PINs), but most subscribers do not bother.

Mobile phone subscribers have tended to believe that their phones are secure, but this is changing. Surveys by Javelin Strategy & Research have shown that the number of consumers who rated mobile banking as 'unsafe' or 'very unsafe' increased by 54 per cent between 2009 and 2010. Interestingly, consumers believe that browser-based mobile banking is safer than using mobile banking apps. Javelin blames these security concerns for the lack of growth in mobile banking in the US, despite a considerable rise in the number of smartphone owners.[ci]

Chapter 10 – Other channels

ROLE OF OTHER CHANNELS

In the previous four chapters, we have discussed the four most important channels in the distribution strategy. Banks do use other channels. The most important of these are: mail, cards, cheques, mobile sales forces and partnership distribution.

MAIL

Banks mainly use the mail for marketing or for sending out information that is important but not urgent. Direct interaction with customers through the mail – customer correspondence – remains important although a lot of routine communication now goes through other channels.

The following table shows how banks expect their mix of marketing communications to change over the next five years. Note that mail channels currently account for more than two-thirds of such communications, but are expected to fall to less than half in five years' time.

Channel	Current	In 5 years
Statement inserts	38 per cent	21 per cent
Other direct mail	33 per cent	27 per cent
Email	20 per cent	33 per cent
SMS	9 per cent	18 per cent

Source: EFMA/Atos Worldwide Survey quoted in the EFMA report Expanding role of e-channels in CRM May 2011

Direct mail marketing

Banks use direct mail marketing to reach large numbers of customers or prospective customers with a marketing message. The direct mail marketing process involves the following steps: select, extract, validate, distribute, monitor and follow up.

Select. The select step involves deciding the target group for the mailing. Based on the product that the bank wants to market, a profile is drawn up to describe the target group. This may contain demographic information (age, salary etc.), information about product usage (mortgage holder etc.) and geographic information (where does the customer/ prospect live?).

Extract. The extract step converts the profile into a computer file listing names and addresses. Many banks market primarily to their existing customers (cross-selling and up-selling). The profile can be converted into a query and run against the bank's central customer database.

Marketing to prospective customers who have no existing relationship to the bank involves buying a list of names and addresses from a third party.

Validate. The validate step involves checking the list. The list must be checked to remove duplicate names and addresses, and to make sure that it does not contain any customers or prospects that are deceased. It must not contain anyone who is registered with the Mail Preference Service (MPS) or any customers who have indicated that they do not want to receive marketing material.

More sophisticated checks can improve response rates. Customers who already have the product can be excluded, as can customers who have recently been approached but have declined it. Some customers ignore all direct mail marketing – they are said to have a low propensity to purchase through this channel – and they can be excluded.

Distribute. Banks usually send direct mail marketing through a mailing house. Mailing houses have the capacity to send out very large numbers of letters at a very low rate. Small mailings might be done in-house.

Monitor. The monitor step involves tracking responses to the mailing. This allows the bank to assess its success and to learn lessons for future mailings.

Follow up. The follow-up step involves following up all customer responses until the customer either purchases the product or definitely decides not to purchase it.

The response rates for direct mail marketing are notoriously low – generally less than 2 per cent.

Direct mail can also be used for information mailings, such as changes to terms and conditions. Much the same process applies, although the monitor and follow up steps do not usually apply. There is not usually any requirement to exclude customers with 'no marketing' indicators or MPS registration, as these mailings are not for marketing purposes.

Statements

Banks are required to issue regular statements, giving details of transactions on customers' accounts. These are usually sent by mail on a monthly basis, although statements for savings and investment accounts may be sent quarterly, six-monthly or annually.

The confidential nature of the information means that statements are produced in-house, not by a mailing house. The major banks use machines that also put the statements in envelopes and add statement inserts.

Statement inserts can be used to give customers information about new products and special offers. Unlike direct mail marketing, they are not targeted and are sent to all customers receiving a statement.

Messages can also be printed on statements. They can be printed at the bottom of the statement sheet or as a separate sheet. They have less impact than statement inserts but, as they are part of the statement, customers may be more willing to read them.

Sending out statements is a cost to the banks, who are increasingly trying to get customers to convert to e-statements. These are usually in a format such as Adobe's portable document format (PDF) and must be downloaded from the bank's web site – they cannot be sent through the public email system because it is not secure.

Customer correspondence

The way in which customer correspondence is handled has changed greatly over the last few decades. Instead of going to the branch, letters from customers are sent to mail centres where they are imaged and the image is sent to the branch or department responsible for answering it. The imaging process includes the steps: receipt, imaging, indexing, routing, processing and archiving.

Receipt. Mail centres are usually located close to motorways to make sure that there is no delay to mail deliveries. The post room is usually located next to the loading bay to minimise the internal movement of paper.

Imaging. Letters are opened (usually automatically) and the contents are imaged on both sides. Again, this takes place as close as possible to the post room to minimise the movement of paper. The original letter and its envelope are placed in a plastic folder and a document identification number (DIN) is added.

Some letters may contain original documents, such as birth certificates, and these must be kept separate so that they can be returned to the sender.

Indexing. Indexing is arguably the most important step in the process and the mail centre's most experienced staff are often given the indexing role. The indexer is responsible for identifying the purpose of the letter and the customer.

Optical character recognition (OCR) can be used for part of the process. For example, OCR can be used if the letter contains a sort code and account number, or a card number. If one of the documents is a pre-printed form, it may be possible to recognise that by matching the layout of the form to information stored on the computer. However, the indexing process is so important that a human indexer will check if there is any doubt.

The customer information is used to link the letter to the customer record. This is important so that the bank is aware of all past correspondence with its customers.

Routing. The image is routed to the appropriate department or branch using Workflow technology. Workflow integrates human and computer work – the Workflow Management System tells human operators what they need to do and when.

One advantage of using the image, rather than the original, for processing is that different people can work on the same document at the same time.

Processing. The mail centre may be part of a processing centre but this is not essential – images can be routed anywhere in the country through the bank's internal telecommunications network.

If one of the documents is a pre-printed form, OCR can be used to interpret the form. Different confidence levels can be specified, so the OCR interpretation for very important fields (such as account numbers and amounts) is only accepted if the computer has a high level of confidence that the interpretation is correct.

If text is difficult to read, operators can zoom in to make parts of the document larger. They can also reverse the image (so that it appears as white writing on a black background), or make the text lighter or darker.

All of this is managed by the workflow system.

Archiving. Banks have to make a decision about whether to archive original documents or to destroy them. Most banks archive them. The plastic folders are sent to a storage facility (which is usually owned by a third party). If they ever need to be retrieved, the date of receipt and the DIN can be used for this.

Some banks destroy original documents. The advantage of this in the UK is that the image then becomes 'best evidence' and can legally be used in court proceedings. If the original document still exists, it is the 'best evidence' and the bank is required to retrieve it and present it to the court. However, images are less good evidence than the original document and the court may not give the image the same level of credibility as an original. Another disadvantage is that the bank must show that it has a robust process in place to make sure that the image is a true representation of the original document and cannot be altered.

Customer correspondence is not only used for forms. It is also used for general customer queries and for compliments and complaints.

Outbound correspondence – the banks' response to customer letters – is usually produced on a word processor. Standard templates are used to ensure that the letters meet local legal requirements, and to save time. Letters are often left unsigned or a facsimile signature is used. If a letter is personally signed, it is not uncommon for other handwritten changes to be made (for example, crossing out the recipient's title and surname and replacing it with a forename) to emphasise the personal nature of the correspondence.

CARDS

Are cards a channel? Probably not. They should probably be categorised as a product or a token that allows customers to access channels such as the Automated Teller Machine

(ATM). However, they do have some of the characteristics of channels. They are a touch point between the bank and its customers and they are used to deliver a service, payments. Therefore we will include them, but some aspects (security, for example) will be omitted.

Banks can offer a range of cards: credit cards, charge cards, debit cards, Solo/Electron cards, pre-paid cards, electronic cash (e-cash) cards and ATM cards. Most cards use magnetic strip technology, where the card must be placed in a reader so that the contents of the magnetic strip can be read, but an increasing number of cards are contactless and can be used by bringing the card close to a reader. Contactless devices were discussed, in the context of the mobile phone, in chapter 9.

Credit cards are the most flexible for the customer. They allow customers to pay for goods or withdraw funds provided that the customer stays within the limit of the card. There is no requirement to pay the balance in full each month. Cash withdrawals are usually subject to a fee and interest on the cash withdrawal starts to accrue immediately. If a credit card is used to pay for goods, there is an interest free period until the date shown on the next statement. If the balance is not paid, interest starts to accrue on the amount remaining.

Charge cards work in much the same way as credit cards. There are two differences. They cannot be used to withdraw cash and the balance must be paid in full each month, although some charge card issuers have separate schemes that allow customers to spread the cost of large purchases (for example American Express has the Extended Payment Option).[cii]

Debit cards operate against the customer's bank account. The card limit is the amount of money (including any agreed overdraft facilities) available from that bank account. The debit card itself does not have an interest free period, and interest depends on whether the account is in credit. Practice on charges varies widely and will be considered in more detail below.

Solo and Electron cards are debit cards but have the additional restriction that they cannot be used to make a payment that would cause the account to go overdrawn.

Pre-paid cards must be loaded with cash before they can be used. They can usually be topped up on-line and they can be topped up by a third party, which allows them to be used as a way of providing money to people who do not have a bank account.

Electronic cash (e-cash) cards are pre-paid cards but the balance is held on a computer chip in the card. E-cash cards can be accounted or non-accounted. If the card is accounted, the account balance is stored both on the card and in a central record. If the card is non-accounted, the balance is only held on the card.

ATM cards are cards that can only be used to withdraw money from an ATM.

Charges

Charges may be levied for using a card to pay for goods and for using it to make withdrawals from ATMs. Practice varies. Most stores (at least in the UK) do not charge for using a card to pay for goods, although some will make charges for using American Express or Diners Club cards (which charge higher fees to the retailer than MasterCard or Visa). Some Internet retailers do make such charges. The charge is usually highest for using a credit card, a charge card or a pre-paid card, lower for using a debit card and may be waived for using a Solo or Electron card.

Charges for making withdrawals from ATMs are equally complicated. Charges will usually be made for withdrawals against credit cards. Banks will not usually charge customers for making withdrawals against debit, Solo, Electron or ATM cards from one of their own ATMs. Banks in some countries will charge their customers for making withdrawals from an ATM belonging to another bank, so called disloyalty charges. Some ATMs are owned by non-bank organizations, and these will usually charge for withdrawals. Some pre-paid cards are positioned as travel money cards, and withdrawals made using these cards may not be charged. However, this depends on the terms and conditions of the individual card.

Electronic funds transfer at point of sale

Paying for goods and services using a card goes through the electronic funds transfer at point of sale (EFTPOS) system. Five people or organizations are involved in this: the customer, the retailer, the merchant acquirer, the card network, and the customer's bank.

The **customer** either presents the card to the **retailer** who puts it into a reader (magnetic strip cards), or places it near to a reader (contactless devices). Various security checks may be carried out.

The transaction goes to the **merchant acquirer**, which is the bank collecting card payments on behalf of the retailer.

Transactions usually go through one of the four major **card networks**. These are Visa, MasterCard, American Express and Diners Club.

Finally, they are routed to the **customer's bank**, which approves the payment.

Automated Teller Machines

Withdrawing cash from an ATM also relies on networks. Banks may have their own ATM networks, and countries have one or more networks that link these together. The increase in the amount of international travel has also led to MasterCard and Visa providing a global network that allows a card to be used to withdraw cash from anywhere in the world.

Some countries have treated their ATMs as a shared resource from an early stage. For example, all ATMs in Portugal are owned by Multibanco, which is owned by the Portuguese banks. Other countries have adopted a free competition model, in which arrangements between individual banks have evolved into shared networks, which have then competed against each other. Not surprisingly, the UK and the US have adopted the free competition model.

CHEQUES

Cheques, like cards, are not really a channel. However, like cards, they provide a service and we will discuss them briefly.

We can distinguish between three types of cheque: the cheque, the traveller's cheque and the banker's draft.

A cheque is drawn against a customer's account. Banks used to issue cheque guarantee cards, which would guarantee payment up to the cheque guarantee card limit, but this has now stopped in many countries.

Cheques are being phased out in many countries. It had been announced that cheques would be phased out in the UK by October 2018, but the difficulty of finding a replacement for some groups of customers led to this decision being reversed.[ciii]

Traveller's cheques must be purchased in advance and are for a set amount. They can be exchanged for cash at banks, post offices and resorts around the world. They can also be used as cash in some countries, notably the US. If traveller's cheques are stolen, they can be replaced.

A banker's draft is a draft issued by a bank. It is guaranteed for payment. Banker's drafts are also called banker's cheques and (in the US) cashier's checks. Gift cheques, which are used in Hong Kong, are low-value banker's drafts that allow customers with passbook accounts to originate cheques.

Cheque processing relies on the movement of physical pieces of paper. This is inherently more expensive than electronic payment systems, including cards, that only need to move information around. One way of reducing the movement of paper is truncation, in which the physical movement of the cheques is stopped at an early stage, with the remainder of the clearing process relying on the movement of electronic information and images. Many banks have now outsourced their cheque processing operations. For example, most banks in the UK have their cheques processed by either iPSL or EDS.

MOBILE SALES FORCES

Like branch-based relationship managers and specialist sales forces, mobile sales forces are a high cost delivery channel and banks only use them for high-value customers.

There are typically mobile sales forces for products such as cards, invoice finance/factoring and wealth management. There are also general mobile sales forces, capable of selling a number of products.

Branch-based mortgage advisers and financial planners may also visit customers at their homes or places of work.

The main issues with mobile sales forces are cost and security.

The cost of keeping a sales agent on the road is considerable, and can only be justified if the agent is able to produce a high ratio of sales to visits.

Security is an issue because sales agents need to carry equipment, such as laptops and mobile phones, that may include confidential customer information. The loss of these could cause the bank considerable reputational damage and the authorities could fine it.[civ]

One solution that banks have adopted is to store the information on secure servers and allow it to be accessed only through an encrypted Internet link. Citrix is one firm that offers this technology.

PARTNERSHIP DISTRIBUTION

Banks can distribute and sell their products through third parties. We can distinguish between a number of models: supplier, collaborative, retailer, broker and shared service.

In the **supplier** model, a bank provides a service to another financial services organization, which may also be a bank. This allows the first bank to benefit from economies of scale, as it can produce more of the product than it would be able to sell on its own.

One form of this is the white label model. Although the first bank makes the product, it has no involvement after that. The relationship is between the financial service organization and the customer, and the financial services organization is responsible for marketing, distributing, selling and servicing the product.

An alternative, which is often used for investment products, is the marketplace model. The product retains its original branding, even though marketing, distribution, selling and servicing are still the responsibility of the financial services organization. The marketplace model may be used because of the strength of the first bank's brand for that product.

The **collaborative** model usually involves a joint venture between the bank and a retailer. The joint venture is responsible for marketing, distributing and selling the product, although the bank makes and services it. The product is usually sold under the joint venture's brand, which may command more brand equity than the bank's brand.

The **retailer** model operates in much the same way as the collaborative model, except that marketing, distribution and selling take place without the bank being involved, even indirectly. Examples of the retailer model are affinity cards (which are often issued by charities) and consumer finance (which is often provided through the medium of store cards).

Brokers sell products and services on behalf of the bank. An example is a real estate agent selling mortgages on behalf of a bank. The broker model used to be important because brokers were able to add value by their knowledge of the market. This has been undermined by the Internet and the availability of price comparison service.

In the **shared service** model, a number of different banks share a common service. ATM networks are an example of a shared service. Another example is Monolink, which is used to send text messages to customers' mobile phones.

If we look at the provision of financial services in terms of a five-stage process (make, market, distribute, sell, service), we can summarise this as follows:

	Make	Market	Distribute	Sell	Service
Supplier	Bank 1	Bank 2			
Collaborative	Bank	Joint venture			Bank
Retailer	Bank	Retailer			Bank
Broker	Bank			Broker	Bank
Shared service	Bank		Distributor	Bank	

The biggest problem with all partnership distribution models is that the bank has little control over how the service is delivered. There are two consequences of this. The bank may suffer damage to its reputation because of failures by its partners. The bank may incur risk because of poor credit control by its partners. This is a general problem with all forms of outsourcing.

SUPERMARKET BANKING

Supermarket banking in the UK provides an interesting case study as it illustrates a number of different types of arrangement including in-store branches, profit sharing, joint ventures, white label and independent supermarket banks. The first British supermarket to enter the financial services market was Marks and Spencer, which launched St Michael Financial Services in 1985 (St Michael was Marks and Spencer's own label brand). Its first product was the M&S chargecard. It started offering personal loans four years later, in 1989.

1997 was a critical year. Sainsbury's Bank, a joint venture with Bank of Scotland (now part of Lloyds Banking Group) opened in February. Barclays opened an in-store test branch in Morrison's in the same month.

Abbey National (now part of Santander) entered into an agreement with Safeway, launching the ABC Bonus Account in February and opening an in-store branch in July. Midland Bank (now part of HSBC) entered into an arrangement with Morrison's in March that would allow Midland to open in-store branches, ending the supermarket's agreement with Barclays.

Tesco's Clubcard Plus debit card had been operated by NatWest (now part of Royal Bank of Scotland, but independent at that time). That arrangement ended in February 1997 and Tesco Personal Finance, a joint venture with Royal Bank of Scotland (ironically), was formed in July.

Why?

Why did supermarkets enter the market for financial services? And why were the banks willing to partner with them?

The supermarkets entered the market because of slow growth in their core markets.[cv] Financial services provided a way of leveraging their strong brands and the footfall through their stores. They did not need to make a significant investment to do this, as they were able to integrate with the banks' core banking and delivery platforms.

The banks that entered into joint ventures at this early stage were based in Scotland. Although they had a small number of branches in England and Wales, their combined market share was less than 5 per cent and partnering with the supermarkets was a good way to extend their geographical reach. We noted something similar with Internet banking in chapter 6. It also allowed them to sell more products, even if it meant sharing 50 per cent or more of the profits (based upon the typical joint venture shareholding) with the supermarket.

English banks Midland and Abbey National took the more cautious approach of opening in-store branches. The termination of the arrangement between Tesco and NatWest followed the supermarket's expression of a desire to expand into retail banking and insurance, which was in conflict with NatWest's own retail strategy.

This led to two different business models. The joint venture business model, adopted by Sainsbury's and Tesco, was based upon the supermarket selling simple banking products through direct models – leaflets at tills, telephone and Internet banking. These products included savings, credit cards, personal loans and general insurance (motor, home, pet).

The other business model, adopted by Morrison's/Midland and Safeway/Abbey National, opted for an in-store branch approach that also offered current accounts. Many believed that this would deliver benefits to both parties without eroding the bank's brand.

Brand

In the late 1990s and early 2000s supermarket banks were considered as a real threat to banks due to trust in their brands – evidenced by the success of their own brand products and perceived fairness. With over 30 million customers visiting Tesco, Sainsbury's and Asda stores each week and established loyalty schemes running into the millions there was little doubt in many people's minds that supermarkets would change the face of UK banking.

Does being a trusted brand give the right for a retailer to succeed in financial services? Or do customers, who no longer trust banks in the way they used to, fear that retailers are stretching their brands too far?

Since supermarket banking was first introduced into the UK, the market has largely failed to meet the high expectations placed on it by themselves and pundits. This remains true, even after the banks 'shot themselves in the foot' in the late 2000s. Why?

This may be evidence that, whilst customers will buy on price, they also want a multi-channel banking relationship to help them meet their financial goals.

So what happened to date? Has the threat been realised?

The supermarket banks have not had a transforming effect on the UK market for financial services.[cvi] They have tended to offer products that are relevant to their core business, such as credit cards and personal loans, together with savings and insurance products. As we discussed in chapter 4, these have to a large extent been commoditised and do not provide a basis for a long-term relationship. To look at the supermarkets individually:

Tesco

> Pile it high and sell it cheap
>
> Jack Cohen, Tesco founder, business motto.

Tesco bought out Royal Bank of Scotland's 50 per cent share in 2008 and Tesco Personal Finance re-branded itself to Tesco Bank the following year.

2009 was the middle of the financial crisis. Earlier in that year, Tesco announced what amounted to a full assault on UK high-street banking. This included opening Tesco Bank branches in 30 of its stores by the end of the year and selling current accounts and mortgages, subject to approval by the Financial Services Authority (FSA).

Tesco built its own banking infrastructure and migrated its Information Technology systems away from its partner's platform. After this, and lengthy negotiations with the FSA, Tesco announced that it would offer mortgages in late 2011.

However, in March 2011 Tesco announced that it was scrapping the pilot scheme and closing the branches in its Glasgow, Blackpool, Brisol, Long Eaton, Oldham and Coventry stores.

Tesco acquired an 84 per cent share of data analytics company Dunnhumby in 2010. Dunnhumby was responsible for exploiting the data Tesco held on its 15 million Clubcard scheme customers so successfully.

According to CompareandSave.com in August 2010, Tesco Bank operates 6.5 million customer accounts across 28 products and services. It currently holds just 1 per cent of the savings market, 1.7 per cent of the loans market and 7.9 per cent of the credit card market. CompareandSave.com reported that Datamonitor research indicates that when Tesco starts to offer current accounts it could take a 1.5 per cent market share as early as 2013.

Sainsbury's Bank

Sainsbury's Bank grew to about 2 million customers in the mid-2000s, where it has remained fairly static despite efforts to increase its market share through savings account promotions.

Asda

Asda followed Tesco and Sainsbury's into financial services, attaching its brand to products provided by other companies such as Santander and Norwich Union. In terms of the partnership distribution models we discussed earlier, this follows the retailer model. Asda does not sell directly in-store, but uses the supplier's telephone, online or postal application processes.

Morrison's and Safeway

Safeway was sold to Morrison's in 2005 and Abbey National was sold to Santander. Morrison's deal with HSBC ended in 2009 and has not been renewed, and all in-store branches have been closed.

Following the Safeway takeover and end of the HSBC agreement, Morrison's appear to have abandoned the idea of supermarket banking to concentrate on their core business. The only banking service appears to be ATMs located at stores.

Co-operative

The Co-operative Society, who already had their own high-street bank, offered only limited financial services to its supermarket customers. It merged with the Britannia Building Society in 2009 and the Co-operative Bank started to introduce in-store branches into its parent's supermarkets in 2011.

M&S Money

Marks and Spencer pioneered the concept of retailer-based financial services in the 1980s as they introduced their own label store cards, credit cards and other financial services such as loans, general insurance and foreign exchange. HSBC acquired M&S Money in 2004, and have integrated it into their UK operation whilst maintaining the brand. Under the terms of the deal Marks and Spencer became an introducer to HSBC and is entitled to a share in the profits of M&S Money until 2014. M&S Money has around 3.8 million customers in 2011.

The phantom menace?

Supermarket banks have not fulfilled their potential by capturing market share – after 14 years the largest, Tesco, has only had success in the credit card market, where they have the market share of a medium-sized bank. Despite the mass of data all supermarkets gather through their loyalty cards they have been unable to differentiate themselves from banks and have resorted to selling commoditised products on price. To a consumer, many supermarket banks appear to offer only a disparate mix of products compared to that of a full service bank.

In November 2003, IBM Business Consulting Services (in conjunction with Sainsbury's Bank) published a report, Supermarket banking – fulfilling the potential.

This examined the current market and potential for supermarket banks to make an impact on the UK financial services sector. It concluded that supermarket banking had made an impact on the retail financial sector and that it can take a greater market share in the future. It pointed to a number of strengths and weaknesses that supermarket banking had compared to traditional banks:

Strengths

- Strength of their retail brands – very strong and trusted brands with large numbers of loyal customers (supported by loyalty schemes) who appear to be open to being offered financial services products by them. In many cases supermarket brands are stronger than those of traditional financial services brands.

- Low operational costs resulting in highly competitive products – because of their focused business model, the operational costs of supermarket banks were estimated to be around 25 per cent of those of a financial services company.
- Strong access to a large customer base – Sainsbury's, Tesco and Asda supermarkets are each visited by more than 11 million people a week, giving them an opportunity to interact with customers at various times during their visit.

Weaknesses

- Lack of proposition differentiation – supermarkets offered financial products as commodities, rather than more integrated solutions focused on life events, such as buying a car or moving home. The loyalty schemes are not exploited to help differentiate them from the banks.
- Customer insight not exploited – through their loyalty schemes, supermarkets have even more detailed customer data than banks, but have only focused on using this in managing their traditional business.
- Lack of physical presence – in a survey by Sainsbury's, conducted in 2003, 55 per cent of its supermarket customers and 71 per cent of its banking customers said that they would be more likely to use the bank if some sort of counter service was available in-store.

However, when you examine supermarket banking initiatives and progress since 2003 it is evident that they have failed to capture market share. Is it because they cannot get the service element right? Most Sainsbury's customers indicated that they'd like some sort of counter service available in-store, but individual supermarkets' business models haven't successfully met their customers' clearly stated need. Most supermarkets have implemented and withdrawn some sort of manned branch or kiosk concept.

After all, providing a counter service is where retail high-street banks incur most of their costs and offer customers this service. Supermarkets who wish to extend their product range into more complex products, such as current accounts and mortgages, may need to implement innovative alternatives to the more traditional manned branches in order to gain their customers' trust

Customers – whom do they trust?

In moneysupermarket.com's 2010 industry service rankings, supermarkets were 6th out of 16, whereas the banks were 14th out of 16. This might suggest that customers trust their supermarkets more than their banks.

But another moneysupermarket.com survey, conducted in 2009, tells a different story. The study found that traditional banking brands still hold a far greater sway with the public's finances and that supermarkets face a different set of consumer challenges.

Only 4 per cent of people surveyed by moneysupermarket.com in 2009 would trust a supermarket brand more than a bank to look after their finances, compared to 27 per cent who said they would trust a traditional banking brand more than a supermarket. A further 20 per cent say that they would not trust a supermarket brand to look after their finances. 14 per cent simply don't trust any big company with their finances.

Just 10 per cent think a supermarket would provide a better service than a bank when looking after their money. 24 per cent would take out a credit card with a supermarket brand – but only 5 per cent would take out a mortgage.

Consumers are deeply divided on supermarkets. 11 per cent of survey respondents felt that 'supermarket brands are taking over our lives and should stick to more traditional products', and a further 30 per cent felt that these brands 'have already gone too far and should stop expanding'.

On the other hand, more than a third (37 per cent) were quite happy with the growth and expansion of major supermarket brands, with one in five saying they could get a cheaper deal for a range of products with a supermarket and 17 per cent happy to be able to get everything from one place.

The research uncovered the area in which supermarket banks are perceived as being better than traditional bank brands – providing good value products (e.g. cheaper insurance premiums, higher savings rates and [eventually] lower mortgage rates). One in five of those surveyed felt a supermarket bank would offer better deals on their products than traditional high street banks. This compares to just 9 per cent who felt a bank would be more likely to offer the better value products. But good value rates are obviously not key as the vast majority said they are unlikely to go to a supermarket brand for any financial product.

Competing with banks?

Of all financial products, people would be most willing to take out a credit card from a supermarket brand (24 per cent) closely followed by general insurance (23 per cent).

Only 15 per cent would be willing to take out a savings account, 11 per cent a current account, 10 per cent would buy life insurance and 5 per cent would buy a mortgage.

In addition, supermarkets trail their rivals in the key area of customer service. Just 10 per cent think a supermarket would provide a better service than a bank when looking after their money, with 20 per cent saying the bank would do better (18 per cent think neither would give good service and 28 per cent think both would give good service).

Attack of the clones

It is clear that Tesco has successfully driven other supermarkets to provide financial services. And they've raised the bar again by assembling the components of a fully-fledged bank. It remains to be seen how Tesco's supermarket competitors and the traditional banks react to their strategy.

United States

The United States opened the first supermarket (King Kullen, which opened in New York City on 4th August 1930). It is also credited with originating supermarket banking in the early 1990s. However, supermarket banking in the US during the 1990s adopted a different trajectory from the UK, being driven by the banks not the supermarkets.

US banks recognized the opportunity to reach more potential customers with their products, whilst reducing the cost of opening more traditional units (in 1996 it was estimated that a traditional branch could cost up to US$1,500,000 to build, while a supermarket branch typically cost US$200,000). In addition, the total expense of an in-store branch was estimated at about two-thirds that of a traditional branch. In 1990, it was estimated that by 2000, 1 in 10 bank branches would be in supermarkets.

Supermarkets gained by renting the banks space for their units – in line with what banks thought were 'reasonable' rates, based upon their existing experience. But supermarket economics are quite different from bank economics and it is reported that many massively overpaid.

Perhaps the banks' biggest mistake was not to recognize that supermarket banking was different from traditional banking and needed a different sales culture to translate their exposure to a large number of new customers into sales that would support the cost of the additional branch. As a result, supermarket branches tended to open mainly low-balance, secondary, convenience checking accounts and rarely secured the customer's total banking relationship.

It was reported in early 2011 that the total number of in-store branches for US banks and thrifts had fallen 2.2 per cent to 6,051 since June 2009, and in-store deposits had dropped by 3.4 per cent. The driver for the change is believed to be the banks refocusing on more profitable businesses.

So what are the supermarkets doing? After all, Walmart is the largest grocery retailer in the US.

It appears that US retailers and supermarkets want to offer financial services to their customers, but face strong lobbying from traditional banks and, as a result, are currently restricted to the 30 million US households who are either unbanked or underbanked (defined as people who have checking or savings, but rely upon alternative financial services such as payday lenders and check cashing services). Supermarkets and retailers like Walmart, Kmart and Best Buy are restricted to providing cash checking, pre-paid credit card issuing and bill paying services and cannot take deposits or make loans.

In addition to providing a valuable local service, they hope that their customers will spend the money in their store. However, it does not bring this population into the mainstream financial services market. Walmart has been trying, unsuccessfully, to get a banking licence since 1999 and recently failed to get permission to buy a Utah-based bank that would have allowed them to fully enter the market. Walmart does have experience in supermarket banking – it has banking licences in both Canada and Mexico (where it has operated since 2010 and 2007 respectively).

In the UK, Walmart's subsidiary Asda acts as an introducer and is not a bank.

Canada

The story of in-store banking has been somewhat similar, with banks such Canadian Imperial Bank of Commerce (CIBC) implementing in-store branches in Canadian and US supermarkets (with strong on-line support) during the period of expansion and now closing down units to refocus on more profitable businesses.

CIBC also operates a joint venture, President's Choice Financial, with supermarket chain Loblaw Companies.

Conclusion

Supermarket banking has, to date, failed to become a dominant force in UK financial services, failing to gain significant market share in any product range except credit cards, despite the perception that supermarkets offer better value for money on many products and that banks are no longer as trustworthy as they were.

Part of the reason may be that consumers fear that supermarkets are overstretching their core competencies with financial services, or that they are becoming too big. Another reason is that, despite the vast quantities of data at their disposal, supermarkets have failed to differentiate themselves and remain providers of commodities. Supermarkets sought to offer selective products rather than aiming for the customer's banking relationship.

Generally, their failure to offer current accounts because of cost has reduced their ability to offer themselves as credible rivals to banks. By not offering current accounts they have denied themselves the opportunity of realizing a competitive advantage over banks. By combining the rich insight they have from their loyalty schemes with the wider current account data, supermarkets would be in a position to understand their customers' behaviour and offer relevant solutions that might rival or surpass many smaller banks capabilities.

Tesco's acquisition of a majority share of Dunnhumby gives them the capability to do just that – and probably denies competitors (supermarkets and banks) access to this source of insight.

Finally, given that consumers continue to want the opportunity to have a face-to-face interaction with their bank when they need one (which is why bank branches will survive), it is probable that the failure by supermarkets to either successfully provide the service or to replicate the experience without incurring the associated costs is a handicap.

This makes Tesco's plans very interesting. By providing current accounts (and thereby the means to understand their customers better) and mortgages they are closing the gap as they see it. However, the banks are 'moving the goalposts' by focusing more resources in serving more affluent customers with wealth management services, including dedicated channels such as branches and relationship managers.

Chapter 11 – Non-bank competitors

Banking is necessary – banks are not

Dick Kovacevic

INTRODUCTION

Banks are not the only actors on the financial services stage. We have already discussed many of the factors that have allowed non-banks to enter the banking market, which had traditionally been closed. These include deregulation, reduced entry costs and the availability of direct channels.

The first attempt to break into this market, by the pure play Internet banks, achieved limited success at best. We discussed this in chapter 6. Later entrants have learned from this experience and have adopted a more focused model. Instead of trying to deliver a wide range of services through a single channel, most of them deliver a narrow range of services through a single channel – the monoline model.

The next attempt to intrude on what the banks regarded as their territory was the price comparison services. Price comparison is not a service that the banks had traditionally offered, so it was probably not picked up as a threat. However, it had the effect of increasing price transparency. This represents a direct threat to the traditional banking model, which relied on cross-subsidising services. A further development of this is the cashback service.

Another development has been social lending, or peer-to-peer lending. The banks have traditionally acted as intermediaries between depositors and borrowers. Developments such as the commercial paper market have affected this role in the wholesale markets, but these rely on the borrower being sufficiently well known and credit worthy to borrow without the involvement of an intermediary. The social lending model allows retail depositors and retail lenders to connect directly, without the involvement of the banks.

Personal financial management (PFM) is another development. PFM has been around for many years, but early versions had limited functionality and limited ability to take information from banks. A merger between traditional PFM and account aggregation poses a significant threat to the banks. In the worst case, they could relegate the banks to a position of being 'white label' suppliers to the PFMs. We discuss the white label model in the next chapter.

Mobile devices, which we discussed in chapter 9, present another threat. The problem with mobile devices is that they can be used as a method of payment even if the subscriber does not have a bank account. This allows third parties, in particular the telecommunications companies (Telcos), to provide financial services for the unbanked and the underbanked.

This was a potential threat with Internet banking, but the Telcos did not attack the market at that stage. The mobile market is different.

This threat faces the banks with a dilemma. Banks are, in spite of the experience of the credit crunch, risk averse – it is part of the genetic make-up of the industry. The security risks associated with mobile devices are, as yet, unquantified. This makes the banks reluctant to commit themselves fully to this channel. But competitors, in particular the Telcos, do not show such restraint. The banks risk losing the mobile market before they even commit themselves to it. The critical areas of competition are Mobile commerce and Mobile payments.

In spite of the failure of the pure play Internet banks to break through into the mainstream, there are non-banks who are prepared to offer an approximation to a full banking service. They include supermarket banks, many of which have banking licences but which we will regard as non-banks because their main business is supermarket operation. They also include a small number of pseudo-banks, which act as intermediaries between white label suppliers and consumers. We will discuss these in the next chapter.

Price comparison services

Price comparison services allow individuals to see prices charged by different suppliers for the same (or a comparable) product, and to click on the listing to obtain more details or to purchase the product. These listings are usually ranked. Financial products are usually ranked by price but other services, such as travel, may also offer rankings by 'our recommendation'.

Price comparison services can take their information as a direct feed from the retailer or can access the retailer's website and get the information from it. There are third party data providers who will aggregate data feeds from a number of different retailers and sell them on to the price comparison services.

Price comparison services usually earn their income from the retailers. This can take the form of a flat fee to appear as a listing, a fee whenever the user clicks the retailer's listing, or a fee whenever the user completes an action such as purchasing a product or registering an email address.

One of the most important uses of price comparison services in the financial services industry is for insurance products. These require the users to enter additional information, including contact information, which may be used by the price comparison service or the retailer to contact the customer at a later time.

Price comparison services are particularly significant for insurance. In December 2009, 81 per cent of people wanting home insurance quotes and 89 per cent of people wanting motor insurance quotes used a price comparison service.[cvii] Not surprisingly, customers who use one or more price comparison services are more likely to switch supplier. Using one price comparison service increases the probability that the customer will switch provider from 31 per cent to 47.5 per cent, with a further increase in probability of 3.4 per cent for each additional price comparison service used.[cviii]

One reason for the popularity of price comparison services is that they reduce search costs.[cix] Searching is one of the pre-purchase activities discussed in chapter 3. The need to enter detailed information to get quotes for motor insurance and home insurance means that the search costs of approaching a large number of different suppliers directly are high. Using a price comparison service reduces these.

Some major insurers have excluded themselves from price comparison services. High profile UK examples include Directline and Aviva (Aviva in effect operate their own price comparison service by showing quotes from their competitors on their website)[cx]. In spite of this, the number of brands appearing on price comparison service websites continues to increase.

Price comparison services are another factor that reduces the entry cost to the financial services market. Price comparison service websites treat all suppliers equally, whether they are established firms or new entrants. Of course, customers may well take account of brand when they decide which product to purchase.

As we discussed in chapter 1, price comparison services increase price transparency. They also emphasise the role of price as a product differentiator. Therefore they are of greatest importance to motor insurance and home insurance, which, as we saw in chapter 3, are the most commoditised financial products.

Banking products are less commoditised and less vulnerable to competition from the price comparison services. However, as we noted in chapter 3, commoditisation is likely to increase in future.

Cashback services

Cashback services, like price comparison services, take commission from the retailer for sales made through the website. Unlike price comparison services, they share the commission with the customer.

Social lending

Social lending or peer-to-peer (P2P) lending uses the Internet to allow lenders to provide money to borrowers without the banks being involved.

Traditional bank lending relied on banks taking deposits from customers and lending the money on to other customers. Social lending 'disintermediates' the process by taking the banks out of the picture. Social lenders do not take deposits – which would require a banking licence – but provide an environment that allows borrowers to post requests for funding and potential lenders to see these requests and to provide the funds required.

There are some disadvantages of social lending. There is evidence of discrimination on the prosper.com website.[cxi] It should be noted that the reason that prosper.com is frequently cited in academic research is because it has been very open in making information available to the academic community, and it can be assumed that other social lenders suffer from the same problem. It is perhaps also worth noting that such discrimination on the part of a bank would be illegal in the US under the Equal Credit Opportunity Act (ECOA).

Social lending websites do not need to follow standard default criteria such as 90 days past due, and the lender has no recourse in the event of the borrower defaulting. One way of managing this risk is to limit the exposure of any one lender to any one borrower.

Important social lending websites include zopa.com in the UK, and prosper.com, lendingclub.com and lendingtree.com in the US. They establish the borrower's identity and check the borrower's credit score. They also formalise the legal agreement between lender and borrower.

The market for social lending in the US was $118 million in 2005 and was predicted to reach $5.8 billion by 2010.[cxii] A significant proportion of this growth may have been due to the credit crunch and the difficulty of obtaining bank finance. This is an example of adverse selection and may explain prosper.com's high reported default rate.[cxiii] In the UK, zopa.com claims a very low default rate of 0.8 per cent.[cxiv]

Social lending is not a channel currently used by banks. It is a significant competitor (zopa.com had a 1 per cent share of the UK loans market in 2010)[cxv] – although the prediction made in 2008 of a 10 per cent share of the worldwide market for retail lending and financial planning in 2010[cxvi] seems to have been overly optimistic.

Personal financial management

Personal financial management (PFM) systems help customers to manage their finances by keeping a track of their accounts, investments, income and expenditure. The antecedents of PFM were account aggregation and standalone products such as Microsoft Money.

Account aggregation allowed customers to bring all of their accounts, irrespective of where they were held, together onto a single screen. They were seen as an important new product in the year 2000, when services such as Citigroup's My Accounts were introduced.

The disadvantages of account aggregation were that the customer had to give security information for the account to the aggregator and that they provided few financial management capabilities. Citigroup withdrew its account aggregation service in 2005.

Standalone products had better financial management capabilities by, for example, allowing customers to diarise regular payments and to enter one-off payments. Early versions did not have the same capabilities to get account data as account aggregation.

PFM brings these two aspects together and adds a few features such as bill payments. The problem in the UK has been that two factor authentication, which we discussed in chapter 6, made both account aggregation and PFM much more difficult. This has not been so much of a problem in the US, where PFM services such as Quicken, Mint.com and Yodlee have become very popular. These started as Internet applications but can also be used on mobile devices.

Most banks' Internet banking and Mobile banking propositions provide the customer with the raw data, for example product balances and transactions, but leave it to third parties to add value for the customer through PFM.

There is a danger that the banks will be disintermediated from their customers by an organisation that is not a bank, but uses technology to provide customers with the information and customer experience they need.

Mint.com is probably the most widely used PFM. Intuit, who also own Quicken, have owned Mint.com since 2009. Since April 2010, Mint.com has been able to connect securely to and download transactions from virtually every bank, credit union and credit card account in the United States with an online banking capability – more than 16,000 US financial institutions.

Mint.com has grown from having more than three million users in April 2010 to having more than five million users in May 2011. It supports more than 17 million individual financial accounts and was recently introduced in Canada.

Yodlee has developed an account aggregation 'engine' and the web-based PFM Yodlee MoneyCenter. Yodlee's account aggregation engine is widely used by banks[cxvii] and PFM providers such as MoneyStrand. Mint.com has stopped using the Yodlee account aggregation engine since its takeover by Intuit.

A few banks, such as ANZ, are providing their customers with value-added PFM capabilities. The question is, will others follow before their customers switch to third party PFM providers? And, if that happens, will the banks become nothing more than white label suppliers to the dominant PFMs?

Mobile phone as an entry point

The acceptance of the mobile phone, particularly the smartphone, opens banking to new large well-known competitors who are looking for new income streams based upon the mobile phone.

Frequently mentioned new competitors are usually technology-based companies who have invested heavily over the last few years in hardware and communications technologies, often having a huge base of owners or users of their technology. Companies mentioned include Apple, Google, Amazon and Microsoft. Rogers Communications, a Telco company in Canada, is currently filing for a banking licence.

However, most of these new competitors will not be full banking propositions, instead they focus on delivering technology that, by joining with a card issuer, facilitates a banking function, such as contactless payments or the mobile wallet. This strategy potentially disrupts the bank's position in the payments value chain. We discuss the potential risks and options for banks in chapter 18.

Other new competitors include start-ups, such as BankSimple and MovenBank who aim to disrupt the traditional banks by focusing on payments and money management rather than full banking. Their proposition is based around Mobile banking and Mobile payments functions and will not have a branch network, Telephone banking or ATMs.

Chapter 12 – New channels

There is nothing more difficult to carry out, nor more doubtful of success, nor more dangerous to handle, than to initiate a new order of things.

Niccolò Machiavelli

LAUNCHING A NEW CHANNEL

One of the problems with the multi-channel world is that nothing poses a greater threat to the brand than launching a new channel. Why would a bank expose itself to this risk? Common reasons include cost reduction, customer demand, competitive pressure and opportunity.

Cost reduction

Banks may launch a new channel with the intention of reducing costs. New channels often have a different cost structure to traditional channels such as the branch. They may have quite high capital costs (equipment etc.), but their operating costs for each transaction are usually much lower. Recent research shows the following cost comparison:

Channel	Cost
Branch	$4.00
Call centre	$3.75
IVR	$1.25
ATM	$0.85
Online	$0.17
Mobile	$0.08

Source: TowerGroup and M-Com research[xviii]

An example of launching a new channel for cost reduction is the telephone call centre. Offering a telephone banking service in-branch required the banks to allocate staff time at every one of the bank's branches to answering the telephone. In practice, staff were either attending a telephone that was not ringing, or customers were unable to get through because the line was engaged or the telephone went unanswered.

The call centre allowed banks to put a much smaller number of staff in a few centralised sites. Technology could be used to monitor and manage the calls. This allowed considerable cost savings within the branches.

In practice it was not quite that simple. There were problems with forecasting the level of demand, which are discussed later in this chapter. There was customer resistance to moving from a branch-based service to a call centre.[cxix] It was not possible to reduce headcount in many of the branches because telephone banking was only a part-time activity in all but the largest of them. However, it is generally accepted that the introduction of telephone call centres did reduce costs.

Customer demand

Banks may introduce a new channel in response to customer demand. This usually occurs when there is a clear customer need that cannot be satisfied through existing channels, except at unacceptable cost.

An example of launching a new channel in response to customer demand is the Automated Teller Machine (ATM). In the 1960s and 1970s, the UK banks extended their customer base from their traditional middle-class customers to the working class. There were a number of reasons for this. Rising wages left the banks facing higher costs, but also meant that the traditionally 'unbanked' working classes had sufficient money to be a valuable customer segment. There was government pressure to replace cash with bank giro credits for paying wages. Deregulation and the end of the interest rate cartel increased competition within the industry. The failure of some Hire Purchase companies during the secondary banking crisis in the early 1970s left credit demand from the working class unsatisfied.

The problem was that UK banks were only open from Monday to Friday, until 3:30 in the afternoon. This was acceptable for the existing middle-class customers, who were usually able to get to the bank during their lunch hour, but not for the new customers. The banks started to open on Saturday mornings, but this increased their costs and still did not provide a level of service that would meet the needs of this group.

The biggest single problem was cash withdrawal. Customers were prepared to accept banking hours for other services, but they needed to be able to get access to the money in their accounts at other times.

The banks had already been interested in deploying ATMs as a method of reducing costs. ATMs would take cash withdrawal transactions away from the branch counter, freeing staff time for other work. However, the ATM also met a very real customer demand that could not have been satisfied by the banks in any other way at an acceptable cost.

Competitive pressure

Banks may introduce a new channel in response to competitive pressure. If there is a risk that a competitor – either an established bank or a new entrant – may gain significant market share by introducing a new channel, the banks will respond by introducing that channel themselves.

An example of banks launching a new channel in response to competitive pressure is Internet banking. Although banks had introduced online banking at an early stage (Chemical

Bank's Pronto home banking service was introduced in 1982), they were reluctant to use the Internet because of its perceived security weaknesses.

The commercial failure of the Videotex system, which many of the early online banking systems relied on, forced a change of plan. However, banks were still not prepared to deploy a browser-based solution and instead implemented a thick client personal computer (PC) banking solution.

This changed in 1995, when Security First Network Bank (SFNB) became the first true Internet bank in the modern sense. It has been argued that SFNB was never intended to compete in the banking market (it was used as a live trial of the security software), but it was followed by other new entrants such as the Atlanta Internet Bank (later NetBank) in 1996.

The banks felt compelled to respond, and launched their own Internet banks shortly thereafter. Their success can be judged by the fact that, in spite of their cost advantages, none of the pure play Internet banks ever broke through to establish a major market presence.

Opportunity

Banks may introduce a new channel to take advantage of an opportunity. There are two types of opportunity: technology trigger and new infrastructure.

An example of banks launching a new channel in response to a technology trigger is electronic cash (e-cash).

Banks and retailers dislike handling cash. It is heavy and difficult to move. It needs insurance against fire, theft or loss. Both banks and retailers devote a lot of staff time to the task of exchanging one denomination of cash for another by, for example, giving change to customers.

How much easier would it be if everyone paid electronically, using a card?

The problem was that the card authorisation process required the retailer to connect to the merchant acquirer over a telecommunications link. This was expensive in the early 1990s, and was not economically viable for small purchases.

However, the cost of computer chips was coming down. This provided an opportunity to introduce a new channel, in which the account balance and the identification and verification (ID&V) information would be stored in a chip on a card. The retailer would still need to connect to the merchant acquirer, but this could be done once, at the end of the day.

Mondex was developed by the National Westminster Bank (NatWest) in the UK in 1990.[cxx] NatWest realised that the best way to get retailers to accept Mondex was to use existing infrastructure and to make sure that the potential customer base was as large as possible. Therefore they formed a joint venture with BT and the Midland Bank (now part of HSBC) and launched the first Mondex trial in 1993.

It is fair to say that neither Mondex (which is now owned by MasterCard) nor its Visa equivalent VisaCash has been a runaway success. There are a number of possible reasons for this.

Although the price of computer chips had fallen, they were still quite expensive. This was particularly true of the high quality chips needed for Mondex and VisaCash. The only way for the banks to recover the cost was to charge for the cards. Neither Mondex nor VisaCash offered customers sufficient advantage to be worth paying for.

In addition, the price of telecommunications connections over the Internet fell dramatically. 'Always on' broadband connections, which would have been very expensive in the 1990s, are now very cheap. Therefore there is no longer a requirement to carry out ID&V on the card to save telecommunications costs. The role envisaged for e-cash cards is increasingly being filled by the contactless card.

An example of banks launching a new channel in response to new infrastructure is mobile banking.

The commercial potential of third-generation – 3G – mobile telephony was recognised by governments around the world, many of whom conducted auctions to sell bandwidth for this. In the UK, for example, the auction was held in 2000 and raised more than £22 billion for the government.

The launch of 3G services was more expensive and took longer than expected, but 3G is now well established and widely used. In the UK, for example, more than 25 per cent of mobile phone users were using 3G smartphones by May 2010.[cxxi] 48 per cent of mobile phones sold in the first quarter of 2011 were smartphones.[cxxii]

This has provided a platform on which banks have been able to launch new services. Nordea launched a mobile banking app in Norway and Sweden in 2010. Turkish bank TEB launched a version of its Internet banking service specifically designed for smartphones, with larger buttons to accommodate the smaller screen size.

Marketing research

Marketing research is essential, whatever the reason for launching a new channel. There are two reasons for this.

The first is to establish what the customers want. A good example of this is the First Direct telephone bank.[cxxiii] Midland Bank, First Direct's parent, did not want to set up just another telephone bank. There would have been no point in doing this. Instead, they decided to target First Direct at customers in the ABC1 demographic groups – better off customers – and used marketing research to identify what these customers wanted.

The second is to establish the demand for the new channel. As we will see later, establishing the demand for channels such as the call centre based on the demand for a branch-based telephone service is unlikely to be successful. Marketing research is essential to find out how many customers will use the service.

UK start-up Metro Bank has estimated its target market customer base at seven million people, 80 per cent of whom come from London.[cxxiv] Metro Bank's business model is based on branch-based banking and superior service, and, according to research, London-based account holders are the most dissatisfied with their banks. Metro Bank is also targeting business customers who have seen their credit supply reduced since the credit crunch.

Pilot

With any new channel, the first stage is a small pilot. The purpose of this is to make sure that there are no problems with the new technology or with the training of agents.

Staff are often used for the pilot. If they are not suitable, for example because they are not typical of the broader customer base, the bank may ask some of its customers to take part. The pilot may be extended, by adding more customers or making more services available, as the channel is proved.

Roll out

Once the pilot has been successfully completed, and any lessons from it have been learnt and incorporated into the channel, the next stage is a roll out. This may be limited in extent, or it may be a full national roll out.

A limited roll out can be restricted to specific customer segments. An alternative is to limit the roll out to a region. The disadvantage of a regional roll out is that customers in other regions may hear about the channel from the news and try to use it themselves. This can overload the service. Egg suffered from a problem similar to this when potential customers tried to access the web-site before it was ready for national roll out.

The final stage is the full national roll out, accompanied by an advertising and publicity campaign.

Risk

We have said that launching a new channel is risky. What are the risks? They include:

- The risk of failure
- The risk of success
- The risk of fraud
- Data security risks
- Poor service levels
- The risk of cannibalisation
- The risk of adverse selection

The risk of failure

This is the risk that customers will not use the new channel. In terms of the brand, this is a relatively benign risk. It may be embarrassing and expensive, but it does little damage to the reputation of the bank in the eyes of its customers.

A particular problem with failure is that it is very difficult for a bank to decommission a new channel. If the channel gains any customers at all, these customers may be unhappy if it is closed down. Therefore the bank is faced with a choice between upsetting some of its customers and accepting the ongoing costs of operating an unprofitable channel.

It is important to recognise that the demand for a channel is likely to start slowly. This is described as the S-curve – demand starts slowly when the channel is introduced, grows rapidly during a growth phase, and then slows down as the demand for the channel becomes saturated. This is discussed below.

The risk of success

This is the risk that the take-up of the channel will be much greater than predicted. This will overload the infrastructure set up to support the new channels. Servers will be overloaded and may crash. Staff will not be able to cope with the number of customers. This will lead to a perception of poor service.

It has been said that an organisation is judged by its weakest channel. Poor service in one channel will damage the reputation of the brand as a whole.

The risk of fraud

This is the risk that fraudsters will take advantage of the new channel. A large element of fraud detection is behavioural. It uses technology such as expert systems to develop an understanding of normal patterns of customer behaviour. A departure from these normal patterns is an indicator of potential fraud.

The problem with a new channel is that the bank does not have sufficient information to determine what constitutes a normal pattern of customer behaviour. Therefore these channels are more vulnerable to fraud.

Banks have a choice as to the level of fraud risk that they are willing to accept. All fraud detection systems produce a mix of false positives and false negatives. Taking a cautious approach upsets customers, whose legitimate transactions are rejected. Taking a less cautious approach increases the risk of fraud.

Data security risks

There is a risk that confidential customer information will be released, either by accident or on purpose. This may be a result of errors in the design of the underlying systems or a failure of data security systems.

One example relates to Internet banking. A British bank validated customers' identity by checking the name and address. This created the risk that someone of the same name, living at the same address, could access another customer's account details. This might happen if, for example, a father and son had the same name and lived at the same address.

It has also been alleged that a call centre employee, working in an overseas call centre, copied and offered to sell customer details.

This can cause serious damage to a bank's reputation.

Poor service levels

We have discussed the problem of poor service levels as a result of unexpected success, but the same problem can occur because of inadequate planning. Telephone call centres are an example.

When the banks first deployed call centres, they were surprised to receive a much greater number of calls than they had planned for. This affected the level of service, because the services that call centres can deliver are very sensitive to the number of calls.

The number of calls that they had expected to receive was based on the demand reported by the branches. There were two reasons why these estimates were too low: the M25 effect and strangled demand.

The M25 effect has also been described as 'build it and they will come' or 'channels create their own demand'. Customers will use a channel if it offers them convenience and a good level of service.

Strangled demand is a result of demand being under-recorded in the branches. Branch staff dealt with customers physically present in the branch in preference to telephone callers, leaving telephones unanswered and calls unrecorded. In addition, many customers were reluctant to call the branch because of the long wait and the risk that the call would go unanswered.

The lesson of the telephone call centre is that demand for a new channel cannot be predicted based on the recorded demand for existing channels, even if the new channel is a direct replacement.

Another problem is uneven demand. During the pilot phase, the channel is little used and service levels are good. As the new channel is rolled out nationally, it is used more heavily and the service level can easily fall to an unacceptable level. Banks try to avoid this through modelling and volume testing (testing how well the computer systems cope with very large transaction volumes), but it can still occur.

The converse can also occur. The national roll out may produce abnormally high levels of customer demand. Some of these customers may stop using it after a short time, either because they have just been trying the service or because they have been put off by poor service levels or a poor customer experience. If the bank increases resources to meet the initial level of demand, it might find that the channel is under-used.

The risk of cannibalisation

All channels compete against each other to a greater or lesser extent. This is because channels are alternative ways of satisfying demand. If customers choose to use one channel, then they are not using another channel.

This is not a zero sum game – an additional million transactions going through one channel does not translate into a million less transactions going through other channels. We showed this when we discussed the M25 effect and strangled demand above. However, there is likely to be some reduction in activity on other channels.

The problem is that this reduction in activity can affect the financial viability of either the channel as a whole or, more usually, individual outlets. Branches are an example of this. Branches are an expensive resource and need a significant number of customers if they are to be profitable. If new channels, such as the telephone call centre and the Internet, are introduced, this will push some branches into unprofitability.

This does not necessarily mean that these branches should be closed. This is discussed further in chapter 17.

The risk of adverse selection

We have said that new channels are more vulnerable to fraud. But they also attract customers that the bank does not necessarily want. The main problems are rate chasers and customers who are a poor credit risk.

Most new channels are capital intensive. They require a high initial set up cost and have low operating costs. Therefore, banks want to attract as many customers as possible to repay the set up cost. This may involve offering higher rates to savers. This can be justified both in terms of attracting customers and because the lower operating costs ensure that these products remain profitable.

Some of these customers will be rate chasers – customers who are only interested in the product because of the high interest rate. If this falls, these customers will move their accounts. This makes it very difficult for banks to make a significant profit from these customers and may mean that the profit earned is insufficient to cover their recruitment costs.

Customers who have been rejected for credit in the past may also decide to try the new channel. If they are new customers, the bank will not have the behavioural information that is usually used in the credit scoring process and may not be in a position to assess the credit risk accurately. In addition, new channels might be associated with changes designed to make the application process easier, for example self-certification of income, that can also result in the acceptance of customers who are a poor credit risk.

INNOVATION

If launching a new channel using established technology is risky, it may be thought that launching a new channel using experimental technology would be unwise in the extreme.

The justification usually given for trying to be first to market with a new channel is the attempt to secure first mover advantage. The first organization to bring a new channel to market is believed to gain an advantage as a result of technological leadership, pre-emption of scarce assets and switching costs.[cxxv]

Technological leadership is the ability to exploit a technological breakthrough by bringing a product to market that other organizations are unable to copy. Intellectual property legislation is often used to prevent copying. Even if competitors can copy the product, the first mover will have gained an advantage by going through the learning curve of developing and deploying the technology.

Pre-emption of scarce assets is the ability to buy up resources at a time when they may be very cheap. For example, some banks have entered the Internet Service Provider (ISP) market. If this had been successful, other banks would have wanted to follow and the resources required (such as bandwidth and telecommunications capacity) would have increased in price.

Switching costs is perhaps the advantage that applies most obviously to banking channels. Customers who start to use a new channel invest time, effort and money in that channel. Changing to a different provider imposes switching costs, at least in terms of time and effort and sometimes in terms of money. In addition, organizations attempting to follow the first mover need to invest resources to persuade customers to switch.

Innovation can come from two sources: start ups and established organizations. Both sources have their own record of successes and failures. For example:

	Success	Failure
Start up	Directline	Internet-only banks
Established bank	First Direct	Mondex

There is no real evidence that being first to market with a channel can give banks a sustainable competitive advantage. One reason for this is that banking is a service and it is very easy to copy innovations in service industries.[cxxvi] The intangible nature of banking also facilitates the free rider effect, in which the first mover shows its competitors how to make the new channel a success and what pitfalls to avoid. They are then able to enter the market quickly and at a lower cost than the first mover.

In spite of such first mover disadvantages, some established banks seem to be willing to take the risk of launching innovative channels. We have already discussed the Midland Bank and First Direct, but other examples from the UK include the Woolwich Building Society (now part of Barclays) with its Open Banking multi-channel service, and the Nationwide Building Society, which has introduced a number of innovations in Internet banking and virtual branches.

Spanish bank BBVA is another example. The bank has a specific department for innovation and development and asserts "innovation forms a cornerstone of BBVA's strategy".[cxxvii]

ADOPTION OF NEW CHANNELS

We have already said, in chapter 2, that customer adoption of new channels follows an S-shaped curve, starting slowly, accelerating, and finally tapering off. Why is this?

Customers can be classified into five groups, depending on how quickly they are prepared to adopt an innovation such as a new channel.[cxxviii] Innovators, who make up about 2½ per cent of the population, are the first to adopt it. They are followed by early adopters, about 13½ per cent of the population, and the early majority, about 34 per cent of the population. The late majority, about 34 per cent of the population, follows, with the laggards, about 16 per cent of the population, being the last to adopt the innovation.

The S-curve is a result of this pattern of adoption. Adding the percentages for each group, to give a cumulative percentage, gives an S-curve as shown:

Figure 9 – Adoption of new channels and the S-curve

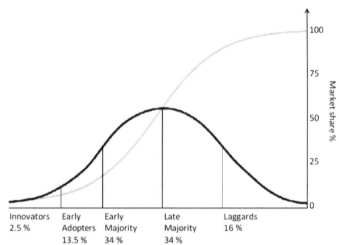

Source: http://en.wikipedia.org/wiki/File:Diffusionofideas.PNG last retrieved 30th July 2011

As we said earlier in this chapter, this makes it very difficult for banks to assess the success or failure of a new channel early enough in the process to take corrective action.

One way of managing the risk is to introduce new channels in three phases:[cxxix]

- The informational phase. The bank provides basic information and contact details.
- The transactional phase. The bank provides transactions and more complex information such as loan and mortgage calculators.
- The relationship phase. The bank uses the technology to offer specialised and customised solutions.

DILAPIDATING CHANNELS

We have already said that it is very difficult to decommission an unsuccessful channel. Why is this? The problem is that even the least successful channel is likely to have some users. These users might be quite happy with the channel. They are likely to be 'early adopters' and, as such, valuable to the bank. Note that the same argument applies to decommissioning products.

Therefore many banks follow a process of dilapidating channels. This includes four steps: Close to new customers, develop a substitute channel, incentivise customers to switch and decommission the channel.

The first step is to **close the channel to new customers**, and to stop advertising. It will appear on rate cards as a closed channel.

The second step is to **develop a substitute channel** or channels. These may already be available. This was the critical issue with the plan to decommission the use of cheques in the UK, which was scheduled for October 2018 but was halted because no suitable substitute was available.

The third step is to **incentivise customers to switch** to the new channel. This is usually a mixture of carrot and stick. Customers who switch to the new channel may receive various incentives, including cash. The level of service on the old channel may be allowed to deteriorate, for example by reducing staffing levels. Or additional charges can be levied.

This can backfire spectacularly. Abbey National, now part of Santander, attempted to persuade customers to make bill payments through virtual channels, instead of the branch counter, by levying a charge for bill payments at the counter. This resulted in their receiving some very negative publicity.

The fourth step is to bite the bullet and **decommission the channel**. In practice, many banks are unwilling to risk the damage to customer goodwill and public relations and remain stuck on the third step.

An example of failure to decommission a channel is the passbook account. Passbook accounts are expensive to administer (because of the need to install and maintain passbook readers) and they usually have low balances, which means that the bank gets little benefit from holding the funds. But they are still used because a large number of customers still have them and many banks are unwilling to take them away.

An example of successful decommissioning is online banking. Many of the early attempts at online banking used Videotex, a system that used a keyboard and set top box in conjunction with the television and a telephone line.

As we said in chapter 1, videotex was not very successful. The banks were reluctant to move to browser-based Internet banking, because of concerns about Internet security, and introduced personal computer (PC) banking. This used software installed on the customer's PC to provide the necessary level of security, using the Internet to carry encrypted messages (this is called a thick client solution, because it depends on software installed on the customer's 'client' PC).

The main disadvantage of this was that the customer could only use the channel from a PC on which the software was installed. This made online banking from work, for example, more difficult.

As Internet security improved, a number of pure play new entrants started to offer a browser-based Internet banking service. Therefore the established banks withdrew their PC banking offerings and replaced them with browser-based Internet banking.

Why did they succeed in decommissioning this channel? One possible reason is that each successive channel offered a service equal or superior to the previous channel. Therefore there was little incentive for customers to remain with the old channel.

Chapter 13 – Channel integration

The vision of most banks is to provide their customers with a seamless, fully integrated and uniform experience across all channels. Many banks are still years away from achieving this.

John Kirkbright[cxxx]

WHAT IS CHANNEL INTEGRATION?

As we said in chapter 1, banking used to be very simple. The branch was at the centre of the relationship, so channel integration was limited to making sure that the other channels reflected what the branch was doing.

However, we now live in a multi-channel world. The branch is no longer at the centre of things. Life is much more complicated.

A diagram might help to explain the difference:

Figure 10 – Branch-centred vs. multi-channel banking

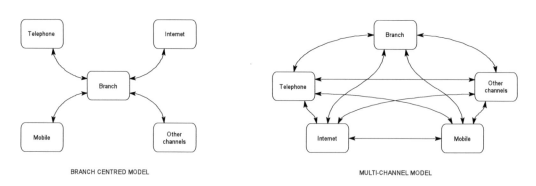

The greater complexity of the multi-channel model is obvious. There is another problem. In the branch-centred model, the branch controlled the relationship. The information held by the branch was the definitive view of the information about the customer. In the multi-channel world, none of the channels controls the relationship.

What do we mean by channel integration? What do our customers expect from channel integration? Research has shown that customers expect their channels to give them consistent information and a consistent experience across channels.

We also know that customers expect to be able to carry out multi-channel transactions. This implies a third requirement. This is for a corporate memory that spans all of the channels and records all previous contacts between the bank and the customer.

CONSISTENT INFORMATION

"A database is an organized collection of data for one or more purposes, usually in digital form."[cxxxi] Therefore banks can ensure that they get consistent information about their customers by taking it from their central database. If only it were so simple!

In practice banks have many databases. There are a number of reasons for this. Banks' Information Technology (IT) systems are built piecemeal, as new requirements arise, instead of all being built at one time. Banks acquire new IT systems and databases as a result of mergers and acquisitions. Banks may buy package software, systems that have been developed by a third party and have their own databases.

The information in these databases will usually be different. Sometimes this is because different systems need different information – a mortgage system needs to hold much more information about the property than a current account system does, for example. Sometimes it is because of mistakes when the information was entered. If the piece of information is not very important for the system, any mistakes are unlikely to be noticed and corrected.

Date of birth is an example. One bank was surprised to note that a lot of its customers appeared to have been born on 1st January. The reason, as the bank subsequently discovered, was that tellers had guessed the customer's age as 'about 40' (for example) and put the date of birth down as 1st January in the corresponding year.

It is easy to understand the rationale for this. The date of birth was not usually important for the current account system and it saved the teller from asking the customer a question that might have been regarded as personal or intrusive. This might have become a problem later, if the date of birth was used as part of the identification and verification (ID&V) procedures for telephone banking and Internet banking.

It would also have been inconsistent with the date of birth held on other databases, such as that for a life assurance system, where the date of birth was very important and was recorded correctly.

Therefore many banks went through a data cleansing exercise. The purpose of this was to identify discrepancies between the data, or data that was clearly unreliable (such as dates of birth), to get the correct information and to change the database. Initiatives such as Know Your Customer (KYC), which was introduced to combat terrorism and crime, gave the banks both an opportunity and an additional incentive to do this.

However, this did not solve the problem. As long as different databases were being maintained separately, there was no way of ensuring that the information held was consistent.

The only long-term solution was to use a single source for all information. There were two ways of achieving this: Combining the bank's databases and creating middleware.

Combining databases is a major investment and few major banks have combined all of their databases. However, it is possible to combine critical parts of the database, in particular customer information. A number of banks have done this, although it is still difficult in practice to achieve the objective of a single database for all customer information.

The idea of middleware is that it is a layer sitting between the channels and the underlying systems, as in the following diagram.[cxxxii]

Figure 11 – Middleware

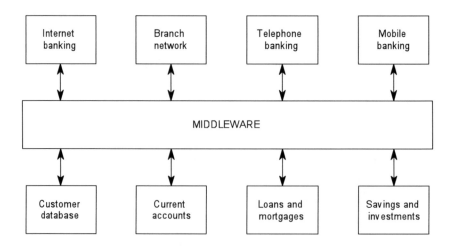

The middleware includes the rules about which source should be used for each individual piece of information, which ensures that customers will receive consistent information across all channels.

CONSISTENT EXPERIENCE

A consistent customer experience means that customers should be treated in the same way irrespective of which channel they use. For example, if a customer applies for a loan product the channel used for the application should not affect the decision as to whether that loan will be granted.

Channels are not completely equivalent, of course. Some products, such as Internet savings accounts, may only be available through one channel. However, if a product is available through multiple channels, the treatment of the customer should be identical.

The way in which customers are treated depends on a number of factors. Some of these are related to the information held about the customer. For example, lending decisions are based on the customer's credit score. Consistent information, using middleware for example, should ensure a consistent experience for these factors.

However, banks also apply treatment strategies. These are the rules as to how customers are treated. For example, there may be a treatment strategy for students that allows the bank to make loans to students even if they do not meet the credit score requirement.

Banks constantly try to refine these treatment strategies. One way of doing this is called champion challenger. Most customers, for example 90 per cent, will go through the 'champion' treatment strategy. The remainder, 10 per cent in this example, will go through a 'challenger' strategy that applies different rules. The bank will examine the impact on indicators such as default rates and customer goodwill over a period. From this analysis, the bank may decide to promote the challenger strategy to be the new champion. Or it may make changes to the challenger strategy to try to improve the results.

To ensure consistent treatment across all channels, the same treatment strategies must be applied. Again, this can be achieved through middleware.

CORPORATE MEMORY

We have said that the corporate memory allows customers to carry out multi-channel transactions. Multi-channel transactions are transactions that go through two or more channels. We have already discussed customer buying behaviour in terms of pre-purchase, purchase and post-purchase activities. There is no reason why the customer should not use different channels for these.

A common example of this is a customer using the loan calculator on a bank's website to calculate repayments before completing the loan through another channel such as the branch.

Banks need to record potential pre-purchase activities such as using a loan calculator for two reasons. First, they signal possible future actions by the customer and can be used as a trigger for marketing activity. Second, they can save the bank time. If a customer uses a loan calculator and then makes an appointment with the branch, it is reasonable to infer that the customer wants to discuss some form of credit arrangement.

This is the role of the customer contact history. All of the bank's contacts with the customer, irrespective of channel, are recorded on the customer contact history and analysed to determine future customer intentions.

USE THE INFORMATION!

"An international bank in Hong Kong responded to a tender for a large piece of business from a major corporation. The customer was visited by two senior managers from different departments in the bank on the same day each with a response to the tender. Unfortunately each was unaware that the other was seeing the client. Although both presented similar proposals with respect to content, the fees they quoted for the work differed by 25 per cent. This resulted in considerable embarrassment at the bank and considerable amusement in the local financial community – neither bid won the business."[cxxxiii]

Consistent information and the corporate memory are not just for the benefit of customers using self-service channels, they are also for the bank's staff. The cautionary tale given above should help to illustrate this point. Banks must use the information they have about their customers and approach them in a coordinated way.

CHANNEL STRATEGY

We discussed what the distribution strategy is in chapter 5, but how is it populated? Banks need to make a number of strategic decisions relating to:

- Changing customer attitudes and behaviour
- The product range to be distributed
- Number of channels to be offered
- Their attitude towards innovation
- Their attitude towards automation
- Channel segmentation
- Competition between channels

CHANGING CUSTOMER ATTITUDES AND BEHAVIOUR

By far the biggest factor in considering your third-generation channel strategy is your customer, in particular their attitudes and behaviour.

Factors to consider include:

- Attitude to security and risk – in addition to the countermeasures that banks and customers can use to deter unauthorised access and fraud, customers assess their personal security when considering which channels to use. For example, even though most consumers have not used their mobile phone as an electronic wallet, research amongst potential users has revealed concerns about security, as they believe that they are more likely to lose their mobile phone than their wallet.
- Convenience of access – we have discussed one of the challenges for branches being their convenience to access them for counter service or advice. One of the factors that increased Internet banking adoption was 'always on' broadband connectivity that speeded up logging in and therefore completion of the task in hand. Mobile banking will replace Telephone banking for day-to-day transactions as it does not require the same degree of privacy to conduct transactions and is available when most Telephone banking services are closed.
- Ability to access channel – banks must consider whether customers have, or will acquire within a short period of time, the right technology to enjoy the service. Mobile banking penetration is around 10 per cent and is dependent upon smartphone penetration of the market, which in many countries is approaching 50 per cent. Most banks have introduced some form of Mobile banking app to facilitate access. So, why the gap? We believe that it is partly down to consumer concerns about security,

a subject that eventually Internet banking overcame.

- Changing payments behaviour – the last 30 years have seen a massive switch away from cash and cheques as the core payments vehicles to debit cards, credit cards – the next stage will offer mobile electronic peer-to-peer payments, near-field communications (NFC) devices (plastic card or mobile phone based). Banks must consider how customers use money to ensure that their channels are fit for purpose, or risk losing part of their business to more agile competitors who meet the need.

- Changing demographics – a rapidly ageing population, with a greater life expectancy is becoming a feature of most economies. There is some evidence that suggests that Baby Boomer and Gen X channel usage behaviours differ from Gen Y. The former are said to be heavier users of traditional channels, such as branches and Telephone banking and even Internet banking. Gen Y, the Digital Natives are more likely to adopt Mobile banking, contactless payments and social payment methods. Banks need to consider the future of channels, such as branches, that require a significant investment, given falling transaction volumes and profitability.

- What customers want – an obvious statement, but one that is sometimes overlooked. In the past some banks have simply followed 'the herd' where new channels or social media are concerned. First- and second-generation thinking was 'bank-in' and focused on cost reduction, not the customer experience or relevancy. Customers have views on what their banks should provide, and how they should do it. As they ultimately pay for the channels, they should have a say!

- Social media – many banks continue to struggle with a social media strategy. Any consideration of a multi-channel strategy must include social media in the mix, as it is increasingly where your customers are when they are on the Internet and very relevant to them.

- Consumer financial education and marketing – in a world where consumers are bombarded with marketing messages, have access to price comparison information and peer-to-peer recommendation, banks must consider how they better equip customers to manage their finances.

PRODUCT RANGE TO BE DISTRIBUTED

Financial services providers can choose to operate a very narrow product range. This is called the monoline business model. Common examples include organisations specialising in motor insurance, credit cards, remittances and foreign exchange.

Start-ups often choose the monoline business model and then expand their range of services later. Directline started as a monoline seller of motor insurance but has since diversified and now sells a wide range of non-life insurance products.

Monoline providers also usually operate through a very limited range of channels. This makes their distribution strategy very straightforward.

To use Directline as an example, it started with one channel, the telephone call centre. It successfully managed the transition from a telephone-based service to an Internet-based service, retaining the telephone call centre channel both as a secondary sales channel and as a channel for dealing with claims. It does not have branches.

Specialising in a narrow range of products delivered primarily through one or two channels allows monoline providers to operate with very low costs.

NUMBER OF CHANNELS TO BE OFFERED

Financial services providers can choose to operate a small number of channels. The term that is used for this – the monochannel business model – suggests that they only operate one channel. This dates back to the time when the telephone call centre was the only virtual channel capable of operating a banking service. In practice most monochannel providers use the Internet as their main channel, supported by telephone call centres and the mail.

As we discussed in chapter 10, the choice of channel has a major impact on the cost of a transaction. The cost of carrying out a transaction through Internet banking is about four per cent of the cost of carrying out the same transaction over the branch counter.

Therefore it seemed likely that a monochannel Internet bank would have an unbeatable cost advantage over its traditional rivals, and this was widely expected to be the case when the pure play Internet banks first appeared in the mid-1990s. Academic and industry commentators were aware that the established banks would bring out their own Internet banking offerings, but thought that the cost of the branch network would prevent them from achieving the same efficiency as the monochannel providers.[cxxxiv]

This belief lasted for a remarkably short period. By 2001, it was generally accepted that the Internet-only banks had performed poorly.[cxxxv] Michael Porter, one of the leading academics in the theory of competition, pointed out something that other commentators had missed. The established banks had other competitive advantages, such as economies of scale, which were sufficient to outweigh pure transaction cost.[cxxxvi]

Few of the monochannel banks have made the breakthrough by acquiring a customer base of sufficient size to allow them to enjoy economies of scale comparable to the traditional High Street banks. In the UK, and disregarding the supermarket banks (which are something of a special case), only First Direct and Cahoot have acquired a large customer base and they remain a long way behind the traditional full service banks.

Although the monochannel model reduces costs, multi-channel banking may lead to more sales and increased revenues. There are two reasons for this.

First, customers have channel preferences for purchases. In other words, some customers prefer to use one channel for purchases, other customers prefer to use a different channel. Monochannel providers are limiting their customer base by restricting it to customers who prefer to use one particular channel. Multi-channel operation has the additional benefit of appealing to customers who prefer to use one channel (the Internet, for example) for research while using a different channel (the telephone or the branch) for the purchase.[cxxxvii]

Second, there is a correlation between the cost of a sale and its complexity.[cxxxviii] Given that complex sales generate greater profit and improve customer loyalty, multi-channel banking would be expected to generate higher revenues.

The most important factor is to provide the right mix of channels to satisfy your customers, and target customers, needs. Failure to provide the right mix of channels to sell the product and maintain it conveniently and easily will discourage customers from choosing you in the first place.

ATTITUDE TOWARDS INNOVATION

Banks must decide how innovative they want to be in the introduction of new channels. There are often considered to be three choices of strategic position: Leading edge, fast follower or laggard.

Organisations at the **leading edge** adopt and deploy new technology at an early stage. One reason for taking a leading edge position is the ability to secure first mover advantage although, as we discussed in chapter 6, it is not clear that this is a source of sustainable competitive advantage in banking.

One disadvantage of adopting a leading edge position is that it can be very expensive. Indeed, the leading edge is sometimes called the bleeding edge because of the way in which it consumes cash. However, banks are often able to moderate this by partnering with universities or suppliers.

One advantage of adopting a leading edge position is that banks may benefit by developing expertise in deploying new technologies. This 'learning curve' effect may allow them to respond to changes in technology faster and more effectively than their competitors.

Fast followers monitor technological developments and the activities of their competitors. Instead of attempting to be first to market with a new technology, they plan to deploy a response before the leading edge organization is able to use its technological lead to build significant market share.

One disadvantage of the fast follower position is that they can fail to identify technological innovations that do not originate from their traditional competitors. PayPal is an example. PayPal was a start-up and few banks would have been monitoring it. PayPal has succeeded in taking a dominant position in its market.

The advantage of the fast follower position is that the costs of imitation are lower than the costs of innovation. The fast follower can learn from someone else's mistakes rather than its own. As was shown by the pure play Internet banks, late entrants can usually catch up provided that they can leverage their existing advantages.

Laggards wait until the technology has been proven and deployed across the industry before adopting it. Some small banks adopt a laggard position, either because they do not have the resources to monitor developments in technology or because they do not believe that their customers are interested in innovation.

One should also determine the attitude to technology of one's customer base. Customers have their own attitudes to technology. The five groups of technology adopters outlined in chapter 12 are theoretical groups, but they emphasise that customers have attitudes to adopting new technology and a mis-match between the bank's attitude towards technology innovation and its customers' technology adoption rate, or the pace of introduction of new technology, could have dire consequences for the bank.

It is important not to assume the distribution when planning channel strategy; actual research of your customers is required. Due to a number of historic factors, such as acquisitions, mergers and market positioning, banks do not have the same demographic profile and their customers' attitude to technology may differ from each other and from the above model. We would expect the profile of First Direct and a smaller high street bank or building society of a similar size to be different, with First Direct attracting more Innovators and Early Adopters, but probably few Late Majority and Laggards. To retain its Innovators and Early Adopters First Direct must continuously innovate in new channels, such as Mobile banking and social media – which is what we see in real life.

ATTITUDE TOWARDS AUTOMATION

We discussed the role of automation in reducing costs in the context of telephone banking call centres in chapter 8. Although automation reduces costs, it produces a less satisfactory customer experience and banks must decide what balance they want between efficiency and customer satisfaction.

Another example of automation is the virtual branch. Lloyds TSB, now Lloyds Bank, ran a pilot in the Reading area in which it replaced the vast majority of its staffed branches with virtual branches. As we said in chapter 7, these are unstaffed and use a mixture of self-service and virtual channels to serve customers. This provoked strong local and national opposition and the bank reverted to the previous arrangement of staffed branches.

Whatever the bank's attitude, the channels themselves have characteristics that affect the degree of personalisation or automation that is possible. The following diagram illustrates this.

Figure 12 – Personalisation vs. automation

More personal ← ———————————————————————— → More automated

Relationship management	Branch	Call centre	Call me	Web chat	Avatar	Automated telephone service	Web site	ATM

CHANNEL SEGMENTATION

We introduced the idea of channel segmentation in chapter 5, giving branches as an example, and discussed it in more depth in the context of the telephone banking call centre in chapter 8. As with automation, channel segmentation requires banks to decide on the correct balance.

The advantage of making channels open to all customers is that this makes the most efficient use of the assets. A branch may have only a few hundred private customers in its catchment area, whereas there may be thousands of premier, mass market and basic customers. Setting this branch aside for the exclusive use of private customers will result in its being used less than opening the branch to all customers.

However, setting the branch aside for the exclusive use of private customers will give these customers a better experience. In addition, by setting aside a small number of branches for private customers the bank will be able to concentrate the expertise needed to deal with these customers in these branches. This is much cheaper than training people in every branch to deal with the occasional private customer.

Most banks reserve a small number of branches for private and corporate customers. These customers have different banking needs from other customers, which justifies setting branches aside. Concentrations of private banking customers are often found in particular locations, such as the West End of London, which allows banks to locate private banking branches in places where they will achieve a satisfactory level of footfall.

Some banks set aside branches for the exclusive use of premier and business customers, but it is more usual to set space aside in branches for them. If counter positions are reserved for these customers, they can be used for other customers at busy times, when no premier or business customers are waiting.

Telephone banking can be segmented. Higher value 'premium' customers may receive a differentiated service that reflects their value. For example, having completed the automated security as all customers do they may be routed to a human customer representative who will greet them by name and handle their enquiry personally. Lower value customers may be greeted by an automated menu-driven IVR that offers little or no opportunity to speak to a human customer service representative.

Internet banking is sometimes segmented for 'premium' proposition customers; providing them access to additional functionality, such as having a consolidated view of products held in different countries and the ability to make real-time transfer of funds between the accounts. 'Premium' customers may also receive a differentiated service if they ask for help whilst using Internet banking. One example is to route their request to a highly trained specialist (or Virtual Relationship Manager) who can initiate a videoconference with the customer (customer technology permitting) should they wish. Lower value customers may be routed to a contact centre representative who provides voice support only.

CHANNEL MIGRATION

One way for banks to reduce their costs is to migrate customers away from expensive channels, such as the branch, and towards cheaper channels, in particular the Internet and mobile devices.

The factors that persuade customers to switch from another channel, for example the branch, to the Internet are not the same as the factors that lead to high customer satisfaction amongst customers who already use Internet banking.[cxxxix] Although banks only offer one Internet service, they need to promote it in different ways to existing Internet banking customers and to customers they wish to migrate.

Convenience is the most important reason for customers to adopt Internet banking and is also the most important factor for existing Internet banking users. However, other factors that are important for Internet adoption include making the system easy to navigate round, making sure that the information is accurate and up-to-date, providing online help, and providing feedback for complex transactions, to reassure the customer that it has completed correctly. These are not important for customers who already use the service.

COMPETITION BETWEEN CHANNELS

The branch-centric thinking of the first-generation led to the idea of customers being 'owned' by a branch. The development of direct banking through virtual channels such as the telephone and the Internet gave rise to the idea that a channel could also own a customer. It has been pointed out that this concept of ownership can result in income relating to that customer being incorrectly allocated, distorting the profitability of channels and branches.[cxl]

The question that banks face is how much competition to allow between channels. Academics have suggested that competition between channels can be managed in three ways coordination, free competition, managed competition: [cxli]

Coordination means that all channels work together in a coordinated way. Executive management makes decisions about the distribution strategy centrally.

Free competition means that channels are able to compete freely against each other. Each channel has its own profit & loss account.

Managed competition means that channels are able to compete against each other, but do so within a firmly agreed set of standards. Transfer pricing is used to allocate costs and revenue from customers who use multiple channels.

It is perhaps worth noting that this analysis was written in 1998, at a time when it was still believed that the cost advantages of the pure play Internet banks would give them an unbeatable competitive advantage. However, it is still useful as a framework for our analysis.

The authors noted that the coordination model was best suited for customer-centric organizations. However, the weaknesses of the coordination model are that decision-making takes longer (leading to slower response times by management), the complexity of developing coordinated processes makes them more costly, and there is a lack of clear accountability.

The free competition model is best suited for organizations with product and channel based value propositions. The weaknesses of the free competition model are the risk of confusing customers by sending mixed messages, and the inability to take advantage of opportunities that require a consolidated view of the customer relationship. It was also noted that the efficiency gains that could be achieved through clearer accountability would be partly offset by the duplication of overhead activities such as Information Technology (IT).

The authors saw the managed competition model as the golden mean, offering greater accountability but through the use of standards, protecting the brand by showing a consistent corporate image to the customer.

More than ten years has elapsed since that paper was written, and banks have moved away from a transactional view of their customers and back towards a customer-centric view. Nor, given the experience of the pure play Internet banks, does it seem so important that management should be able to react to changing events in a very short time period. And transfer pricing is notoriously difficult to get right.

We believe that it is appropriate for most banks to adopt a mixed model. The coordination model, which is the best suited to a customer-centric value proposition, is the right model to use for the bank's established channels. The size and complexity of many of the channels means that banks need channel managers, but they need to act in a coordinated way and compete against other banks, not each other, if they are not to undermine the customer experience and the customers' confidence in the bank.

The managed competition model may be appropriate when a new channel is first introduced. It gives management more freedom to respond to problems as they arise and protects the bank's brand, as the new channel remains within an agreed set of standards. Banks may also have some activities that are completely peripheral to their main customer base. Examples include share registrations and auctions. These have no impact on the brand and can operate under the free competition model.

Chapter 15 – Third-generation thinking

THIRD-GENERATION THINKING

In this chapter, we summarise the central themes of third-generation thinking. The three generations of thinking can be summarised as:

Automation – 1980 – driven by bank to reduce cost, undifferentiated approach, branch-centric;

Connectivity – 2000 – (but not always connected), driven by bank to leverage new technology to reduce cost, segmented approach, channel-centric;

Intelligence – 2011 – driven by the customer, personalised approach, customer-centric.

Third-generation thinking has become necessary because the banks have lost control over their channels. There are a number of reasons behind this, including: banks failed to appreciate or predict changing customer attitudes, behaviour and demand; increased competition; new competition from non-bank organizations; reduced entry barriers; increased regulation and the rise of the social media.

As a result, banks increasingly face disintermediation and pressure on revenues.

Third-generation thinking requires bankers to adopt a completely new mindset. This involves working with customers and third parties in order to develop new solutions that are relevant to customers and mutually beneficial to all parties.

It also requires bankers to reject some cherished models of how banks operate. These include the branch-centric model, traditional approaches to marketing and a belief that the automation of existing processes is the only way to deliver services effectively.

THE AGE OF THE CUSTOMER

Third-generation thinking has become necessary because the environment that banks operate in has changed. There are a number of reasons for this, including:

- Customer attitudes and behaviour towards banks has changed significantly since the start of the financial crisis. Customer trust reached all time lows and as a result banks are having to work hard to rebuild trust through genuine improvements in the customer experience to prove that they are relevant;
- Through technology such as the Internet and social media, customers are more connected, knowledgeable and empowered and are demanding more from their bank – and they can 'punish' if they don't get it. We have seen the rise of the self-directed customer since the start of the financial crisis;
- Customers have more choice of financial service providers and products than ever before and it's more confusing than ever. Because they created relevance to customers, price comparison services now dominate decision making for certain sectors of the

market, and the criteria are no longer about price alone. Social media allow consumers to share information on the wider customer experience when they have bought the product;

- Post-crisis governments are increasing regulations around banking and encouraging competition by lowering some of the barriers under their control. One example is the recommendation from the Independent Commission on Banking to introduce simplified current account switching between banks. This threatens to increase banks' operating costs whilst reducing revenue streams;

- New technology, such as the Internet, mobile phones and social media, is encouraging non-traditional competitors to enter the 'banking' market. As they do not offer full banking they avoid most of the regulatory barriers and costs to entry. Their business model is to target parts of a bank's business from which they can skim off a proportion of income, for example payments.

The following diagram sums up the three generations of thinking and the drivers.

Figure 13 Three generations of thinking

Age of the branch
- Branch saturation post-70s consolidation creates inflexible, inefficient and expensive branch network
- Mass customer acquisition strategies require processing economies of scale and new distribution channels
- Switch away from 'cash economy' as new money transmission methods accepted, starts to impact branch traffic
- Banks unable to offer same level of personal relationship to best customers

Age of the channel
- Channel proliferation, but the customer experience fragments because they are not always connected
- Cheques decline as more payments made by plastic or electronically, further pressure on traditional distribution
- New monoline competitors gain market share, but 'full banking' proves more difficult, further consolidation during crisis
- Price comparison sites encourage 'disintermediation' based on price

Age of the customer
- Empowered, connected, knowledgeable and demand more from their bank – and can 'punish' if they don't get it
- New technology and social media encouraging non-traditional competitors to attack valuable 'full banking' niches
- Post-crisis regulatory pressure and competition driven by government threatens traditional revenue streams
- Banks increasingly face disintermediation and pressure on revenues

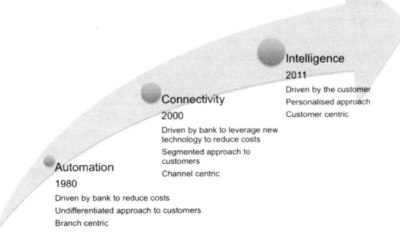

Intelligence
2011
Driven by the customer
Personalised approach
Customer centric

Connectivity
2000
Driven by bank to leverage new technology to reduce costs
Segmented approach to customers
Channel centric

Automation
1980
Driven by bank to reduce costs
Undifferentiated approach to customers
Branch centric

Source: Intelligence Delivered (Asia) Limited 2012

JOURNEYS

Journeys are not just multi-channel transactions. The problem with journeys is that they are multi-channel transactions that involve steps that are outside of the bank's control.

The Internet has been the enabling technology that has made journeys a reality. The Internet allows customers to keep control of the journey and to make side trips, for example to price comparison sites, review sites or the social media, without having to leave the transaction and start again.

There are three main issues for the banks.

- The first is how to make sure that customers return to the bank to close the transaction.
- The second is how to make a profit out of the transaction. The Internet has increased price transparency and put pressure on margins.
- The third is how to support customers through the journey. This is similar to the role the banks must adopt in supporting customers through their pre-purchase activities, discussed in chapter 3.

COLLABORATION WITH CUSTOMERS

The Internet has provided customers with a vast range of financial service providers from which to choose. Why should they choose your products?

One reason might be that your products are a particularly good fit for their needs. You can only achieve that by being relevant to them and you do that by listening to them.

Banks' traditional marketing efforts, based on propensity modelling alone, 'pushed' products at customers by direct mail or outbound telephone contact without any real understanding of what the individual target customer actually needed. This was very ineffective, with less than a 2 per cent sales rate, and caused customer dissatisfaction as they were often bombarded with irrelevant offers.

A more effective approach is to listen to your customer describe their current and future financial needs and agree with the customer to discuss solutions at a mutually agreed time. By recording this information in your CRM system as a set of codified needs, with contact dates, you are able to use the 'corporate memory' to contact the customer at the right time, with the right solution. Where the customer's situation has changed the need can be rescheduled or cancelled and new needs identified and followed up. Sales rates can be 20 times higher than direct mail and builds the customer relationship as the customer appreciates the more mutual and individual approach. Research revealed that customers were happy to provide the information provided it was used for mutual benefit.

The Internet, and in particular the social media, is an effective mechanism for this type of collaboration. If banks can set up communities for key groups of customers, they can work with these communities to develop new products for them.

THE VIRTUAL ORGANIZATION

The virtual organization has impacted the banking industry in three main ways.

First, it has reduced entry costs. This has made it much easier to start a new bank, or for a non-bank to offer what would traditionally have been thought of as banking services.

Many banks outsource their disaster recovery arrangements – the contingency sites that they will use if their main site becomes unavailable – to third parties. If they did not do this, they would have to lease, equip and maintain a contingency site themselves. They have converted an entry cost – the cost of setting such a site up in the first place – to an operating cost – the ongoing cost paid to the third party.

Second, it has reduced exit costs. This has allowed banks to be much more flexible. They are no longer forced to continue to provide unprofitable services because they are unable to redeploy the staff and equipment used for them. They are still not able to stop offering these overnight, because they are under a contractual commitment to their outsourcing partner, but they are able to plan to exit that particular line of business within a reasonable timescale.

Cheque processing exemplifies this. Cheque processing centres are large buildings that are equipped with cheque reader/sorters – machines that have no function other than to process cheques. They employ a large number of people who specialise in that one function. Outsourcing cheque processing has given the banks much more flexibility.

Third, it has made it much more difficult for banks to control the quality of service delivery where this takes place through a third party. The banks have some control. This is partly contractual and partly because a large bank will be a major customer, who outsourcers will not want to upset. However, banks cannot deal with service delivery in these channels themselves, they have to go through the outsourcer.

Call centres are a good example. Although banks were happy with the cost savings that they were initially able to realise by offshoring and (in many cases) outsourcing their call centres, customer complaints have led to many of them repatriating their call centres and bringing them back into the bank.

Governance is the critical issue. Banks must make sure that the contract between themselves and the outsourcer gives them sufficient control and that a governance system is in place to resolve problems as they arise.

THE CUSTOMER-CENTRIC DISTRIBUTION STRATEGY

All of this leads us to the idea of building the distribution strategy round the customer. This may not be possible at the individual customer level – yet – but analytics and communities can allow banks to achieve this.

It may seem odd to suggest using Metro Bank as an example of this. Surely Metro Bank is an example of an old-fashioned, first-generation, branch-centric bank?

Not quite.

The problem with old-fashioned, first-generation, branch-centric banks was that the lack of flexibility in their human and Information Technology systems made it very difficult for them to operate in a multi-channel environment and led to the mis-allocation of resources. The branch became a bottleneck that inhibited the free flow of information within the bank.

Metro Bank is seeking to avoid this by using modern Information Technology systems that are designed for the multi-channel world. The branch is the most important channel, but that is because the bank believes that its customers want it that way, not because that is the only way in which the bank can function. The branch is the first channel amongst equals, not the bottleneck through which everything should flow.

Or, at least, that is the theory! Metro Bank is still very young. We wish it success and will follow further developments with interest.

WHERE NEXT?

So where does the third-generation bank go from here? A good question. We will suggest some directions.

Overall, there needs to be a shift from volume to value. Banks need to concentrate more effort on the customers that create value for the bank. These are not necessarily the richest customers – research shows that premium customers create more value than private banking customers.[cxlii] Lloyds TSB has targeted the expatriate Indian community with its India Banking Service, working in partnership with India's ICICI Bank. The needs of expatriate communities are often very simple – remittances usually being critical – and can be met profitably through a strongly-focussed product offering.

This does not mean that banks should simply abandon all their non-profitable customers. "No company ever shrank to greatness."[cxliii] Instead of eliminating unprofitable parts of the business by hollowing out the company, third-generation banks should talk to these customers to make these parts of the business profitable.

The Internet needs to move up the value chain, away from a transactional role and towards a relationship role. The banks failed to achieve this with account aggregation, but personal financial management may be one tool that will help them towards this.

The social media are critical. They are a listening post to the views of an increasingly important demographic segment, and the banks must make sure that the listening post is attended. They are also a means of engaging with customers, through communities and otherwise.

The future of the branch remains unclear. Many of its roles – engaging with customers, collecting information, acting as a point of presence – are valuable but do not generate income directly.

The consensus view in the industry is that the branch revenue stream will come from the sale of complex products. The problem is that the increasing regulatory burden and regulatory risk undermine the profitability of such sales and create a risk of future liabilities through mis-selling. The third-generation bank must engineer its processes for the sale of complex products in such a way as to maximise its conversion rate while minimising the risk of mis-selling. This is likely to require greater use of non-branch channels, in particular the Internet, in the fact find and sale. It will also require a more detailed understanding of customers' financial positions and financial needs.

One point is clear day-to-day counter transaction levels in branches are falling rapidly as Internet banking and other payment systems reduce the need for customers to visit branches to pay in and withdraw cash, pay-in cheques, transfer money between accounts and pay bills. For most customers the branch is too inconvenient compared to virtual and self-service channels.

The call centre, once condemned as the battery farm of the electronic age, has a key role in support of both the Internet and the branch network. The third-generation bank must remain acutely aware of the balance between cost control and service quality.

Mobile banking remains an enigma. This is an area of the market in which the banks' position is under serious threat from third parties, but the issues surrounding the security of mobile devices are yet to be resolved. Third-generation banks must be seen to be taking an initiative in this market but need to be fully aware of the risks to which they might be exposing themselves.

Much the same could be said of contactless payment technology and third party providers are an increasing threat in this market. For example, Telcos or technology giants such as Google are able to enter the market without a full banking licence and threaten banks' traditional revenue streams. Although security is a concern, the issues may be better understood and third-generation banks should be better equipped to deal with them.

Above all, the third-generation bank must have a coherent distribution strategy that joins up its channels and provides customers with consistent information and a consistent customer experience whichever channels they use.

Chapter 16 – In search of relevance

What is 'relevance'? The Merriam-Webster dictionary[cxliv] defines it as 'relation to the matter in hand' or 'practical and especially social applicability'.

Third-generation thinking is the shift to relevance: 'service with a purpose that is in the customer's interest'. In this chapter we will discuss what it is and why it is important and lay the foundation for following chapters where we will discuss how banks can adopt a different approach to deliver it.

INTRODUCTION

Relevance: it is one of the great topics for debate in the late 20th and 21st Centuries. Technology, changing economic situations and future uncertainties are causing people concerns about the 'meaning of life' and they are questioning the relevance of work, governments, economics and financial institutions in their lives.

As we discussed earlier, the relationship between banks and their customers is changing and the customer is gaining more control of the relationship. As a result, they are no longer grateful for what their bank gives them, they want more – something that benefits them individually, or helps them solve a problem. They are searching for the relevance of their bank in their lives. If they don't experience it they will find a bank that delivers it.

At the same time, many banks are searching for differentiation, something that distinguishes them from their competitors in a crowded market. Maybe it's the striking colour of their branding or a snappy brand-marketing message. But this misses the mark with many customers who have a totally different real-life experience of the brand.

A bank that is looking at these solutions to differentiate them in the market is not necessarily thinking about customers and it is an example of 'bank-in' thinking. Banks should be thinking about their relevance to customers as one of their differentiators. This will unify the many disparate customer experience and business process re-engineering initiatives into a common customer-centric and practical solution that differentiates them from the competition.

WHAT CUSTOMERS WANT

We first highlighted the extra dimension, beyond the purely transactional, of what customers want in chapter 3. To recap, research carried out by HSBC[cxlv] into what customers want identified the following needs:

- Recognise my value to you
- Know me and treat me as an individual

- Provide expertise I can get at
- Be on my side (and reassure me that you are)
- Leave me in control
- Be my trusted advisor
- Notice what I need
- Be easily available

This is no mistake. They are looking for relevance.

THE NEED FOR RELEVANCE

Since the mid-to-late 2000s the need for relevance has increased due to a number of factors largely outside of the banks' control:

1. Customers, as a result of the financial crisis, have become more demanding and we have seen the rise of the self-directed customer;
2. Consumers are suffering from 'ad fatigue' from the proliferation of media, such as TV, the Internet, press comment, blogs, comparison sites and social media. Many consumers no longer hear the message; if they do hear it, many don't believe it;
3. From a challenging market where there is intense competition; financial services products are becoming increasingly commoditised; comparison information is freely available; customers are actively encouraged by governments to switch provider and finding it increasingly easier to do so in reality.
4. In the face of this instability banks have two options. They can continue to try and 'out-shout' the competition, which is difficult when marketing budgets are flat or cut. Or they can use the resources that they have to be more relevant to their customers. This does not mean massive investments in technology: in the main it requires a change in thinking and application of that thinking in the customer's interest.
5. Relevance is the cornerstone of the shift from Industrial Age 'make and sell' thinking that was typified by depersonalised mass marketing to Information Age 'sense and respond' thinking that adapts to individual customer needs and demands. We will discuss these fundamental changes later in the text.

CREATING RELEVANCE

We defined relevance as 'service with a purpose that is in the customer's interest'. What exactly does that mean?

This third-generation thinking means that the products and channels that you provide customers and the interactions that you conduct with them have a clear purpose and benefit primarily from the customer's point of view (not just the bank's). Channels such as Internet banking or Mobile banking are not designed to reduce costs by migrating customers and transactions away from more costly channels such as branches or Telephone banking. They are designed to offer and deliver real tangible benefits to the customer in terms of convenience, accessibility and security that naturally draws them to use the channel. It means that to always be relevant, interactions with customers, irrespective of channel or media, conform to a 'right customer, right message, right time' framework.

As an example, we outlined earlier in the text how banks implemented outbound marketing calls in the evening in an attempt to increase sales leads or sell simple products. But, in many cases, the call and product is irrelevant to most customers on the list, often poorly executed, and simply irritates customers, or at worst, causes them to disconnect from the bank's messages. To emphasise the points, here are two scenarios using the same channel but with different results.

The first is the traditional outbound call from a call centre when it's expected the customer will be home. This means calling the customer at 7:30pm, whilst they are relaxing or having dinner, to offer the customer a new credit card. To achieve economies of scale it is an automated approach where the call centre agent follows a script when a call is connected and has little opportunity for the agent to have genuine empathy or build rapport that motivates the employee. The customer may well ask "what is the benefit of another credit card?" Apart from its low contact and success rates it is an irritation that the customer might dismiss once. However, frequent irrelevant interruptions leads to customers disconnecting from all marketing messages from the bank (but, remember, not necessarily from competitors who take a different approach). Customers see it for what it is, a marketing 'push' call. Not the desired result. This is first- or second-generation thinking.

When might a call at 7:30pm that disturbs them be relevant in the eyes of the customer?

Imagine this scenario. Every day thousands of your good, creditworthy customers go overdrawn without an overdraft facility or exceed an overdraft facility, and you are happy to allow the excess because the customer is creditworthy and you're confident the overdraft will be repaid. However, it may take a few days for the customer to realise that they are overdrawn and they will be liable to penalty rate interest and fees. Contacting the customer that evening to alert them to the situation and to re-assure them that you can help, even though you may be disturbing them, will usually be seen as positive by the customer as the outcome is in the customer's favour – the customer avoids penalty rate interest and fees because they are able to transfer funds to cover or you will organise an overdraft, new credit card or loan then and there. This is 'service with a purpose in the customer's interest'. It is third-generation thinking.

In our experience, these service calls lead to a deepening of the relationship as in most cases the customer's explanation of the situation leads to future sales (for example, the customer may have recently changed jobs, and his new employer wasn't able to pay the customer on time). This will not only allow the bank to update its customer information, but may lead to a conversation about future financial needs. This more friendly and customer-centric approach was very popular with one bank as it encouraged employees to show empathy and build rapport and was more satisfying for them when there was a positive outcome. So much so, that they actually asked for more leads; however, we found it difficult to make more customers go unintentionally overdrawn! It had become their most effective lead generation tool (from a customer experience and sales perspective). One might question the wisdom of giving up some penalty rate interest and fees in the short-term, for long-term customer satisfaction, retention and future sales potential. We don't.

From 'product push' to 'customer pull'

In first- and second-generation thinking products were 'pushed' at customers, just like in the first scenario above. That is, the bank decided which products should be offered to which customers based upon their propensity models. Customers with a profile that matched customers who had a particular product were subjected to direct marketing, such as direct mail or outbound calling, until they bought the product, they complained or the bank had filled its quota for that product at that time. In addition to not being very effective (less than 2 per cent sales rates) it forced many customers to turn off marketing from the bank.

Third-generation thinking uses the principle of 'customer pull' to create relevance with the customer. The second scenario is an example of 'customer pull', where the initial conversation (an overdrawn account) frequently leads to an opportunity to review the customer's finances, or the provision of a solution (an overdraft) then and there.

Even after the financial crisis, banks still enjoy a unique relationship with most of their customers. Whilst the proportion of self-directed customers has risen in the last few years, there are still considerable numbers of 'validator' and 'delegator' types who look to banks to help them manage their finances and wealth. Many customers will share their needs with the bank provided it's relevant and there's mutual benefit.

The 'honeymoon period' – relevance from the start

It's a common belief that the customer is most open to cross-sales in the first 90 days of the relationship, sometimes called the 'honeymoon period'. However, the desire to achieve cross-sales without being relevant may result in a poor customer experience.

If you are relying on your customer contact during the 90-day 'honeymoon period' to build your relationship through cross-sales then either you failed to understand the customer needs in the first place or sold the wrong products during the original sale.

The contact during the 90-day 'honeymoon period' should be relevant to the customer: for example, helping them complete the account opening and transfer procedures (from their old bank) so that their initial expectations of you are met and their decision to switch to you justified. This would ensure that post-sales processes are completed satisfactorily, e.g. standing orders and direct debits set-up correctly, bill payment instructions set-up (to fully migrate them from their previous bank). If the customer identified other needs during the initial sale then these should be followed-up as agreed. It may include contacting the customer to establish needs if this was not part of the original sale. It may also include a satisfaction survey, that relates specifically to the sale (the recent memorable event), provided the customer has agreed to it and it is relevant to improve that customer's service.

Making a service call to 'tick a bank box' during the on-boarding process is 'bank-in thinking'. The purpose of the call should be relevant to the customer, not just the bank, and have a context that the customer can understand.

Due to their nature, direct marketing campaigns during the initial 90-day 'honeymoon period' may be crude as you may have insufficient reliable behavioural data and is little more than 'push marketing' and so they should be avoided. The best technique is to gather needs at the initial sale that can be followed up as mutually agreed ('sense and respond'). This requires forethought and an account opening process that includes some degree of needs gathering without an 'inquisition'.

CHANNELS

'Channels exist for one purpose: to deliver relevance'. In other words, to deliver service with a purpose that is in the customer's interest.

In the past channels were launched to reduce costs, migrate customers from high-cost to lower-cost channels, copy the market or competitors. Now that the customer is in control of channels, distribution needs to understand the purpose of each channel based upon relevance to the customer.

This may mean that long-cherished beliefs have to be re-assessed or abandoned. One such belief is the relevancy of branches to customers. Branch usage for day-to-day transactions is in terminal decline because customers are using channels, such as Internet banking, that are more convenient when they are undertaking those transactions. More product enquiries and sales are being completed through Internet banking, with the potentially more complex sales moving to Internet banking, as it is more convenient, and to simplify regulatory compliance. So, the question to ask is: "what is the relevance of branches to customers?"

Another question might be "what is the relevance of Relationship Managers to self-directed customers?" Are they valuable or an expensive irritation?

"What is the relevance of call centres when Mobile banking reaches a tipping point in terms of adoption and usage, as it surely will in the next couple of years?"

The question of how your channels are relevant to customers is key to defining and implementing a multi-channel strategy that will meet the needs of your customers.

CUSTOMER MANAGEMENT SYSTEMS

It follows that all customer relationship management (CRM) and sales systems should be designed with a single purpose: 'to create and deliver relevancy'. This approach helps bridge the gap between data and the customer (whether or not there is a human intermediary) and means that their design focus must be 'bank-out' and designed around the customer, not a specific channel or product.

To do this banks will need to re-assess how their CRM systems generate and manage leads and opportunities from traditional propensity-modelled direct marketing campaigns in favour of event-driven 'sense and respond' processes that are more relevant, timely and personalised.

ORGANISATION

Whilst most customers do not interact directly with the internal organisation, they do with individual channels they manage. Are your internal organisational hierarchy and responsibilities relevant to the customer? Or is it a maze of complex teams or groups operating independently or in an uncoordinated fashion? How close or remote are executives and decision makers from the customer?

Chapter 17 – Real-time shockwave

FROM THE INDUSTRIAL AGE TO THE INFORMATION AGE

No new theories on which a big business can be built have emerged.
But the old ones are no longer dependable.

So Peter Drucker reported in a Wall Street Journal article in 1992. He was concerned about an increasing inability to forecast what customers want, a trend that had been evident for many years. The industrial age theory of predictable market conditions was no longer true.

The industrial age

Leaders of the industrial age, such as Henry Ford and Frederick Taylor, formulated the concepts and principles that became institutionalised as the industrial age 'make and sell' managerial framework. To Frederick Taylor businesses were not *like* machines, they *were* machines. The managerial challenge lay in designing ways to make the machines more and more efficient.

The logic of scientific management of business led to innovations such as the assembly line, time and motion study, business process design, and, most recently Six Sigma. Scientific management found its way out of manufacturing and into financial services and typified the first-generation thinking of automating processes to cut costs.

Taylor's model leveraged the fact that marketplace change was usually gradual enough to make incremental organisational change an efficient way to cope with it. Phrases such as 'plan your work, work your plan', 'optimisation' and 'chains of command' are examples of industrial age 'make and sell' vocabulary that reveal how deeply the concepts of stability, efficiency and predictability remain embedded in today's corporate DNA (being found in the organisational structures, marketing process designs, measurement and reward systems) – even in those that proclaim responsiveness, speed, agility, resilience, variability and adaptability to be institutional qualities they seek.

The principle that the financial services market changed gradually was true in the 1980s and internal factors, rather than external forces such as customers or new technology, drove banks to introduce new products and channels.

The trouble is: in the 21ˢᵗ Century, marketplace change is neither gradual nor predictable.

The information age

We have moved from an industrial age that dominated the 19th and 20th Centuries to the information age, but many organisations still operate on the old model.

Since 2006, a combination of the Internet and web-based technology, changing customer attitudes and behaviour, the continued uncertainty concerning the economy, the pace and variety of financial product introduction and increased regulation have created a state of 'discontinuous change' – that is the "non-incremental, sudden change that threatens existing or traditional authority or power structure, because it drastically alters the way things are currently done or have been done for years."[cxlvi]

As a result banks find that it is increasingly difficult to predict demand for financial products and services next year, never mind two or three years out. They find it difficult to offer the right product to the right customer at the right time (and through the right channel). One reason is that their organisation and processes are out of step with customers.

If the concept of the industrial age was to 'make and sell' physical products, its banking equivalent is to market products based upon what banks think customers want and offer them for sale through direct marketing.

A fundamental disconnect happens if a bank operates a 'make and sell' model and the customer wants a 'sense and respond' bank (such as more self-directed customers, or higher net worth individuals). Customers will reject offers that don't meet their needs as irrelevant, badly timed or not personalised.

The concept of the information age is 'sense and respond': a radically different way of thinking about why the business exists to do what they do and how they do it to be successful.

SENSE AND RESPOND

'Sense and respond' is an adaptive managerial framework developed by Stephan H. Haeckel at the IBM Advanced Business Institute.[cxlvii] It is an internally consistent and scalable re-organisation of strategy, structure and governance for environments of unpredictable change.

Comparison of industrial and post-industrial managerial frameworks

	Industrial age – Make and sell Demise of efficiency managerial framework	Post-industrial age – Sense and respond Emergence of adaptive managerial framework
Purpose	Enterprise-centric	Customer-Centric
Strategy	Strategic plan OF action	Strategic design FOR action
Structure	Functional hierarchies of authority	System of modular roles and accountabilities
Governance	Command and control	Context and coordination

Source: Leading on demand businesses – Executive as Architects, Stephan. H. Haeckel, IBM Systems Journal

The transition to the information age requires a radically different business strategy, structure and organisation capability. Sense and respond provides the framework.

In rapidly changing environments leaders can no longer rely on planning, process designs, hierarchies of authority and command and control. Instead of operational excellence in executing plans and processes, the core competencies of an enterprise are to:

- Know the meaning of what is happening now;
- Dynamically dispatch modular capabilities to respond;
- Express the strategy as a system design of roles and outcomes.

Each role in the design is accountable for producing outcomes for the other roles. The design specifies the interactions between the roles, not their activities. Sense and respond is a foundational business model framework for on-demand or real-time businesses.

Sense and respond is a change in business orientation from 'firm forward' or 'make and sell' to 'customer back', from actions to outcomes, from prediction and optimisation to knowing earlier and improvising in context.

Sense and respond calls for four new core competencies:[cxlviii]

- **Knowing earlier** – this is not predicting what will happen. It is rapid sensing and interpreting the meaning of what is happening now. Data or events known to be relevant must be captured earlier and made sense of faster.
- **Managing by wire** – knowing earlier is only useful if the organisation can act upon that knowledge appropriately, and in time. Managing by wire is the business equivalent of fly-by-wire that enables pilots to fly airplanes that travel much faster than planes in which the pilot directly controls the plane's hydraulics. It incorporates and extends 'knowing earlier' capabilities by translating managerial decisions into operational action.
- **Dispatching capabilities from the event back** – operations in a sense and respond organisation are driven from the customer request (and event) back, rather than from a company's plan forward. This means that capabilities must be modular and easily recombined. They should be linked, or chained, at the latest possible moment – when the specifics of the customers' present need is discerned.
- **Designing the organisation as an adaptable system** – adaptive organisations need to adopt systems design principles as managerial tenets. Systems designs produce synergy and align every element of the system around a common purpose – customer value creation. Designing a business as a system means specifying the interactions among, rather than actions of, organisational capabilities. It means designing a business from the purpose down, not from the capabilities up. The result is a role and accountability design that serves as a structure for action and becomes the central strategy document of the organisation.

The adaptive loop – sense-interpret-decide-act

The four competencies are used in a model that enables signals from customers and the market to be processed quickly and effectively to take advantage of the rapidly changing environment and internal resources.

Sense – gather a wide range of signals, from hard data and reports to conversations with customers, that are used to spot impending change in your business environment and your customers' needs. Internally, hard data and customer conversations should also track breakdowns in your organisation's performance.

Interpret – use a variety of technologies and techniques to understand the meaning of what you are sensing, and why performance has broken down.

Decide – with a clear understanding of what is happening, and why, translate managerial decisions into operational action.

Act – commitments between roles with accountability will be renegotiated and the operational action implemented. The impact of the action will be gathered through the 'sense' stage.

How do these principles apply to real-time multi-channel?

These principles help traditional banks compete with the new, more agile, competitors who are not hampered by legacy organisational structures and data silos.

One example of a process that is stuck in an industrial age 'make and sell' paradigm is contact management. Examples include:

- Propensity-modelled direct marketing campaigns – where demand is not known, but by using statistical analysis of customer data to determine the likelihood that a customer will buy a particular product and manufacturing the offer that is made to the customer is 'make and sell';
- Campaigns that require a 13-week lead-time to construct – are 'make and sell'. If it takes that long the organisation is not making use of 'sense and respond' principles such as modularity;
- TV commercials or advertising of products – that reach mass markets of consumers are 'make and sell' as, again, demand is not known and media hopes to catch a percentage of customers who had a need at that moment.

Promotion of the bank's brand is not usually 'make and sell' as it usually portrays the beliefs and values of the organisation, raising awareness, and not a specific product. Of course, brand advertising can result in an increased interest in the bank's products.

Benefits

After transforming to a 'sense and respond' organisation, businesses will be able to:

- Manage unpredictable variations in demand;
- Improve their cycle time by an order of magnitude;
- Achieve an increase in revenue growth.

NEW REALITY – REAL-TIME MULTI-CHANNEL CONTACT MANAGEMENT

The prime purpose of customer relationship management and analytics is to optimise the organisation's contact capacity to create maximum sustainable value by sensing and responding to customers needs and wants.

The purpose of this section is to discuss how the need for real-time multi-channel 'conversations' that engage customers requires a change in thinking and organisation.

Why 'real-time multi-channel' contact management?

Because, it's 'reality' – it is the world that your customers now live in. Due to changing consumer attitudes, behaviours and technologies such as the Internet, 'always on' connections, 3G, mobile smartphones, email, SMS Text, chat, iTunes, YouTube, Facebook and Twitter, consumers live in a 'real-time' world, where conversations, news, information and services are always immediately available. Content now streams 24x7. Consumers now expect immediate fulfilment. The real-time world is a 'sense and respond' world.

In a 'sense and respond' world it's no longer acceptable to take a week to follow up a quotation on the Internet; to take three months to prepare a direct marketing campaign or not to synchronise offers across channels so that the customer isn't offered the same product tomorrow that they rejected yesterday.

Never has 'right customer, right offer, right channel, right time' been so important. Many customers are connected 24x7 by mobile smartphone and there's evidence that many Gen Y customers' attitudes are different to Baby Boomers. As they're always connected they're more accepting of relevant, timely and personalised contact from organizations that they do business with during their leisure time.

First-generation contact management thinking was dominated by automation that resulted in centralised mass direct mail marketing with little differentiation developed around simple propensity models because customer data was often out of date or missing. It was typified by 'make and sell' mentality from the industrial age.

As customers were selected on propensity to buy, rather than their need, most campaigns failed to achieve more than 2 per cent response rates, as they were irrelevant, not timely nor personalised in the customer's eyes.

The end-to-end processes involved manual data extraction and modelling, offer letter and application form design, product pricing, advertising control, compliance and legal. In all, most direct mail campaigns had a 13-week lead-time.

As a result, customers could have already bought the product between the data being extracted and receiving an irrelevant direct mail. It was not unusual for customers to receive up to four or five direct mailshots a month from their bank: for example, credit card; personal loan; home insurance and mortgages because the data was in silos and mined independently for different product managers with no prioritisation across offers.

Customers could only respond to campaigns in one of two ways: return a completed paper application form to the branch or a central back-office unit for processing or visit the branch and ask to buy the product. Branches often did not know that a customer had been mailed and so the conversation was often an embarrassing one. Application forms were rarely personalised, that is pre-completed with known information, to help the customer. Personalisation was non-existent as all customers received the same offer.

Second-generation contact management thinking resulted in fragmentation of the customer experience as new channels came on stream and marketed independently.

Firstly, the call centre offered the opportunity to outbound call customers using automated call technology that offered productivity gains and the ability to contact customers after branch opening hours at home. However, calling customers at home with unsolicited offers, often whilst they were having dinner or relaxing was not popular and customers asked banks to turn off this channel.

Email was seen as a replacement for direct mail as it offered a lower unit cost; however, it suffered from security issues such as 'phishing' and these concerns prevented many customers from clicking on the link embedded in the email. Email is fundamentally insecure in terms of the right person being at either end, and so it was dead on arrival as a way of sending personalised information. Banks have tried to get over this problem by creating secure email based behind their security wall, but customers don't know a relevant, timely and personalised message is waiting for them. Because of the volumes of 'spam' emails many customers have become immune to email messages that are not immediately relevant and personalised.

And finally, Internet banking offered the opportunity to revolutionise the customer experience, but fell short. Offers conflicted with off-line channels – they were either different or not synchronised. Straight through processing of products offered was limited, even for existing customers, forcing them to the branch to complete the sale.

Because there were now four channels: branch, direct mail, Telephone banking and Internet banking, this increased the pressure on customers. Often, campaigns were uncoordinated, with conflicting campaigns on Internet banking and in the branch, for instance.

In some instances banks had separate 'direct' marketing teams who managed Internet banking and email campaigns. This lead to a disconnected multi-channel contact management and sales process, with the customer frequently required to download application forms and process them through the branch or centralised unit. Initially, little STP existed as branch processes were adopted and not designed for the channel.

This was a continuation of industrial age 'make and sell'.

Third-generation 'intelligent' thinking recognises that the customer demands three things: relevance, timeliness and personalisation. In a world where the customer is bombarded daily with advertising, most of it irrelevant, your message has to be relevant to get the customer to look at it once, never mind buy the product.

It also has to be timely, that is, you make it at a time that coincides with a customer need. This sounds complex, if not impossible, unless you are able to detect 'events' that connect need to a solution or develop an understanding of your customer's future needs and respond at the appropriate time. We call this 'sense and respond contact management'.

Finally, customers demand a more personalised service. This means not only making the offer in the most relevant or stated preferred channel, but also providing the customer with the right information to meet their needs.

What does it take to achieve third-generation thinking?

It involves building an organisational and delivery model – a 'sense and respond' model that is designed for the information age.

Real-time multi-channel contact management is a 'sense and respond' process by which all customer contact, irrespective of proposition, segment, product, channel or media is created using a single engineered process, with the objectives of improving the customer experience; optimising channel capacity and delivering sustainable value.

Re-engineering the multi-channel contact management process

All existing channel and product marketing must be re-engineered using 'sense and respond' competencies:

- **Designing the organisation as an adaptable system** – the process is designed with one purpose in mind – customer value creation. The roles and interactions of the players in the table below are aligned to that purpose. The players' role is to ensure that decisions to respond to customer demand or behaviour are actioned into relevant, timely and personalised contact.
- **Knowing earlier** – supported by IT, the marketing analytics team is responsible for rapidly sensing and interpreting the meaning of what is happening now.
- **Managing by wire** – means that the process is linked by a tracking and reporting information system that enables management to understand what is happening now, make decisions that can be translated into actions for the contact management team to deploy and tracking it through to presentation to the customer. Real-time management information ensures that multiple 'sense and respond' offers are processed at the same time, yet the team manages to control all of them.
- **Dispatching capabilities from the 'event back'** – this means how the contact management team action and deliver the decisions using modular components such as marketing messages, banners and internal communications, that can be reused or recombined to assemble or modify contact and offers quickly and effectively, without having to have all aspects re-approved. Management information is modular allowing new information to be added without delay or significant cost.

To this end a new contact management process model is required. This model must clearly define capabilities, roles and responsibilities at every step of the redesigned process.

The following outlines the typical CRM and Analytics functions, capabilities, roles and responsibilities (using a RACI model) that are required to design a multi-channel customer management model that delivers relevant, timely and personalised offers that differentiate your customer experience.

Sample multi-channel contact management process RACI model

	Head Office management	Local management	Analyst	Segment	Product	Marketing	Finance	Advertising control	Legal	Compliance	Distribution
Analysis to support 'chain of thought' and strategy	A	C	R	A	R	R	C	C	-	-	C
Propensity model building/scoring	A	C	R	A	A	-	-	-	-	-	-
Event detection	A	R	R	RA	RA	I	-	C	C	C	C
Contact/offer assembly	A	C	R	RA	R	I	I	C	C	C	C
Contact deployment and channel capacity management	A	R	R	R	I	I	I	-	-	-	RA
Contact/offer modification	A	C	R	A	R	I	I	C	C	C	C
Result assessment, appraisal and learning	A	R	RA	C	CI	I	I	-	-	C	C
MI development	A	C	R	A	C	C	C	-	-	-	C

© *Intelligence Delivered (Asia) Limited 2012*

RACI model: R = Responsibility to deliver; A = Accountable; C = Consulted (actively taken into account); I = Informed (not taken into account)

Core CRM/Analytics functions and responsibilities

Core functions of CRM/Analytics	Summary of responsibilities
Analysis to support 'chain of thought' and build strategy	Provide insight to drive strategic proposition development (product, channel, pricing) and customer segmentation, includes ad-hoc for region and countries not available in standard MI cubes
Propensity model building/Scoring	Building and managing scoring modules
Event detection	Working with customer teams to detect and manage library of customer/product events and their detection
Contact/offer assembly	Working with CVM/contacts to cut lists and load offers
Contact deployment and channel capacity management	Deploy offers/contacts to channels and manage capacity (ultimately moving to real-time)
Contact/offer modification	Moving towards real-time modification through strategy engines
Result assessment, appraisal and learning	Campaign and strategy assessment. 'Champion/challenger' etc
MI development	Design, build and maintain analytical customer data cubes for use by region and locally

Chapter 18 – The future of channels

Prediction is very difficult, especially if it's about the future

Niels Bohr, Physicist

Having a deliberate multi-channel strategy means understanding customers, their behaviour, their satisfaction and value more holistically and not through one lens such as Internet banking or branches. All channels are connected in customers' eyes and what happens in one channel has an impact in another. Delivering a successful multi-channel strategy requires banks to understand what customer service improvements to make where, and directing resources to achieve the desired result.

We believe that fundamental changes to banks' distribution channels will continue, and accelerate – driven by changes in customer attitudes and technology adoption.

What was the big shift in customer attitudes and technology that changed things?

We believe that The Internet caused a paradigm shift in banking, opening up access to information and new ways of interacting with a bank through Internet banking, but was mainly 'internal' to the industry, few new entrants achieved market share – a second paradigm shift is emerging, no less powerful, but more threatening to banks.

Mobile banking is the leading edge of a fundamental change in what it is to be a bank. We believe that Mobile banking opens up a core part of the bank's business and revenue from the payments market to new and nimble competition that isn't interested in being a bank, but just wants a big bit of the bank's lunch. Disintermediation follows.

In this new reality the importance of the Internet as a technological and cultural phenomenon cannot be underestimated.

The concept of channels shifted too. Once a bank regarded its channels as the ones it owned – these were operated by the bank and closed to others. Now customers are driving banks to adopt new more collaborative channels such as social media or mobile payments-related channels. To reflect these different perspectives we've split our assessment of the future of channels into the next two chapters:

- Bank-owned channels – those channels that the bank owns and manages, such as branches, Internet banking and Mobile banking;
- Bank-collaboration channels – those channels where the bank collaborates with others, such as social media and mobile payments.

This allows us to consider how banks can proactively manage their own customer journey destiny by reengineering their processes and motivating employees to deliver the highest levels of customer service. Banks have a different challenge on the level playing field of collaborative sites where the bank is just another financial service provider on someone else's platform. How do you differentiate yourself to your existing customers and prospects?

Banks must consider both aspects when considering truly multi-channel experience, including how a customer might start a journey on the bank's social media channel (because that's where they happened to be at the time they have a financial need) and transition to complete the transaction on a bank-owned secure channel without the need to repeat or rekey the information or conversation initiated on the social channel.

The Internet is more than a channel: it is the technology for all channels

Whilst this is not a technology text, we believe that we should consider how banks will be able to use the Internet to deliver a more relevant relationship with customers.

First- and second-generation thinking has left banks with a mixture of different technologies for their channels. For example, Internet banking, obviously, uses the Internet as its operating platform – but there are differences between Web 1.0 and Web 2.0 technologies; branches may use a different, older technology (or use Web 1.0 when Internet banking uses Web 2.0); call centres may use a third technology that isn't Web 1.0 or 2.0 at all. Early Mobile banking solutions are based upon SMS Text and do not use the Internet, introducing a fourth technology platform. Mobile banking via smartphone uses the Internet either via WAP or the same platform as Internet banking. A bank's social media site, or Facebook or Twitter, will use Web 2.0 technology that may be at odds with Internet banking and Mobile banking. And so forth.

All of this adds layers of complexity and silos of data that make it difficult for banks to offer a seamless technology interface to its customers, requiring them to adapt every time they use a different channel. The result is also not transparent to either the customer or the bank. Individual channels have different process designs to accommodate different underlying technology. All of this makes it difficult for customers to easily interact with their bank, for even the simplest transaction, and does nothing to make banks more relevant to customers.

In the present, and the future, consumers will continue to drive banks towards an operating model that suits them and not just the bank, and punish banks that don't comply.

The proliferation of channels and technologies is also another cause for concern for the bank: new channels get introduced, but none of the old channels are being phased out or replaced, the M25 just keeps on getting wider but some lanes have little traffic. Internet banking is yet to have significant impact on branches, they've reduced day-to-day traffic, but many sales or service transactions can only be completed in the branch and so they are closing at less than 5 per cent per year; call centres failed to remove all service enquiries from branches as planned and are under threat from Mobile banking, but won't be replaced entirely so long as 50 per cent of the population don't have smartphones.

As a result, banks will have to maintain all channels indefinitely, even if transaction volumes fall – some banks may be overwhelmed by the cost of doing so.

Banks will need to respond with third-generation thinking and solutions.

Build once for the Internet and deploy everywhere.

We believe that the solution is to embrace the Internet as the core infrastructure for all channels. We do not believe that the current mixed infrastructure is sustainable.

By building once for the Internet and deploying across all channels the bank will be able to design functionality around the customer, ease of use and convenience. Because it is built around the customer, or millions of them, it will need to be intuitive as the bank is not capable of or cannot afford to educate customers.

Core functionality, irrespective of channel, such as bill payment, inter-account transfers and person-to-person payments will be designed and built once and deployed across branches, ATMs, Internet banking and Mobile banking with little increase in development costs. In effect they will become an application and maintaining them, or making compliance changes, will be significantly reduced.

Sales processes will become unified and customers will be able to easily switch between channels to complete sales themselves. Manned and unmanned channels will be able to collaborate more effectively for the customer as branch or call centre employees will be able to screen share and will pick up from where the customer left off – not on another system. Interfaces to core banking, risk and payment systems will be built and maintained once.

Channels, such as branches and call centres, where bank employees conduct transactions for customers, will use the same underlying intuitive functionality as customers, but with an 'on behalf of' layer (accessed by employee identification and password) that allows access to the customer data and tracks activity for regulatory, compliance, monitoring, reporting and incentive reward purposes. Having the same intuitive interface and functionality as customers (remember, employees are customers too!), will reduce training when the system is implemented or upgraded.

The bank's social media platform will be directly integrated into the single version of customer information, allowing employees to interact more quickly, transparently and effectively with customers through this channel.

Overall, the bank's relationship with the customer will become more transparent to both the customer and the bank. It will also make banking more simple and relevant to the customer.

Chapter 19 – The future of bank-owned channels

As we discussed in the previous chapter there is no doubt that customer behaviour and technology, especially the Internet, has changed banking and will continue to do so. This has been the subject of much debate and conjecture in the financial services industry, with all sorts of projections about the future – and the occasional emotional outburst concerning the future of certain channels.

Banks have invested millions, sometimes billions of dollars in their own channels to attract and service the segments of customers that they want to acquire and grow.

Banks' own channels are a manifestation of their brand personality – look no further than First Direct's progression from a Telephone bank without any branches to a predominately Internet bank that is now focusing on Mobile banking. They have successfully maintained the same brand personality across all of their channels to differentiate themselves from their competitors no matter which channel the customer uses.

Banks must consider how to match the customers' needs and expectations with actual channel capabilities and direct their resources to ensure that their most valuable customers have the best experience on any channel.

Bank-owned channels offer the best opportunity for them to differentiate themselves – in time all banks will have a Facebook or Twitter presence (one might argue they're now mainstream and dull!) and it will be difficult to tell them apart as presentation and functionality will be determined by the underlying platform. Equally, Mobile payments may be determined by players other than the banks, with many banks providing a vanilla proposition without the ability to innovate to differentiate.

In this chapter we've grouped channels differently from the first half of the book to reflect the new reality:

- Branches – including tellers, customer service teams, self-service (ATMs) and relationship managers to reflect how new branch thinking is more closely integrating these elements to deliver a differentiated customer experience;
- Telephone banking – to reflect the repositioning of this channel to support both branch and Internet banking propositions;
- Internet banking – ubiquitous and now the cornerstone of many banks' customer propositions. Many banks have some way to go before they are able to fully realise the channel's capabilities and the benefits;
- Mobile banking – the convenience of a bank in your pocket for the customer and reduced transaction costs for banks is a heady combination for many bankers. The new reality is that Mobile banking will potentially disrupt all channels, including Internet banking, through its convenience to customers. However, bankers will only realise the cost saving benefits if customers overcome the barriers to adoption. On

the other hand, Mobile banking potentially leads banks into disintermediation from their customers as banks are not typically leading the Mobile payments propositions.

THE FUTURE OF BRANCHES

> The reports of my death are greatly exaggerated
>
> Mark Twain

Introduction

There was a time when banks 'shooed' customers out of branches by any means possible; that's all changed and they are now 'wooed' into the branch for entirely different reasons.

During the latter half of the 20th Century branch location and design were driven by different factors from today – the way we were paid and how we spent our money influenced branch purpose and design: most people were still paid in cash, and the government paid benefits and pensions in cash. Spending money also meant using cash; cheques were for the wealthier, and usage grew in the '60s and '70s as banks expanded their business into the middle classes. This also meant that retailers and the service industry had significant demands for cash and cheque handling that local branches satisfied. Even 10 years ago 22 per cent of UK workers were still paid in cash or by cheque.[cxlix] This invariably meant at least a weekly trip to the branch and made them relevant to customers.

As a result of these fundamental social changes the need to visit a bank on a regular, weekly or monthly basis has diminished significantly. Banks accelerated and compounded the change through their desire to reduce branch, cash and cheque handling costs, increase customer convenience and access to their money through ATMs, debit cards, standing orders and direct debits, Telephone banking, Internet banking and more recently Mobile banking.

Diminishing branch profitability

According to Dave Kaytes at BAI, 40 per cent of US bank branches are unprofitable ('Transfer to the new model – before its too late')[cl]. The Asian Banker reported that it is estimated that 43 per cent of all branches in emerging markets and 32 per cent in mature markets in Asia Pacific underperform.[cli] It is easy to see why. Traditional branch traffic that brought with it the opportunity to develop the relationship and cross-sell products has fallen dramatically in the last few years due to ATMs and Internet banking.

What happens next?

Many commentators are predicting the demise of branches in the next few years.

We believe that a few banks understand that customer behaviour, based upon emerging technology and attitudes, is changing the way that their customers are using their channels. And as that shift occurs the channels themselves will change – in line with customer needs. Many banks are experimenting with different branch formats – whether it's emulating Apple

Store technology-orientated concepts, improving the experience for their more valuable customers, making branches more family friendly or creating a community space.

The future of branches? We think there is an exciting one.

Tipping point

A 'tipping point' for branches will come, but it won't end in the death of branches. In 2011 Capital One showed the following chart to their investors to gain approval to buy ING DIRECT US business.[clii]

Figure 15 – US consumer channel penetration

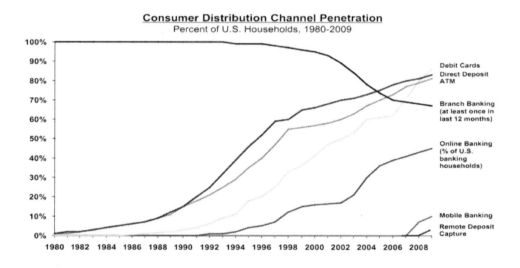

Not much had changed until about 2003 (2005 in the UK). That's when broadband communications and Internet banking finally gained critical mass and started to impact the branch and other channels. Until that point doing basic banking, such as checking balances and transactions, transferring money between accounts and making bill payments had required most customers to visit the branch teller or ATM.

Banks have tried to reduce their network size since the 1980s and are faced with an outcry from the local communities affected by closures – and customers told banks to keep their branches open as they still needed to pay in cheques, transfer money, get cash and pay bills over the counter.

Local small businesses still accept cash and cheques and rely upon the branch to process these items – and now no-one expects cash or cheques to disappear in the next few years. The demand to keep cheques came from customers and would now appear to be under greater scrutiny and their demise this decade is by no means certain.

According to the British Bankers' Association (BBA) there are 9,309 bank branches in the UK as at 2010.[cliii] The BBA reported the number of closures at 3 per week or 2 per cent per year.

We believe that banks will continue to close underused and unprofitable branches and re-configure their branch networks to meet the needs of the next generation of customers who will require branch counters even less than the previous generations.

Alternatives to underused branch counters

There are alternatives that banks should consider. Most small or rural branches are used for their counter service – cheque and cash processing, transferring money or paying bills. Alternatives proposed include:

- Post Office Counters – there are around 11,000 Post Offices in the UK. However, this network itself is undergoing a fundamental change and would need to financially justify the proposal. Some banks have already set up arrangements.
- Utility bank – a service funded by the high-street banks to retain 'the last branch in town' for counter services. Banks already have the Inter-bank Agency Agreements that are used by banks to provide certain branch counter services to each other's business customers.
- Collection service – for retailers, such as pubs, local shops that no longer have a local branch. This would use the sort of security carrier services that larger retailers use to get cash and cheques from their stores to banks for smaller businesses. However, this service is unlikely to help personal customers.

Cash and cheque secure processing, transport and storage have always been relatively expensive and relied upon economies of scale to cover the cost. The continued reduction in the number of cheques being written and cash transactions (being replaced by debit and credit cards), diminishes the economies of scale and makes the provision of counter services in every branch less profitable.

But on the other hand it is the majority of customers who are driving the change. Once they reach a tipping point it will be difficult for the people who don't use the branch for day-to-day transactions to claim that they want one.

Perhaps we need to consider why customers say that they still need branches, and how banks might respond.

WHY DO CUSTOMERS STILL NEED BRANCHES?

Branches have been described as 'big, expensive comfort blankets'. And there's evidence that suggests that's exactly how customers see them. Customers want branches for comfort and the important points in their financial life when many need and appreciate the 'human touch'.

Empathica Consumer Insights Panel research indicates that customers have a broad idea about how they currently want to use channels. (We believe that Mobile reflects its current position on adoption S-curve.)

Preferred channel	Routine transactions	Account issues
Branch	32.6%	60.0%
Online	41.4%	6.0%
ATM	23.3%	n/a
Mobile	1.5%	n/a
Telephone	1.3%	34.0%

Empathica Consumer Insights Panel, Analysis of US and Canadian Consumer Behaviours in the Financial services Sector Wave 2, 2010.

The research also revealed that customers preferred to visit branches to complete high-value transactions, such as home loans (no other high-value products such as investments or retirement schemes were surveyed, but we anticipate a similar result).

Home loan preference	
Visit branch	78.7%
Internet	18.5%
Telephone	2.5%
Mobile	0.3%

Empathica Consumer Insights Panel, Analysis of US and Canadian Consumer Behaviours in the Financial services Sector Wave 2, 2010.

Customers are not ready to abandon the branch just yet

Research by Deloitte and Vlerick Leuven Gent Management School in Belgium concludes that both Belgian and Dutch retail customers demand face-to-face contact and continue to visit their branches, However, they are not satisfied with the services provided by their current bank and branch.[cliv]

- **Branches are still visited** – 79 per cent of personal and 89 per cent of business customers visit the branch at least once every six months against 59 per cent and 84 per cent for Internet banking and 65 per cent and 44 per cent for self-service banking.
- **The Internet is used for getting information on financial products while visiting the branches is the preferred channel for buying and getting after-sales service** – 71 per cent of personal and 79 per cent of business customers

consider the branch as their preferred sales channel.

- **Advice provided at the branch fails to satisfy 1 in 3 customers** – 27 per cent of personal and 30 per cent of business customers are not satisfied with the quality and the promptness of the advice provided.
- **Access to the branch is too limited** – 38 per cent of personal and 41 per cent of business customers consider the opportunity to make appointments after closing time as the main area for improvement for branches (Note: Most banks are open Monday to Friday from 09:00 to 16:30 and a few banks are open on Saturdays. Many smaller branches may close at lunchtime, often between 13:00 and 14:00).

All of this prompts us to ask the next question.

What will branches of the future look like?

"Like retailers" is a frequent answer. But why? Is getting a mortgage the same as seeing a pair of shoes in the window of the high-street retailer and going in and buying them? How many 'impulse-banking purchases' have you made recently? It's not a commonly used phrase, so not many we'd guess.

Predictions and ideas range from wall-to-wall technology or picking up a 'box' from the shelf, swiping it over a bar-code reader to café environments that serve cool smoothies and lattes whilst you relax and do your banking.

Certainly, branches will have a more relaxed environment – the latest designs for premium and affluent customers have a different layout as they are designed for service and advice, not counter transactions (as they had been for the last 150 years).

However, as every bank appears to want to be a 'retailer', just as all bank branches ended up looking the same in the '80s there will be little visible differentiation as the physical design will end up looking the same: the same concierge desks, lots of big advertising screens, touch-screens in booths, comfy chairs in the 'affluent' section, scents and chill-out music. Banks are herd animals. You'll only be able to tell them apart by the branding colours.

What will the experience be?

We think that the great retail experience that everyone should emulate is 'being customer focused', that is the customer experience when interacting with employees.

When thinking about what branches might be like in the future, there will be three branch characteristics to consider:

1. Service – providing some transaction processing capabilities and a point for the resolution of more complex service enquiries, where the customer wants a face-to-face conversation. Many customers are comfortable with self-service equipment that processes cash and cheques, makes transfers and bill payments, prints statements and passbook updates and even dispenses foreign currency. Banks will need to consider the mix of self-service and human transaction processing that they provide in the

branch of the future, to meet customer needs and expectations and ensure that interactions with humans have the time and space to meet customer expectations.

2. Advisory – providing face-to-face financial advice, either for managing finances, wealth management or seeking advice on more complex needs. Not all customers are confident 'self-directed' decision makers yet. By far the greatest percentages are 'validators' and 'delegators', who value advice, good service and a trusted relationship.

3. Relationship management – premium and affluent customers say that they appreciate a relationship manager, but as we've seen not all RMs service all of the customers in their allocated portfolio. Switching more employees from transaction fixers to advisors will allow more time with customers to build a relationship. This will be based upon CRM systems to maximise the amount of time that the customer-facing advisers have with customers, removing manual tasks, interfacing with product systems and channels to provide a consistent 360° view of the customer (this same information will also be viewed by the customer online). Banks might need to reconsider whether it's productive to put 'self-directed' customers into a traditional relationship manager's portfolio, or whether 'help when its needed' can be delivered in a way that would satisfy them more.

The design and technology will provide the convenience, accessibility and privacy that will help the customer get done the job they came to do quickly and efficiently and will increase satisfaction, but won't build or strengthen loyalty.

The availability of accessible and knowledgeable experts is even more important. This means eradicating most, if not all, administrative tasks from front-office employees job descriptions (and not letting them creep in informally) – currently, up to 60 per cent of their time can be spent this way. Employees should be freed from their desk, in the front office as well as the back-office, by using hand-held devices such as tablets or netbooks.

Branch managers won't have a permanent desk as their role will be to manage the customer experience in real-time, using their tablet device to understand who is in their branch, what the customers are doing and directing their team to meet customer needs.

Even relationship managers and product specialists should be more mobile. Customers say that they appreciate having a relationship manager, but only 50 per cent know who they are. Relationship managers, due to their administrative burdens, are often unable to service more than 50 per cent to 75 per cent of their designated portfolio. Hand-held tablets, linked to RFID chips in customers' plastic cards would alert them to customers who were visiting the branch with whom they'd had little contact with recently. Saying 'hello' is more powerful in building a relationship than you would think. With more active branch front office employees' banks can consider how they manage portfolios, particularly the mass affluent, who may not have a dedicated relationship manager, but deserve a more personalised relationship.

It will require banks to consider very different front-office employee to customer ratios, and will probably require more of the right employees in the front office. However, as the branch is now primarily a service, sales and advisory unit, where everyone has sales targets increased staffing levels should correlate to increased customer acquisition, sales and retention. Customers will like more accessible staff too.

'The right customer, in the right channel, for the right interaction'

We first introduced the following 'rules' in chapter 3 – The Customer. Because they are about what customers say they need, whether it's a human or digital channel we believe that they still hold true: 'recognise my value to you'; 'know me and treat me as an individual'; 'provide expertise that I can get at'; 'be on my side (and reassure me that you are)'; 'leave me in control; be my trusted advisor'.

Customers have different attitudes towards a number of different factors that need to be considered: what defines good service; convenience and access; taking advice; managing risk and using technology. Those attitudes drive how a customer interacts with a bank's channels, not the latest gadget, although some customers will naturally place higher values on some attributes than others – so, a proportion of customers will simply want to use the latest technology and channel combination.

Branches will provide customers with high-quality interactions that other channels cannot replicate. Our prediction is that whilst 'self-directed' decision makers will likely polarise towards Internet banking financial management and investment functionality, 'validators' and 'delegators' will look to branches to provide the face-to-face advice and relationship. That does not mean that 'self-directed' will not use the branch or that 'validators' and 'delegators' will not use Internet banking or Mobile banking. It merely points to how customer characteristics may, with attitudes towards technology, put 'the right customer, in the right channel, for the right interaction'.

What will happen to branches?

Banks, if they take the necessary steps, are better positioned than the pure-play Internet and Mobile banks, as customers still want branches. Will branches close? Will new ones open? Yes, certainly, many are in the wrong place and like smart retailers they'll relocate to where their customers are, on the high street, in the mall or near the office complex to get the right traffic.

Transforming the branch

As the purpose of the customer using the branch changes from transaction to interaction, how the customer navigates the services of the branch will change too and existing designs may not meet the needs of customers. Third-generation thinking demands that a more customer-centric approach is required and both employee and customer research and involvement will be key to designing branches that meet the needs of customers. Prototype and pilot branches provide good models for allowing employees and customers to contribute to designs and branch navigation modelling to ensure that every branch visit is a productive and positively memorable experience.

From transactions to interactions

Steve O'Neill, Head of Branch Marketing, HSBC Bank plc in an interview with Finextra[clv] outlined his organisation's thinking on the future of branches. He stated that branches have a critical role to play as channels converged and that there would be a shift to advice and relationship management. Part of this would be to improve the experience, for example, recognising that for parents who decide to visit a branch to discuss their finances, it often meant taking the kids along too. HSBC is looking at ways of improving the experience for families so that parents could concentrate on financial matters and that the visit would leave a good impression on the children.

Branch design – a few examples

Almost all banks are experimenting with new branch design, trying to find the right environment for their customers that also encourages prospective customers to walk in to find out more about the brand and what it can offer them.

Standard Chartered

New branch design in Korea and Singapore that incorporates new technology to improve customer differentiation and service.[clvi]

This includes issuing RFID tags to selected affluent customers of its newest branch in Korea (issue based upon frequency of branch visits, approach to technology and those who have a strong relationship with the bank). When a RFID holding customer walks into the branch the branch manager and relationship manager are alerted in real-time, allowing the customer to be personally greeted and provided with a priority service that avoids unnecessary queuing.[clvii]

ING DIRECT Cafés

Originally a branchless direct bank, ING DIRECT opened 7 US and 5 Canadian Cafés from 1997 onwards. These cafés are definitely not traditional branches. Visitors can't perform any traditional teller-based cash transactions at ING DIRECT Cafés. The Cafés' primary purpose is to reassure consumers and build the brand. Guests are welcome to open an account online using ING computer terminals and can get information about the bank products from the Café staff, pick out items from a wide range of ING DIRECT merchandise or just relax and enjoy a cup of fresh coffee while surfing the net on Wi-Fi terminals. Each location features a meeting space that can be used for bank-sponsored financial seminars, or by local community groups. Some locations have a dual-purpose area that allows the bank to quickly and easily switch from café seating to seminar seating.

The cafés even have a small menu of food and brew quality teas and coffees. Bright orange cups, mugs and straws are used to reinforce the brand.

Of course, as you would expect, you can follow ING DIRECT Cafés on Twitter, Facebook and YouTube. But don't look for 'ING DIRECT'' – try looking for something 'less bank' – '@SuperStarSavers' is their social media branding!

If you can't beat social networks, join them

In a multi-channel world branches can become part of the social network themselves. GPS-based or cellular-positioning location software, such as Gowalla, Google Latitude, foursquare and Facebook Check-ins can put the branch into the 'social network'. These services allow people to tell their friends, via their social network application, where they are and sometimes what they are doing. Some banks are experimenting with ways of integrating branches and social media.

DBS Bank, based in Singapore and operating throughout Asia, recently ran a promotion using Facebook Places (now Check-in) in Hong Kong, India, Indonesia, Singapore and Taiwan, with 20 locations in each country where participants can earn points, with the top scorer in each country winning a three day holiday in an Asian city of their choosing. Users can see how many points they have accumulated and how many check-ins they've made through the DBS Facebook application, where statistics are updated in real time. Whilst the outcome for DBS strategically is not clear (did it strengthen the existing relationship? did non-DBS visitors open accounts?), it demonstrates the potential to link traditional and social channels to strengthen engagement.[clviii]

Dupaco Credit Union, based in east central Iowa, northeast Illinois, and southwest Wisconsin launched a non-traditional reward system for loyal credit union members who stop into its locations for service.

Rewards to members who check in while at a Dupaco branch range from free 'koozies' (a foam or neoprene bottle or can holder – we had to look it up on Wikipedia!) to valuable gift certificates from Dupaco business partners, and to registration for weekly $50 gas card drawings and an opportunity to be featured on a digital billboard.

"For Dupaco, the value in participating in the foursquare social circle is engagement with people in a unique, viral way," said Jennifer Hanniford, Dupaco's Assistant Vice President of Interactive Marketing. "When people check in to Dupaco, their foursquare friends know they're here. They can tip off the foursquare community about their experience. It's a genuine tool for user-generated reviews on venues."

She added that social circles are a natural part of Dupaco's unique cooperative structure. "Through a credit union, members come together and pool deposits, and then responsibly provide their friends and neighbors low-cost loans for cars, homes, education, funding for small businesses, and more."

Dupaco has extended the reach of its foursquare efforts by promoting it on other interactive channels including Facebook and Twitter, and highlighting it on area billboards.

"foursquare players have the opportunity to become 'mayor' of any venue based on the frequency of their check-ins. Dupaco is paying homage to our foursquare mayors by featuring them on digital billboards in markets where digital billboards are available, like Dubuque and Cedar Rapids," said Hanniford. "The public sees the foursquare mayor names in lights and it generates more excitement to play and compete for the coveted mayorship position."[clix]

Transforming branch employees

It's no good transforming branches if what the branch employees do is not considered. The biggest overhead of a branch is usually the cost of its employees. Compared to other industries like manufacturing, the understanding amongst banks of their most expensive resource is poor.

As the branch transforms so must the roles of the employees. As day-to-day transactions are migrated to Internet banking, Mobile banking or in-branch self-service equipment so the number of teller positions will be reduced. Online and self-service account maintenance and query resolution will reduce the volume of non-cash simple transactions (such as changing an address, cancelling a standing order etc.) that customer service representatives (CSRs) normally handle.

According to Finalta[clx] currently as much as 40 per cent of a CSR's time is spent on non-customer activity, for example, back office, training, management and 'other' activity. Whilst there will also be a percentage of time required for other tasks, such as training (typically 5%), banks must decide what is appropriate. For example, is 5 per cent of time spent on training adequate?

Banks will need to re-evaluate all branch roles and eradicate the 'time-bandits' that prevent employees from devoting as much of their time as possible to productive customer service and sales activity.

The pressure is on now

The bad news is that 'time bandits' are increasing. New non-sales activity as a result of increased regulatory requirements will inevitably infringe on sales time-spend. Unless activities such as credit monitoring and collections have been centralised and automated there will be a significant impact on time-spend during periods of economic instability. Sales meetings are getting longer as banks deal with the financial crisis and direct a lot more attention to deepening the relationship and focus on needs-based selling. Finally, the post-financial-crisis focus on cost reduction means that there is pressure for branch staff to take on tasks that eliminated roles used to carry out.

Eliminate the 'time-bandits'

CSR and teller activity should be identified, measured and assessed:

- Can the activity be eliminated altogether?
  Has the process become obsolete or automated, but do branch staff still do it out of habit? For example, using the CRM system to manually data-mine which customers to contact, despite the fact that they already have a daily list of prioritised multi-channel originated contacts generated by the system.
- Can the activity be migrated?
  Completing the next stage of self-service migration, e.g. migration of change of address, standing order amendment to secure online channels.
- Should someone else be doing this role?
  This may, in fact, simply shift the 'time-bandit' without overall benefit and requires closer inspection of individual employees' activity, particularly where an activity should be a minor part of their duties. For instance, less commercially-orientated CSRs may be filling up some of their time with a disproportionate amount of non-

sales activity e.g. support teller activity, to mask their lack of confidence or ability.

- Can this activity be automated or centralised?
  There are often processes that creep into common use that start to diminish employee effectiveness and can be either eliminated, automated or centralised. Sometimes a temporary manual process is implemented as a short-term fix to quickly launch a new product, but is not automated when critical mass is reached. Periodic reviews are required to stop such processes becoming 'time-bandits'.

Make the gains stick

Elimination, automation and centralisation will rarely fully achieve the gains predicted in any business case. It is crucial to ensure that any additional time is used for service and sales related activities (including training). Far more important are the cultural, communication and management activities that explain why the measures are being put in place and that an increase in commercial activity is expected.

Banks with more developed sales activity measurement and management culture will be at an advantage because they can combine time-spend gains with an increase in targets for weekly customer contacts and sales activity.

Having a robust employee incentive scheme in place would further encourage and reward the right behaviour.

THE FUTURE OF ATM/SELF-SERVICE EQUIPMENT

We believe that banks will use ATMs and self-service equipment more strategically in their branch designs to offer the convenience of Internet banking with the personal service of branches. Whilst banks will continue to install self-service equipment in non-branch locations it is their strategic use within branches as part of a well-thought-out and integrated customer experience that will form part of the branch network strategy.

We anticipate that ATMs will continue to provide a similar range of services as they do now for the foreseeable future. Although UK adults will start to use digital cash and mobile wallets more and more in the next few years, the demise of cash is some way off yet. The move is towards a 'less cash' not 'cash less' society. What banks will see is a reduction in the number of visits to ATMs for cash, and therefore other services (if you have a mobile phone you will use Mobile banking for the non-cash transactions).

There will be a few technology and service function advances for ATMs from the most sophisticated, the most likely will be to add NFC communications capabilities to facilitate withdrawals from mobile devices rather than via traditional plastic cards.

ATMs and self-service equipment will continue to provide a valuable service to consumers who still require to deposit or withdraw cash, pay in cheques or undertake day-to-day transaction as smartphone penetration (and the desire to use them for banking) is still growing, and may not fully penetrate some social groups, such as the elderly.

Product sales or offers over ATMs will continue where they have already been established until replaced by wider-spread Mobile banking adoption. In other countries, such as Mexico,

ATM will continue to support sales of simple pre-approved products such as personal loans.

We expect to see further 'free ATM' restrictions (LloydsTSB and RBS) being imposed on lower value basic account holders to reduce the cost of providing services.

THE FUTURE OF THE RELATIONSHIP MANAGER (RM)

The effective relationship manager only exists in the marketing department's mind.

Graham Flower

It is our opinion that the future of the traditional RM model is not sustainable in the face of increased regulation and rapidly changing customer behaviour.

Let's think about why RMs were really created; they came about largely to provide a differentiated service level for 'better customers' (defined initially as large borrowers) and to hunt for new business. This was when there was only one channel, the branch, and most processes were carried out in the branch with the exception of large lending decisions. Few if any processes were automated and the RM provided the single point of entry to help these better customers navigate the bank.

Most research that claims customers seek a relationship manager is flawed in that it does not balance this against the cost to the customer. When given the cost at typically £200-£300 per annum for Premium banking few tick the box! So this has led to a 'dumbing down' of the RM role to reduce cost, an increase in portfolio sizes and the average tenure in the job of 18 to 24 months. Hardly the marketing department's dream and nothing like the customer's need. The key requirement in offering a 'relationship service' is not an inept relationship from somebody ill-equipped to service your financial needs, it is 'easy access to expertise' and a feeling that 'they are on my side'.

Most mass affluent RM models are first-generation thinking where the primary role is to push product rather than any attempt at truly partnering. Customers often comment that they hear relationship management, but experience salesman. The only exception is often to be found in the 'dynastic model' adopted by the top end of Private banking. This is a very long term model.

We believe that the impact of these two forces will reduce the viability of traditional RM propositions, by increasing the operating costs of RMs and reducing revenue opportunities that they can generate, as more and more self-directed customers use the more sophisticated wealth management tools emerging on Internet banking.

Regulation

The biggest impact on this cohort of employees will be driven by regulation that is designed to prevent the 'mis-selling' of products. Increased regulation, and the increasing costs of compliance, will force banks to reconsider how they deliver a face-to-face RM experience.

Changing customer behaviour

Changes in how different generations of customers use the bank's channels and the rise of the 'self-directed' consumer as a result of the recession will require banks to re-evaluate this part of the branch channel. Whilst it's clear that branches will be visited less and less for day-to-day transactions, it is obvious that many customers will continue to visit for the 'human touch' or for advice that the Internet can't provide.

Many banks believe that having RMs is essential in managing the relationship with their customers. We believe that this is not necessarily the case. Customer behaviour is changing with the rise of self-directed customers who prefer to manage their relationship with the bank on their terms. Many customers do not require RMs, but do require help when it is needed.

Relationship management in the past has been somewhat paternalistic and driven by the bank. Membership of a RM's portfolio was at the bank's discretion, whether the customer wanted it or used it. In order to achieve the level of profitability to justify the RMs and their support structure, banks set individual Premium portfolio sizes at anywhere between 400 and 600 customers.

However, many RMs were unable to service portfolios of this size with a quality customer experience and it is estimated that up to 70% of customers fail to receive the experience promised by the bank.

The options of increasing the number of RMs and/or reducing portfolio size are not viable economically and banks will need to reconsider their RM-based propositions.

From relationship managers to relationship management

Customers are looking for a number of features in their RM proposition:

Competence – RMs must be able to demonstrate expertise to gain customer trust.

Attitude – customers want access to expertise when they need it. RMs must be able to demonstrate that they are there for the customer when they need them.

Empathy – understanding the situation from the customer's point of view.

Customers need relationship management, they do not need RMs. Some banks are already successfully moving down this route.

First Direct have demonstrated that you do not need RMs to manage higher value customer relationships and achieve high levels of satisfaction. First Direct are always available, able to create empathy through Internet banking and provide access to experts, through online chat or video conferencing when the customer needs it.

Hargreaves Landsdown have demonstrated that it is also possible to provide wealth management without RMs. Customers manage their investments online and are able to access help using online chat when they need it, with access to Independent Financial Advisers (IFAs) for more high quality advice.

The transition from RMs to relationship management starts with understanding what your most valuable customers want from their bank. Customer attitudes to financial and wealth management are changing rapidly due to the financial crisis and new technology.

In many cases RMs are a hangover from a time when the bank was less connected and less capable of providing the customer with the right experience. Channels such as Internet banking are closing the gap and increasingly replacing the traditional branch. It will replace many customers' needs for contact with RMs on a regular basis.

Undoubtedly, there is a customer need for access to expertise and banks can achieve it in a number of ways that may actually give RMs the time and opportunity to improve the customer experience and act as the financial 'co-pilot' many customers want their bank to be.

Joining up channels to provide better support for the customer is essential, for example, existing call centres can be repositioned to provide online chat and video conferencing sessions that help the customer complete investment transactions or ask questions (where advice is not given). Where advice is required the customer can be seamlessly transferred to a regulated adviser.

THE FUTURE OF TELEPHONE BANKING

One question on our minds is the future of call centres. Internet banking and Mobile banking adoption are steadily eroding the core call centre functionality – providing balances, transaction queries, transfers and bill payments.

The call centre is not the customer's best-loved channel. In particular, customers hate IVR-based Telephone banking propositions and most banks have recognised this and delivered human-based Telephone banking as part of their affluent customer proposition, using the IVR to front security. Some banks have recently on-shored their entire offshore call centre operations.

But now, Internet banking and Mobile banking can provide a more accessible and easy-to-use service for those simple day-to-day transactions – providing balances, transaction queries, transfers and bill payments – that justified the first call centres.

What is the future of Telephone banking?

Banks need to understand what customers want from their channels in the new multi-channel environment. For example, this should consider aspects such as the access and attitude to technology (smartphone versus basic mobile phone), access to Internet banking and how all segments of customers (age and value) use the call centre and anticipate using it in the future. One important aspect to consider is the social inclusion responsibilities a bank may have (either by choice or legislation). How might the 'Law of Unintended Consequences' work in this situation? The last thing most banks want is their lowest value customers flooding branches with non-cash day-to-day transactions such as checking balances and transactions, transferring money and paying monthly bills!

Banks need to consider how their call centres fit with the new channels, particularly Internet banking and Mobile banking, both of which will outstrip the call centre in terms of day-to-day transaction processing (if they haven't already). How do they fit with the new service and advisory branch? The first call centres were implemented to move simple non-cash transaction traffic away from branch counters.

Banks need to understand which bits of call centres satisfy or irritate customers most: is it the IVR as a whole? Are they happy with the IVR fronting security and happy talking to a person? Do they want people to handle the security and call? Is it the way calls are handled – the speed of the call, range of services and scripting?

Once banks have understood what call centres do now and how customers might use them they can re-position them.

How might call centres be re-positioned?

There are several options for banks to re-position their call centres:

- Continue as before as Telephone banking, and watch call volumes and employee engagement and customer satisfaction decrease;
- Position the call centre within the Internet banking sales chain. Sometimes customers will have a question that the Internet sales process can't provide a FAQ to satisfy. Many customers may abandon the enquiry or sale never to return (buy from a competitor with a better process). By using online chat or video conferencing technology the call centre could 'pull' the customer through that part of process to avoid the customer abandoning the sale – making it a contact centre;
- Use the 'contact centre' as a new branch feature. This could act as a customer service safety valve for some customer segments (in the mass part of the branch) to alleviate peaks. Some customers may be comfortable using online chat and video conferencing to speak to someone remotely – so long as they can answer the question to the customer's satisfaction;
- Provide a relationship management solution to the mass affluent segment, who are currently not valuable enough to warrant dedicated named relationship managers, but require active relationship management to help them meet their financial goals. Online chat, video conferencing and skill-based routing technologies would mean that customers spoke with people who could help them with queries or non-day-to-day transactions;
- In the new 'social network' world, who tweets back to customers? The PR or marketing department? Perhaps this is a role for the 'contact centre'? After all, many tweets will be about 'how do I' FAQs.

Throw the script and traditional metrics out the window

Call centres are often criticised by customers as being 'rushed, routine and robotic' (the 'Three Rs') in their interactions. Unfortunately, it's what they've come to expect from call centre employees when they call with a problem. According to a 2006 survey by Genesys, 67 per cent of consumers would stop doing business with a company due to poor service from the call centre.[clxi]

The problem is that call centres are marketed as one thing, 'convenience and access' and managed and prioritised by the bank for another (cost savings). This creates four obstacles for call centre employees when talking to customers:

- They depersonalise what should be personal;
- They emphasise numbers that measure everything except service;
- They over-script interactions that beg for authenticity;
- They invoke customer satisfaction without conviction.

Because call centres were set up to reduce costs and not improve customer service, their metrics (and employee motivation measures and rewards) are typically based around operational call handling durations and efficiency.

The new model metrics should focus on the customer satisfaction measures, such as first contact resolution, sales completion rates (where the employee assisted an online sale), overall satisfaction surveys (event-based).

As with branch employees the measurement, motivation and reward aspects will be crucial. Recruit for attitude, train for the job.

THE FUTURE OF INTERNET BANKING

Internet banking now appears to be ubiquitous, with just 3.8 per cent of Americans over the age of 18 claiming to be unaware of it.[clxii]

Despite the widespread acceptance and usage of Internet banking, there are some differences between day-to-day banking transactions (such as checking account balance, transferring money and paying bills) and information and sales functionality. Whilst most Internet banking customers are aware and use transaction functionality, they are often less aware of features such as chat or video conferencing with an agent, or being able to receive SMS Text account alerts. Banks should think about how they can raise awareness and consideration in wider more complex financial services provided over the Internet banking platform.

Most Internet banking sites are the product of second-generation thinking that sought to cut costs by moving lower value customer transactions out of the branch to create more time for more valuable customers. The result was that as many as 90% of transactions are now completed electronically and branch transaction traffic continues to fall quickly, but the more valuable, time-poor customers abandoned the branch as Internet banking offered greater convenience.

The design of Internet banking therefore focused on transaction processing and not on providing customers with a rounded and useful proposition to manage their personal finances, with additional services being added on without rethinking what the overall Internet banking customer experience should be.

Most banks need to upgrade their Internet banking proposition to meet the changing needs of customers that we discuss in this text. This requires third-generation thinking that focuses on the customer experience and not on cost cutting as has happened in the past.

One issue that needs to be fixed urgently is the lack of straight-through-processing that prevents customers from completing sales in Internet banking and requires them to print out applications that are mailed to the bank or, worse still, visit the branch to complete relatively simple product sales. Whilst there are some legal and compliance issues, many of them can be overcome, such as 'wet signatures' for existing customers.

With its ability to consolidate information from external as well as internal sources, the Internet offers the potential for banks to provide its customers with a powerful personal financial management proposition, based around a PFM platform. This would enable customers to manage their day-to-day finances better, but also use planning and simulation tools to research their wealth management needs and execute for themselves, or share the information with the bank if they seek advice.

Third parties are already taking a lead and by consolidating all customer accounts and investment products into an appealing and functional tool, PFM sites, such as Mint or Yodlee, have the capability to disintermediate banks from their customers. One third-party PFM has recently implemented a 'recommendation engine'. Banks remain at a disadvantage, as they typically only consolidate products that the customer has with them and few banks have implemented PFM solutions for their customers. Given the interest in PFM exhibited by customers, and in response to the continued financial uncertainty, banks might be advised to implement a PFM solution.

THE FUTURE OF MOBILE BANKING – 'THE CHIPS ARE DOWN'

We believe that Mobile banking has opened up a new chapter in banking that threatens to displace banks from their traditional position in the payment value chain.

As we discussed in chapter 9 Mobile banking refers to platforms that enable customers to access financial services such as balance and transaction information, transfers and bill payments from a mobile phone. Mobile payments are generally defined as the process of using a hand-held device to pay for a product or service, either remotely or at the point-of-sale and it is this area where banks face competition to their established position in the payments chain from non-bank competitors.

First of all let's look at UK Mobile banking. Like many developed nations, UK mobile banking adoption continues to grow with the Future Foundation/Monetise Emerging Trends in Mobile Banking 2011[clxii] reporting that it had grown from 4.3 per cent in 2008 to 9.0 per cent in 2010, with a conservative estimate of 39 per cent using Mobile banking by 2020.

Growth is being drive by three factors: firstly, the recession has called for many consumers to manage their money more closely, and the simplest Mobile banking features, such as SMS Text alerts offers a simple way of helping customers manage their finances; 85 per cent of Mobile banking users think that it helps them manage their money more efficiently; secondly, the market for smartphones, and particularly the iPhone, that enable Mobile banking has risen spectacularly, with 34.4 per cent owning a device in 2010 (up from 21 per cent in 2009); thirdly, there is strong demand from consumers to use their mobile phone to manage their finances and high levels of satisfaction and recommendation from Mobile banking users.

Impact on other channels

As might be expected when a new channel is introduced there is an impact on established channels and the Future Foundation reported that amongst Mobile banking users, 55 per cent appreciate not having to go into a branch and 43 per cent value not having to use a call centre.

However, the research also shows that Mobile banking users do not use this channel exclusively and still use Internet banking and the ATM, but interestingly, 75 per cent of Mobile banking users also use the branch at least 'occasionally'. But crucially, they are using other channels less, for example, 50 per cent say that they use the branch less and 40 per cent say that they use Telephone banking less. 23 per cent say that they use other channels as often as they did before.

Customer behaviour

The Future Foundation report revealed some differences in how different segments of customers use Mobile banking. Some 41 per cent of 16 to 24-year-olds check their balances before buying an expensive item – compared to 27 per cent of those aged 35 and older. Similarly, 43 per cent of 16 to 24-year-olds use their phone to see if they are near their limit compared to 34 per cent of people aged 35 and older.

Our observation on these statistics is that banks have an opportunity to help customers budget by providing a personal financial management tool on their Mobile banking service as well as on Internet banking (that automatically synchronises, of course).

Barriers to Mobile banking

A number of barriers to adoption are cited in the Future Foundation report:

Security – 20 per cent of people who do not use Mobile banking cited this as a barrier, something that banks can overcome through communications;

No interest/a phone is to text and call – 17.5 per cent – this attitude has been prevalent for some time and it may reduce as phones become smarter and cheaper. It is worth bearing in mind that older people and those on low incomes are more likely to agree that a phone is just for calls and text messages. Banks could introduce SMS Text alerts to provide customers with a basic service that will dispel this notion;

Prefer Internet banking – 17 per cent – again banks need to understand this preference. This response may be explained by the fact that Mobile banking functionality is limited compared to more mature Internet banking;

Cannot do it with their phone – 11 per cent – one interpretation is that some consumers believe that a sophisticated phone is required for mobile banking. Banks could introduce

SMS Text alerts to provide customers with a basic service that will dispel this notion.

Banks can overcome these barriers; in fact, changing consumer attitudes over the next few years may work in the bank's favour. Internet banking suffered from similar barriers and overcame them as consumers relaxed their concerns and recognised the benefits.

Chapter 20 – The future of collaborative channels

We separated the bank-owned and collaborative channels to emphasise the amount of self-direction or control that banks will have over their channels in the future and perhaps, the lack of control and direction in the collaborative channels. This represents a real risk to disintermediation and further pressure on their traditional revenue streams.

Social media are the ultimate collaborative channels – with customers collaborating to provide product or service comparison views and feedback and even to invest or lend and borrow money in some cases – and with banks collaborating with the social media sites to connect with their customers and prospective customers.

The collaborative channels will level the technology 'playing field', allowing small banks to share the same level of technology as larger more sophisticated banks as they all share the same underlying platform. When every bank is on Facebook or Twitter this means that competitive advantage will need to come from the underlying service proposition and how the bank-owned and collaborative channels are integrated to provide an as seamless as possible experience. However, in this environment emulation will be rapid and competitive advantage short-lived, calling for more nimble marketing departments and more relevant, timely and personalised offers to customers.

One might argue that Facebook and Twitter are now so mainstream that they no longer present a competitive advantage for many banks and having a Facebook or Twitter presence is the same as having ATMs, Telephone banking, Internet banking, Mobile banking or even branches!

Mobile payments offer the next challenge to banks' traditional views of channels. A few years ago many banks might have presumed that Mobile payments would be their domain and that collaborators would align to them. It is evident that even the most powerful banks can no longer assume their position, as equally powerful (in the customers' eyes) telecoms and technology companies seek to secure part of the new Mobile payments value chain by creating alliances with payment processors. Given this new and rapid shift in power, many banks face being minor collaborators and further disintermediation from their customers.

SOCIAL MEDIA

Banks should no longer regard the social media as another channel. Third-generation thinking requires that banks become more relevant to customers, who are now increasingly in control of the relationship and demand that the bank is available when and where they need it.

As customers and prospective customers are spending increasing amounts of time using social media, such as Facebook, Twitter and YouTube, banks should 'go to where the customers are' and engage them in the manner that they prefer.

We described 'what customers want' in chapter 3, and these needs hold true for social media. To recap, research carried out by HSBC[clxiv] into what customers want identified the following needs:

- Recognise my value to you
- Know me and treat me as an individual
- Provide expertise I can get at
- Be on my side (and reassure me that you are)
- Leave me in control
- Be my trusted advisor
- Notice what I need
- Be easily available

These should form the basis of a bank's third-generation thinking, strategy and distribution model. They are particularly relevant to social media's role to create more relevance.

HOW BANKS MAY USE SOCIAL MEDIA IN THE FUTURE

The key objective of social media is to make the bank more relevant to the customer, to fit into customers' lives: not the other way around (as in first- and second-generation thinking).

Interactive two-way communication channel

Social media strategies will move away from advertising and getting more 'likes' to focus on benefiting the customer and deepening their relationship with the bank through relevant conversations.

There is almost no limit to the number of social media networks that a customer can belong to. The number is driven by relevance to the customer and there is no reason why a bank could not create its own secure social network to overcome the concerns about security and confidentiality. This would allow customers to securely communicate with the bank using social media-type messaging that would integrate the conversation into the bank's customer system, just like any other contact. Like any other social media channel it would operate 24x7, 365 days a year and become a two-way communications channel. The key, of course, would to make it highly relevant to the customer and easy to use and not just for the bank to cut costs, for instance.

A secure bank social media site might offer banks the opportunity to improve the customer complaints process by making it quicker and easier to complain and receive a response quickly, and build a conversation-like interaction that is more personal than formal letters.

Relevance to customers

Social media will allow the bank to be more relevant by being able to respond more quickly to simple customer questions or queries that do not compromise customer confidentiality. To do this, contact centre employees should be enabled to respond to enquiries or questions that normally arise through Facebook or Twitter directly with the customer or prospect and invite the person into the bank's secure social media network to continue any confidential conversation.

Engage customers in research more directly

Customer market research is often 'lost in translation' and individual customer voices are sometimes lost, making it less relevant. Social media offer the opportunity for banks to gain direct customer feedback to traditional market research questions at a fraction of the cost and more quickly than traditional methods. In fact, social media make it a continuous conversation, allowing the bank to create a panel of consumers who help determine product and service development. First Direct Lab provides a good example of how to engage customers in product and service development.

Access to easily available expertise

To become relevant once again banks need to make their expertise easily available to customers and prospective customers.

Social media allows banks to do this and enter into the conversation about money. For example, using YouTube to explain the importance of planning for retirement, or weekly video round-ups on finance; blogs by investment experts on the state of the market – not monthly paper-based circulars. (Note: this is not advertising or marketing, but provision of expertise that leaves customers in control.)

Improve employee access to information and improve collaboration

By using a social media infrastructure to manage their internal information banks can help customers get access to expertise. Currently information is inaccessible and siloed in rigid hierarchical directories, information databases and Intranets that make it difficult for employees to navigate, even if they know they exist. In addition to making it easier to find information that helps customers, employees will be able to collaborate, share and improve the quality of the information.

Drive customer engagement across all channels

As social media will be regarded as 'just another channel' banks may link social media more closely with traditional channels to help drive engagement with the new multi-channel model. Each branch should have a social media profile that it can use to build and engage its local community, promoting events that benefit customers and determining what customers want through social media feedback.

Engage more directly with investors, shareholders and influencers

Key to using social media to help rebuild relevance with the customer, senior executives must consider how they 'lead from the front'. Many already have Facebook, Twitter or LinkedIn profiles and use social media in a personal capacity.

Senior executives should start using social media as a business tool to engage more directly with investors, shareholders, employees and influencers, not just to be trendy, but to reach a large audience in a relevant and engaging way.

THE NEXT STEP IN THE EVOLUTION – MOBILE PAYMENTS

Mobile banking has three stages of evolution. The table below summarises the three stages, with most banks somewhere between stage one and stage two – new potential competitors (for example Simple, formerly BankSimple, MovenBank) will enter directly into the third stage.

At this point you might wonder why Mobile payments isn't in the bank-owned chapter. That's because we believe that this stage of the evolution is likely to take place, in part or to a large degree, outside many banks mobile banking platform. Banks will need to collaborate with others to remain viewed as innovative and competitive by their customers and to avoid disintermediation as a payment provider or gain new income streams that the inevitable customer behaviour shift offers.

It is the potential new income stream that attracts non-traditional innovative competitors who are often driving the proposition.

Three stages of Mobile evolution

	First stage **Basic Mobile banking**	Second stage **Mobile banking and remote Mobile payments**	Third stage **Mobile payments at physical POS**
Key features	Account access, balance information and internal transfers	Additional functionality such as bill payment and person-to-person payments that replicates Internet banking functionality	Ability to make payments at point-of-sale terminals through contactless technology
Benefits to customer	• Unrestricted and convenient access to banking information and basic transactions. • Helps customers to better manage their money.	• Increases convenience by reducing branch visits to pay bills or make simple person-to-person payments. • Reduces need to write and post cheques for person-to-person payments.	• Improves speed of payment at checkout. • Reduces the need to carry reasonable amounts of cash for day-to-day payments. • Improves convenience by reducing visits to ATMs.
Benefits to bank	Reduced cost to serve.	• Reduced cost to serve. • Reduces branch counter traffic and cheque processing costs. • Improves 'stickiness' of relationship.	• Responds to customer demands. • Positive image as 'innovator'. • Protects existing payment revenues. • Creates new revenue opportunities.

Intelligence Delivered (Asia) Limited 2012

State of the UK market

The Contactless Cards website provides an overview of contactless card activity in the UK and summarised the state of play as at May 2011.[clxv]

In summary, with the exception of Barclays, who are acting as the 'innovators' in the market, most banks are taking a 'fast follower' approach. As we discussed earlier in the text, there are advantages and disadvantages to each approach.

Mobile payments – who will take gold?

Since June 2008 a number of contactless payment initiatives have been launched in the UK by issuers and banks such as Visa, MasterCard, RBS, Barclays together with retailers and fast food outlets, Transport for London (London buses, Tube and DLR), Stagecoach buses (in Liverpool) and London's black cabs.

In June 2011 Visa passed the 13m contactless cards in circulation mark in March 2011, with 20m Visa cards in circulation expected by 2012. There are now more than 70,000 Visa contactless locations where contactless payments are accepted. Whilst many smaller retailers and fast food outlets have yet to join schemes there appears to be sufficient infrastructure in place. So what might be the tipping point?

The 2012 London Olympics and Paralympics may represent a 'tipping point' where Visa (a sponsor) can potentially expose 850,000 ticket holders to the new technology. A modest investment in a nominally charged (say £5) pre-paid contactless card to pay for refreshments inside the arena might have a significant impact on adoption. Such an event is sufficiently high profile to get people accepting contactless payments as a suitable alternative to cash.

If this is the case, the 'innovators' may gain an early advantage over their more conservative competitors.

What are the consumer benefits?

As the UK's payment landscape continues to evolve, Visa Europe released its first Contactless Barometer in August 2011 to benchmark consumer take up of new payment methods and to highlight changing attitudes to the way people pay.[clxvi]

For the Barometer, Visa surveyed 2,000 UK consumers with 85 per cent of contactless users saying that they would recommend contactless to their friends and family and 90 per cent thought that it makes their life simpler. However, 28 per cent said that there aren't enough retail outlets offering the service and over half (57 per cent) say they have never been asked to pay with contactless in a shop. More than one in three (37 per cent) cited this as the main barrier preventing them using the technology.

The research revealed that consumers are most likely to want to use their contactless cards in fast moving retail outlets where the benefits of the technology (speed and simplicity) are most obvious. Fast food restaurants, petrol stations and supermarkets were selected as the outlets where consumers are most likely to want to use contactless over chip and pin. The motivation for using contactless is clear: it is most popular for people in a rush (58 per cent), people with a queue behind them (30 per cent) and those in busy places with lots of people (26 per cent).

The Contactless Barometer found that the main benefits to consumers of contactless over cash or chip and pin cards are: speed in paying via contactless as opposed to cash (31 per cent); 53 per cent like not having to hand their card over to a cashier; 55 per cent appreciate not having to carry cash in their wallet/purse; 51 per cent like not having to carry loose change; 48 per cent like not having to plan to take cash out from an ATM.

There are benefits for the retailer too, including reduced queuing times of between 15-20 per cent and a decrease in the average transaction time of up to 40 per cent.

Barriers to adoption

There are still some barriers to adoption that will have to be overcome. Some of these are technical or require standards to be agreed and can be overcome by the industry. More important are the genuine concerns regarding fraud and security expressed by consumers that depresses adoption and therefore reduces justification for merchants to invest in expensive new terminals at a time of continued economic uncertainty.

Limited places to pay – the opportunities to use contactless payments will be hampered by the availability of places to pay. Whilst numbers of larger high-street retailers and transport companies are joining pilot schemes, the mass of smaller retailers is yet to join and concerns about the economy will depress investments.

Consumer concerns – the Contactless Barometer also showed some lingering misconceptions about fraud and security. 44 per cent of users expressed concern about security if their card gets stolen, suggesting that issuing banks may need to do more to educate their customers about the security measures in place to protect them (for example, in the UK, there is a £15 maximum transaction ceiling imposed – recently increased from £10 and cards can only be used a certain number of times before the PIN is required) and that they have the same levels of consumer protection as all bank issued cards.

Banks not promoting contactless payments – most banks have not started to actively promote and issue cards or join mobile phone schemes. Whilst most schemes are pilots or have geographical restriction (London and Liverpool are the contactless pioneers), most banks are not actively promoting contactless payments. HSBC's information page on their Internet banking site is 'hidden'. This lack of activity from most banks slows the pace of consumer acceptance, as they are unable to experience the benefits, and to satisfy their individual concerns.

Lack of NFC enabled mobile phones – whilst most contactless payments are made by card, the industry anticipates a rapid move to mobile phone wallets when the next generation of NFC enabled mobile phones. MicroSD cards, dongles or stickers for smartphones are available, but they are viewed as temporary solutions.

Standards and interoperability[clxvii] – there are different standards and limits at a UK, European and worldwide level; difficulties in interoperability in mass transit; differences between MasterCard and Visa, which means it is difficult for a retailer to develop an integrated solution into an existing Point of Sales (POS) device; standards need to be developed for mobile contactless payments.

Customer need – some customers simply don't want to use contactless payments, whether by card, token or mobile phone. It's unlikely that 100% acceptance will ever be achieved, meaning that we move to a 'less cash' society that does not allow banks to discontinue a channel, such as ATMs or branch counter pay-in services.

THE RISK TO BANKS

The risk of taking a 'fast follower' approach is the spectre of new, nimble and highly effective competitors taking control of the mobile payments market. In fact, the traditional hegemony of banks over the payment process is certainly not guaranteed and more at risk today than ever before.

Banks will be seen as even less innovative than ever before in part of their core business – payments. Those banks who don't experiment and pilot schemes will be at a disadvantage, particularly when the threat isn't just their established competitors. Banks may already be under threat from mobile network operators (MNOs), mobile phone manufacturers and operating system developers who now control the banks' access to the mobile payments market that they need to be in to avoid erosion of revenues. These competitors don't want to be a bank. They want a cut of the payments value chain in the same way that PayPal did on the Internet (and will do so on mobile).

The danger for banks is that card or token-based schemes may quickly move to mobile wallet-based schemes if this appeals to consumers; banks who don't have an existing base of satisfied contactless users may lose ground in this switch. MNOs with strong brands will partner with equally strong brands such Visa and MasterCard if the banks fail to get on board.

Technology companies, such as Apple, Samsung, HTC and Sony could all enter the payments market in a similar way to MNOs, partnering with Visa and MasterCard to disintermediate banks from their payments business and impacting revenues from their credit and debit cards.

In the US, Google have already done this and launched their mobile wallet in conjunction with Citibank and MasterCard. In the UK, Orange has partnered with Barclays and Barclaycard. Rogers Communications (Canada's largest mobile operator) recently announced its plans to apply for a banking licence for a new bank called Rogers Bank. It would focus on credit card and payment services, and there are no plans to expand into deposit taking and loans.

But as banks struggle to move ahead in this constantly changing technology and competitive environment, it will be critical from them to understand not only their own objectives, but also those of their partners, competitors and most importantly their customers.

THE MOBILE WALLET ARRIVES

In May 2011, Barclays and Everything Everywhere (Orange)[clviii] announced the launch of their contactless mobile phone payments scheme on their 'Quick Tap' enabled handset. The move builds on existing contactless payment technology with 11.6m contactless cards in circulation, 10m of which are issued by Barclays and Barclaycard. There are also already 42,500 live Barclaycard contactless terminals in retail outlets including Pret a Manger, EAT, Little Chef, McDonalds and Co-operative stores.

Barclaycard, Barclays debit or Orange Credit Card users can transfer funds of up to £100 simply and securely onto the handset's Quick Tap app, after which the phone is ready to make payments of £15 and under in a single transaction.

The race for technology supremacy

Many people are expecting some sort of Near Field Communications (NFC) technology to emerge as the winner in developed countries as it would appear to provide a very simple and convenient method for payment for bank customers. However, NFC is also hampered from widespread adoption by a number of critical and massive challenges.

For one, NFC payments will require that merchants, POS systems will need to be updated to effectively interoperate across multiple banks, card types and devices.

Matters are complicated due to the fact that there are several different ways of using NFC for payments, for example, embedded in cards, dongles or tokens, mobile phone stickers, MicroSD cards and embedded in SIM cards, or embedded in the mobile phone.

Each method brings its own unique challenges. SIM cards for example, allow for mobile wallets to be quickly deployed on phones and provide high levels of security, but this method also makes MNOs responsible for managing the technology and thus may require banks to split revenues with new MNO partners. Embedded NFC chips rely upon device manufacturers to deploy, creating a situation where the bank's revenues may be reduced. In reality, the choice of technologies may be out of the bank's hands. It will be consumers who decide on the winning technology. Dongle solutions, where an external 'attachment' is added or stuck to the phone to enable NFC will likely not see widespread uptake with the mass of consumers, but may be a smart interim step for banks wanting to test the market.

SIM Cards and MicroSD cards, on the other hand would require consumers to install a chip on their own devices which may deter the less 'tech-savvy' and those that already use their SIM or MicroSD card slot for other applications.

One thing is clear. If banks can roll out a safe, easy to use and ubiquitously accepted system, consumers will adopt mobile payment solutions in much the same way they have adopted other services such as Internet banking.

Chapter 21 – Organising to succeed

ORGANISATION AND CULTURE

An organisation that wants to implement a successful customer-centric multi-channel strategy needs to look further than the technology and operational aspects.

There are two distinctly 'human' aspects that have a significant impact on the successful implementation: organisation and culture. Organisational structure can be changed, although it takes time, energy and leadership; culture is harder as it's not as if you can easily 'plug in' a new one if the old one doesn't work.

Whilst we'll look at organisation and culture as two separate topics they are intertwined and failure to get one right impacts the other – and they both impact your strategy and customer experience.

- **Automation** – 1980 – driven by bank to reduce cost, undifferentiated approach, branch-centric;
- **Connectivity** – 2000 – (but not always connected), driven by bank to reduce cost, segmented approach, channel-centric;
- **Intelligence** – 2011 – driven by the customer, personalised customer-centric approach.

Organisation

In this section we will:

- Examine how the banks' channels and marketing organisations have evolved
- Offer some insight on how third-generation thinking can be achieved

First-generation thinking

It would be an oversimplification to say that banks had a simple organisational structure when the branch was the only delivery channel. Whilst there was a branch network structure – typically: branch, area, region and head office – other product areas, such as credit cards, insurance (general and life) and wealth management were separate – operating with their own structure all the way to head office level.

During this period the removal of back-office processing had little impact on the organisational structure, although many employees were affected by the changes.

Centralised marketing departments were responsible for the production of in-branch merchandising, such as core product leaflets and brochures. They also included core product management – current accounts, savings, loans and mortgages. Marketing of credit cards, insurance and wealth management was normally handled by units within the separate product lines.

Mail and statement inserts were the primary direct marketing methods used. However, with products in silos and a limited single view of the relationship customers were often offered products that they already held, or had recently been offered. As a result marketing was often ineffective and, in some cases, actually destroyed customer satisfaction.

Most products required customers to complete paper application forms (from scratch each time), data gathered was usually retained in the product system and very often unusable in other systems (due to inconsistencies and conflicts) or simply missing.

Second-generation thinking

When call centres were introduced they usually formed part of the Operations hierarchy of the bank rather than the same one as the branch. After all, they were migrating a 'telephone answering' process, not a customer experience. Product areas such as cards and insurance retained their own data, processes and call centers, meaning that data was separate and disconnected, often in conflict between channels. Channels did not know what was going on in other channels. Sales, retention, complaints and performance management all fragmented as a result.

Internet banking was often integrated as part of the Operations hierarchy as one of its major objectives was to take transactional costs out of the network (branches and call centres).

Four unconnected organisational structures emerged: the branch network, product silos, call centres and Internet banking. All of whom initially thought they owned the customer and fought to justify their independence.

The impact of second-generation thinking often further eroded the customer experience: a focus on cost not customer service; a continued breakdown of the internal processes that supported the customer; a lack of understanding and vision concerning what the customer wanted.

There was a negative impact on the bank's culture – as they found themselves on the receiving end of more and more customer complaints about multi-channel service. Branches resisted change in a number of ways, one example was prioritising their own self-generated marketing leads over those from other channels (even though the customer had generated the request and it was not in their customers' best interests).

Banks realised that the volume of in-bound calls offered an opportunity to offer products. Also that the call centre could act as an out-bound contact centre to follow up or market to the customer. This introduced further customer experience fragmentation where customers could, in the same day, be contacted by a branch and call centre offering different products that might meet their needs, or even worse, the same product.

The customer experience failure often occurred because branches and call centres were not using the same CRM system and customer contact history. There was little if any straight-through-processing capability, which also meant that the branch had to complete the paperwork or it resulted in a lengthy call to complete input. The process also meant sending application and agreement forms to branch or direct to customer for signature and return to the bank. Up to 30 per cent of applications for products from existing customers could not be closed because the paperwork was not returned (customer changed their mind, found a better deal, lack of time to sign etc). This required banks to set up chasing processes that further increased the cost of sales and fragmented the customer experience.

Linking up the branch and call centres via the same CRM system and customer contact history started the joining-up process, improved the situation significantly and reduced the conflicting offers; it also allowed customers to start a conversation about a product in one channel and complete it in another.

Fortunately, the same marketing teams dealt with both branches and call centres and banks tried to ensure that they tailored certain offers for the call centre to facilitate some sort of straight-through-processing (STP).

Internet banking usually set up a separate marketing team due to the perceived need for special 'digital' marketing skills rather than traditional branch marketing skills. The truth was that what they needed was 'customer' marketing skills. Having separate teams caused friction between the channels and affected the customer experience, mainly through a lack of internal co-ordination. Eventually banks integrated the marketing teams into customer-focused groups.

Customer contact preferences (express or inferred) were rarely captured or if they were it was in a limited format. Where the data was available it was often ignored in pursuit of undifferentiated mass marketing. For example, even when a customer had never responded to email marketing (maybe because of phishing concerns, irrelevance of the offer or poor timing), many marketers continued to bombard the customer with 'junk' mail, that was simply cheaper than the paper version, but had exactly the same result – customer dissatisfaction. In response, many customers 'turned-off' all marketing channels as a result. Contact response analysis and propensity modeling should have uncovered the 'right customer, right product, right channel' principles.

Third-generation thinking

A multi-channel strategy requires an organisational structure that can deliver it. Finalta's research indicates that many banks have failed to recognise this and have implemented a 'many-headed beast' that perpetuates the separation of its channels.

What's wrong with this picture?

The question: 'do you have a Head of Multi-channel?' often results in the person describing one of the following scenarios if the answer is 'yes'.

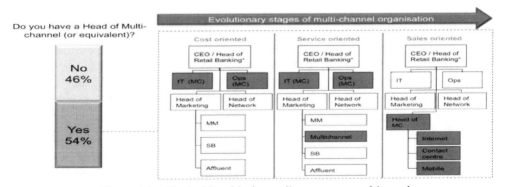

Figure 16 – Typical 'multi-channel' management hierarchy

Source: Intelligence Delivered (Asia) Limited research

On first impression, the answer is 'yes', but it's frequently 'no, not really'. As the Head of Multi-channel sometimes doesn't have responsibility for the branch/sales force network. Many banks still think in terms of branch versus 'alternative channels' (where in reality, customer use in volume terms is predominately 'alternative').

Even in 2011:

- **Legacy accounting systems are not multi-channel** – income from sales originated, and/or closed in 'alternative channels' (and whether the branch is involved or not) is accounted for at branch level (where the customer maintains their account) or where the product is held (e.g. Insurance).
- **Branch-centric, not customer-centric thinking** – continued belief, despite facts, that the branch is the core of the customers' relationship with the bank.

  Customers are multi-channel – they use the channel that matches their need at the task in hand. They consistently say that they still want a branch network – but not for transactions. Some pure-play Internet banks have struggled without a branch network, and even First Direct's success has HSBC's branches available for customers to pay cheques in over the counter and withdraw cash through their ATM network. New technology, such as Internet banking and more crucially Mobile banking (and associated mobile payments capabilities) will continue to change the relevance of the branch in the customers eyes.

  The problem, as described in our chapter on Branches, is that most bank branches were located and designed before 2006 when the Internet paradigm shift occurred. Banks are saddled with an inflexible costly infrastructure that is in danger of becoming even more expensive due to new technology. Many banks are aware of the challenge and addressing it by exploring what a third-generation branch might offer customers that their other channels cannot. In the meantime, with all of that real estate, costs and manpower the Head of Branches/Network is no longer king, but a 'first amongst equals'.

- **Promotion is multi-channel, but the sales process is monochannel** – many banks are unable to fulfil end-to-end in the channel where the customer starts (and presumably often wants to complete) and customers are forced into the branch to complete the process, whether they want to or not. What's the problem? Risk? – No, even non-credit products can't be STP. Regulatory? – No, many banks have successfully dispensed with requiring 'wet signatures' for existing customers. KYC? – No, these are existing customers and surely this information can be collected online for simple products. Lack of customer-centric thinking? – Yes.

  Finalta highlighted this problem in their European multi-channel research conducted in 2010.[clxx] For existing customers: only 24% of Internet banking credit card opening can be completed straight through online. 24% require the customer to print out and send forms to the bank. 36% require the customer to visit the branch to complete the transaction. 16% of banks don't offer online credit card purchase for existing customers.

Only 20% of banks have an online STP for unsecured (personal) loans, 24% must print and send, 40% have to visit the branch to complete and 16% don't offer.

Maybe STP isn't 'straight-through-processing'; but in fact stands for 'straight-to-printer'?

Third-generation thinking – customer paradigm shift

Customers are in control of a bank's channels. They also see them differently from banks. Many banks still see non-branch channels as a cost reduction solution. Customers don't care about the cost of channels to banks, as they simply are a way to get the job of managing their money done and they simply desire convenience and ease of access. They determine how channels will be used (and which survive or die), not the bank; and won't, in the future, be herded down a particular channel as first- or second-generation thinking supposed (or hoped).

Once banks see their channels the same way as customers they can start to be truly customer-centric (most banks say they want to be more, not less).

This requires banks to organise themselves differently. Around the customer, not a product or a channel (first- or second-generation thinking). Organising themselves around 20 million customers sounds difficult, but segmentation and well researched and designed propositions help.

Customer experience is king: and channels and products are utilities (building channels and products is relatively easy; building the customer experience is harder).

Banks will organise themselves around propositions so as to fairly exchange value – premium service for higher value customers for example. Customer propositions do not compete against each other internally as channels or products do. Propositions can also be better aligned to the bank's bottom line than channels or products – and resources can be allocated accordingly.

However, a greater degree of intelligence is required than banks have deployed in the past. By 'intelligence' we mean harnessing all of the relevant data available about customers and using it in a relevant, timely and personalised way.

Third-generation thinking requires a radically different approach to repair the fractures to the customer experience caused by second-generation 'channel think'. Third-generation thinking is dominated by the concept of 'Intelligence' – where the customer drives the relationship, the bank requires a personalised and customer-centric approach.

Intelligence requires a bank to harness its multiple silos of data to: constantly monitor and understand customer behaviour across all of its channels and to use the insight that it derives to anticipate future customer behaviour to take the right action at the right time.

The bank's intelligence must work at two levels: firstly, at a macro-level, to understand how different segments of customers behave and how, over time, the trend is changing; secondly, at a micro-level, to be relevant, timely and personalised to individual customers, irrespective of channel.

How might banks go about managing the customer experience?

Firstly, all distribution channel management, including the branch, must be centralised under one line of business to ensure that information and decisions are taken from a customer-centric, not channel or product silo, point of view.

   Secondly, all relevant customer data must be integrated to provide the holistic view of customer activity and behaviour across your different distribution points. Implement 'robust, single version of the truth' reporting to monitor over time so that you understand what is happening and know when to deploy another strategy. Minimum standards should provide the following insight:

1. Customer activity and behavioural trends by channel;
2. Numbers of customers using the channel, the purpose and frequency of use;
3. Costs to serve in that channel;
4. Revenue allocation to the channel.

Thirdly, you must build a multi-disciplinary management team to manage your multi-channel distribution strategy and implement a process where any new products, marketing initiatives or messages are funneled through this group for approval against a specific set of customer-centric guidelines. The objective is to have a clearly defined multi-channel customer experience at your different distribution points.

   For example, a new in-branch promotion should take into account what information will also be delivered to customers online and what communications and coaching the call centre needs.

   The plan that will arise from this stage can be measured against actual results (including customer research) to improve subsequent customer experience and performance.

Figure 17 – Multi-channel Strategy Management process

Source: Intelligence Delivered (Asia) Limited

Relevant, timely and personalised marketing

Having established the ability to integrate and use customer multi-channel and behavioural data, banks can then embark on delivering a truly personalised experience.

The objective is to be relevant, timely and personalised in every customer interaction, for example, relevant is:

- Following-up a customer originated online product enquiry, such as a loan repayment quotation in priority over another unqualified lead;
- Offering a product to meet a customer's anticipated current financial need;
- Gathering information about the customer's future financial needs to help deepen the relationship with the customer – and do what the customer wants;
- Alerting the customer of a 'risk' to their wealth by identifying detrimental movements in their investment portfolio during a period of stock market volatility;
- Alerting the customer to an opportunity to realise gains in their investment portfolio.

Timely, is about doing it the quickest most accessible way from the customer's point of view. For instance, during a period of stock market volatility there may be a need to alert the customer to a potential investment portfolio risk. Instead of following second-generation thinking and sending a secure email (impractical as you have to be logged into Internet banking to see it!) or asking RM to contact the customer (when they have time): try alerting the customer by SMS and asking them to log into Internet banking or Mobile banking to read the full message and how they may take action (and backing it up with easy straight-through processing).

This approach can only be achieved by being able to do the following three things:

- Understanding what information or events are important to the customer;
- Having the capability to deliver and action the message quickly and easily;
- Having the ability to personalise the message content to individual customers.

This requires robust 'single version of the truth' organisational reporting and strong analytics capabilities to be in place.

CULTURE

Until the 1980s bank culture was relatively simple. There were few competitive or technology threats to employees, and banking was a 'job for life' (unless you dipped your hand in the till!). The branch reigned supreme and the world revolved around the branch and not the customer.

First-generation thinking

The expansion of retail banking during the 1970s increasingly led to a less personalised relationship with customers. There were some differences in branch culture due to regional differences (e.g. typically Greater London versus rest of UK network). Although customers and commentators hark back to a golden period it was one of privilege – the bank was the centre of the high street and it was a privilege to know your local bank manager. Customers often felt that they had to go to the bank to 'beg' for a loan.

Back-office centralization did little to affect the overall branch culture. Although a new culture arose in the operational processing centres it rarely impacted upon customers who continued to interact primarily with their branch.

Second-generation thinking

When banks introduced call centres it required a different approach to culture. After trying, and not always succeeding, with moving employees out of redundant branch jobs to call centres, banks realized they needed a different type of employee, with a different culture to work in a call centre. The shift patterns and working processes did not suit all ex-branch staff and many former back office staff disliked talking to customers. Call centres therefore implemented end-to-end recruitment, profiling and training. They initially focused on performance measurement that was different to branches – based on processing efficiency such as call handling and using techniques such as call monitoring.

As the call centre channel emerged, so did friction with the dominant channel. Because the new and old channels weren't fully connected and synchronised, branches and call centres sometimes struggled to work together effectively, resulting in the first fragmentation of the customer experience and corresponding decline in service quality.

A cultural gap emerged between branches and call centres, which had different recruitment, training, reward and recognition policies. Many branch employees whose jobs were lost in the branch successfully transferred to the call centre environment. Many branch employees feared for their jobs as they saw call centre volumes rise and heard talk of new threats such as Internet banking. Branches and the call centres frequently fought over who was to blame for service failures. In truth, the organisation was to blame as it introduced new channels without fully understanding the implications of introducing new business and cultural models – impacting the same customers. There were now two different customer-facing cultures in the average high-street bank.

This manifested itself in customer complaints that inter-channel actions or messages were not fulfilled properly, one channel did not know what the other was doing, and transactions that required hand-offs between channels were generally poor, using limited technology and often requiring customers to repeat information.

Later, customer experience training was introduced to branches and call centres as banks realised that it was a differentiator in an increasingly competitive, commoditised and price-driven marketplace.

There's something in the First Direct 'Kool Aid'

When Midland Bank introduced First Direct in 1989 it deliberately introduced a new culture to deliver its customer proposition. Not only was this distinct from Midland's branch network culture, but it differed from Midland's call centre culture. The evidence of this was seen in the difference in customer satisfaction scores that First Direct achieved compared to the high-street banks. First Direct's ability to recruit new customers also relied upon the 'word-of-mouth' of existing customers and positive media comment, both resulting from its different culture.

First Direct culture was built around the customer and, although they operated as a monochannel in the early days, it should be remembered that they offered the same core products as a traditional high-street bank and used the same call routing technology as the high-street banks' call centres. Employee recruitment focused on the applicants' communications skills and not just banking knowledge (that can be quickly learnt during the training program). Many applicants had no previous banking experience (other than being a customer) and were recruited from a variety of service sector backgrounds, not just post-graduates trying to get a job. The training program itself was longer than most call centre programs and significantly longer than a branch program. Its content differed too. A traditional call centre program focused on the technical aspects of the job (the bank's products and using the technology). First Direct started with being customer-centric.

Whilst First Direct operated from what could be politely described as an 'aircraft hanger' the culture was evident within this environment, with an approach to work that was orientated towards enjoying what you did and also being totally professional. Status was 'played down' as even the CEO sat at a desk in the main office like everyone else – this meant he was always close to what was happening on the 'shop floor'.

It was notable that at a time when many high-street bank employees had difficulties expressing positive opinions of their employers, First Direct employees were the opposite. Clearly, there was something in the water that they drank in Leeds!

The 'rise of the machines'

The Internet caused another disruption to bank culture. Whilst branch employees were more inconvenienced than threatened by call centres, the rise of the Internet was a different matter.

Here was a technology that put power directly into the customers' hands. They could do more and more without visiting the branch counter – ATMs had already reduced the need for cheque encashment. Although the call centre had introduced bill payments, Internet banking made it more convenient and moved many customers away from the branch counter altogether. Worse still, employees recognised that the Internet 'disintermediated' them from 'their' best customers, as it was these time-poor, more valuable customers who abandoned the branch queue for their home computer.

Third-generation thinking

As banks realised that customers want a joined-up experience they are now working towards instilling a culture that recognises each channel's strengths and how the customer wants the bank to work for them. Banks are starting to complete the centralization of customer information and make it available to any point of contact with the customer in a single view. This reduces friction between channels by joining them up. Banks are starting to retrain employees to work with the channels, e.g. increasingly a relationship manager can rely on direct channels to meet the customers' day-to-day transaction needs, allowing him to focus on their wealth management needs as a 'co-pilot'.

Incentivisition

People respond to incentives. As part of any business and cultural change banks should review their employee incentive scheme to ensure that it still influences the right behaviour.

First-generation thinking incentivised the final sales person for any sale, even if other employees were involved in referring the customer to that sales person.

Just as second-generation thinking saw an increase in unconnected channels, so multiple sales incentives schemes mushroomed and it was not uncommon for employees to belong to two or three: branch core products; credit cards and an insurance product scheme. Because the data was not connected the schemes required manual collation and reconciliation, which resulted in queries and disputes from employees and increased the underlying cost of management of the schemes (it is estimated that the average scheme overpaid employees up to 15% as a result). It was not uncommon for the branch and call centre to have completely different schemes (and rewards), although they were dealing with the same customer!

The schemes themselves were regarded by employees as being unfair by not reflecting the contribution they made to a sale that they did not close. Schemes rarely reflected or supported multi-channel sales activity. Research by Finalta in 2009 revealed that only 8% of European banks were able to allocate the reward across channels according to their involvement; 14% allocated solely to the channel that sold the product; 31% 'double rewarded' the direct channel and the branch; nearly half (47%) allocated the reward back to the branch irrespective of channel involvement.[clxxi]

We must not forget the customer in the way that schemes are designed and implemented. There is evidence that poorly designed schemes can lead to behaviour that does not benefit the customer and creates potential mis-selling. In chapter 3 we discussed how customers currently views banks and their activities, especially their sales culture, which is usually underpinned by the incentive scheme. The Which? Banking Manifesto actually calls for sales incentives to be banned and calls for a switch to rewarding employees for providing high-quality service linked to overall levels of customer satisfaction, complaint levels and regulatory compliance (senior executives only).

Third-generation thinking requires that individual employees and channels are rewarded for the right behaviour – this is more than simply sales, but can include referrals to other business lines e.g. between personal banking and commercial banking, failure-proof servicing, customer needs gathering (to understand the customer's needs), complaint handling and customer retention activity.

This means that banks must have the capability to gather a wide range of information across multiple channels, calculate and allocate the reward across channels accurately according to their contribution. As a result, the true benefit (more than just cost and revenue) contribution for each channel can be assessed, leading to a clearer understanding of where resources should be allocated to maximise customer satisfaction and revenue.

This also means that performance management across the entire range of an employee's duties and their incentives are closely linked, with employees seeing their rewards accrue as their service and sales performance targets are met without any personal negative impact on customer satisfaction.

Chapter 22 – Analytics and contact management

THE EVOLUTION OF MARKETING

There was a time, not too many years ago, when banks did very little in the way of marketing. They had marketing departments, but they were mainly interested in commissioning advertising campaigns and developing artwork for brochures, cheque books and cards – the only physical items that the banks produced.

This form of undifferentiated marketing was taken from the consumer goods industries. It resulted in large, expensive campaigns with very low response rates. Those of us with long memories still recall some of these – remember the bank manager in the cupboard? – but they were not particularly effective.

DATA MINING

Data mining is: "the nontrivial extraction of implicit, previously unknown, and potentially useful information from data."[clxxii] Data mining uses software to analyse data in order to detect patterns, trends and relationships.

Data mining is an automated process and does not require human intervention. Data mining can be directed, which means that the data mining software is instructed to look for relationships between specific variables. Alternatively it can be undirected, which means that the software analyses all of the data available to it.

Data mining establishes patterns based on the data. There may be no obvious reason why the pattern should exist, and a human analyst may be needed to establish exactly what is happening and why. However, data mining can be very useful in establishing the characteristics and behaviours associated with customer decisions. An example of this is: "customers with children purchase savings plans whereas customers without choose a different type of mutual fund."[clxxiii]

Targeted marketing

The banks had failed to appreciate a critical difference between themselves and the consumer goods industries. The banks had a huge amount of information about their customers. They did not need to launch undifferentiated marketing campaigns. They could use this information to target their campaigns.

The thought process was as follows. We can identify the characteristics of customers who hold a certain type of product. Therefore we can draw up a profile of what characteristics a customer who is likely to be interested in that product will have. Therefore we can look through our customer information to identify customers who have those characteristics but do not hold that product. And we can market it to them. We will call this propensity by characteristics.

This was initially quite successful. Consolidation in the banking industry had brought the banks a large number of new customers. Propensity by characteristics allowed them to target these new customers, and to cross sell and up-sell to existing customers. However, the market approached saturation – customers either already had the products or were not interested in them. Therefore response rates started to fall.

The next approach was propensity by behaviour. This came out of behavioural credit scoring.

The banks introduced credit scoring to help them to reduce loan losses. They developed scorecards that predicted the probability of customers failing to repay loans. One type, the demographic scorecard, was based on characteristics.

The other type was based on behaviour. The banks analysed their records to identify how their customers' accounts behaved in the months before a default. They identified certain key behaviours, for example building up an overdraft that was never repaid. They found that these scorecards – behavioural scorecards – were very good at predicting the probability of default.

They extended this analysis to other events of interest. For example, how did customers' accounts behave in the months before they took out a mortgage? They developed scorecards to allow them to predict the probability of customers buying various types of product. We will call this propensity by behaviour.

This is a good point to discuss segmentation. Segmentation and propensity have a lot in common – for example, both can be based on characteristics or behaviour. The main difference is in what they tell the bank. Segmentation is a way of breaking down the customer base and, now, is mainly used for analysis. Propensity is a way of predicting the behaviour of an individual customer and is used, amongst other things, for generating sales leads. We will return to targeted marketing after our short digression.

Segmentation

We have discussed segmentation at various points in this text without really defining it. There are a number of different types of segmentation, of which the two of greatest importance to us are market segmentation and channel segmentation

Market segmentation splits our market – our customers and prospective customers – into groups. These groups can be based on characteristics, behaviours, attitudes or value.

Segmentation based on characteristics is the earliest form of market segmentation and includes techniques such as demographic, geographic and geodemographic segmentation. Demographic segmentation uses factors such as age, sex, income and (in the old days) social class to break the market into groups. Geographic segmentation uses location as a basis.

Geodemographic segmentation relies on the fact that people who live in the same area as defined, for example, by a postcode or zip code tend to have similar characteristics and behaviours. Therefore the postcode or zip code can be used as a proxy for customer information that may not otherwise be available. Large databases of geodemographic information such as ACORN and MOSAIC are widely used. Geodemographic segmentation provides the richest available source of information to banks for non-customers.

Segmentation based on behaviours splits customers by what they do. Examples include product usage, channel usage and lifestage, which considers events in the customer's life such as marriage, first child etc.

Segmentation based on attitudes splits customers by their personalities, values, attitudes, interests or lifestyles. We have already discussed one example of this in chapter 11 when we said that people had different attitudes towards innovation.

We discussed the idea of customer value in chapter 3. Segmentation based on value splits customers by their value to the organization. This can be based on lifetime value or on a combination of current value and future value over a three to five year period, as discussed in chapter 3.

Market segmentation was critical to targeted marketing. The banks divided their customers into market segments and bombarded each segment with offers relevant to their needs as perceived by the bank. The move away from targeted marketing to one-to-one selling and event-driven selling has made this less important.

Market segmentation is still important, however, to help the banks to understand their customers. Segmentation allows banks to monitor and report on groups of customers. This, in turn, allows banks to understand the needs of these groups, and how to extract value from them.

We have covered channel segmentation extensively throughout this text. Channel segmentation involves reserving certain outlets for the exclusive use of specific groups of customers.

Customisation

Targeted marketing was based on the principle of developing a product first, then finding a group of customers that would be willing to buy it. This changed when Peppers, Rogers and Dorf developed one-to-one marketing.[clxxiv]

The principle behind one-to-one marketing was mass customisation. Instead of finding customers for products, banks should be developing products for customers. This was a four-stage process. The first stage, identify, was the accumulation of information about the customer. The second stage, differentiate, was to segment those customers. The third stage was to contact the customers. The fourth and final stage was to customise products to meet the customers' needs, what Irene Dorner, HSBC General Manager for Marketing, described as "building the bank around the customer."

This was *mass* customisation, of course! One-to-one marketing did not involve building products for every individual customer. Instead, it involved developing products to meet the needs of specific market segments.

Event-driven selling

Another source of sales leads is events that affect customers. This comes out of customer segmentation. One form of segmentation looks at customer lifestages, and identifies how customer needs change as they progress through these. For example, the financial needs of a property owner are different from those of someone who is living with parents or in rented accommodation. Buying a house is a life event that changes customers' financial needs.

Another source of leads is customer enquiries. If a customer asks about mortgages, or uses an online mortgage calculator, this suggests that the customer is thinking about buying property. We can show this as a hierarchy diagram:

Figure 18 – Hierarchy of lead conversion rates

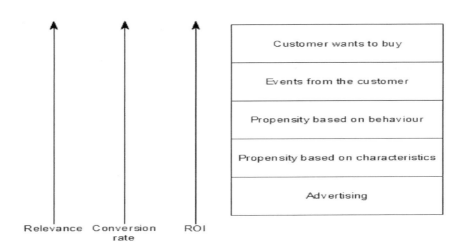

All of the methods that we have discussed will produce sales. The higher in the hierarchy the method, the higher the proportion of leads that will be converted to sales – the conversion rate. The diagram shows two other factors: Relevance and return on investment (ROI).

Relevance

Undifferentiated advertising will be irrelevant to the needs of most of the people who see it. However, if a customer has made an enquiry about a product, the product is likely to be highly relevant to the customer's needs.

Relevance is important for two reasons. It affects the conversion rate because people are more likely to buy something that is of interest to them. It affects customer goodwill.

The fact that undifferentiated advertising is of low relevance is not particularly important because people are very good at tuning out advertisements that do not interest them. However, relevance is important if a sales lead is used to contact people through a medium such as an outbound telephone call centre.

Such contacts interrupt people's lives. They are prepared to accept such interruptions if the contact is relevant to their needs, but not for low relevance contacts. This can produce a loss of goodwill that can damage the bank's relationship with its customers.

The return on investment (ROI) is a measure of the financial success of a marketing campaign. It depends on the cost of the campaign and the number of sales.

Undifferentiated advertising campaigns are very expensive. They reach a large number of people, but the number of sales is very low. Targeted campaigns reach fewer people but are less expensive and produce a higher percentage of sales.

In terms of the hierarchy discussed earlier, moving up the hierarchy (from undifferentiated advertising to customer wants to buy) generates fewer leads and results in fewer marketing approaches, but the higher conversion rate leads to a higher ROI.

INFORMATION AND ANALYTICS

The ability to move up the hierarchy depends on two factors: Information and analytics.

As we have discussed, banks have invested heavily in improving the **information** that they hold about their customers. There have been a number of drivers for this, including the need to ensure consistent information across channels and Know Your Customer (KYC) regulations imposed by governments.

This has resulted in the development of large data warehouses. These are large, centralised stores of information. The rationale of a data warehouse is to provide a 'single view of reality' that holds all necessary information about the bank's customers.

The data warehouse serves the same function as middleware, but there are two important differences. The data warehouse stores a copy of the data, whereas middleware holds the rules about where to get the data. The data warehouse does not store the same information as the operational databases that middleware accesses. We will not go into the reasons for this in any detail, but the data warehouse may store data for longer, may store data in summary form, and may omit data that is needed for purely operational purposes.

Analytics is the application of computer technology, operational research, and statistics to solve problems in business and industry.[clxxv] Analysts use the information held on the data warehouse to identify customer needs. Banks have invested in their Analytics capabilities in recent years to improve the response rate to marketing approaches.

THE SALES FUNNEL

The term sales funnel is used to describe the sales process from the point of view of the bank. This can include a number of stages but we will use a simplified sales funnel with five stages: Lead, approach, fact find, contact and close.

It is called a sales funnel because it gets narrower. The number of leads is greater than the number of contacts that, in turn, is greater than the number of sales. We have discussed the conversion rate as the ratio of leads to sales, for example if it requires ten leads to generate one sale this is a conversion rate of 10 per cent. However, the ratio of contacts to sales is also relevant.

The main source of **leads** for the banks is analytics. Using customer enquiries, customer life events and behavioural information can, as we have discussed, lead to a higher conversion rate than using customer characteristics.

The lead will result in an initial **approach** to the customer. This may be through a dedicated sales channel such as direct mail marketing or an outbound call centre. Or the sales approach may be blended with customer service activity through a channel such as the branch counter or an inbound call centre.

Blending sales and service activities in this way should only be done if the approach to the customer is of high relevance.

As we discussed in chapter 6, the **fact find** stage depends on the customer's response to the initial approach. It is only relevant for some products.

Some banks are reducing the cost of the fact finding stage by using Internet-based advice agents to allow this stage to be completed using a self-service channel. These are computer programs that collect information and can also use expert systems technology to suggest products in which customers might be interested.

The **contact** stage is the stage at which the bank makes a proposal to the customer. If the customer accepts, or an alternative proposal is agreed, this is the **close** stage at which the sale is completed.

The banks have three objectives with the sales funnel.

The first is to obtain a lead to sales ratio as high as possible. They attempt to achieve this by improving their understanding of the customer and the customer's needs through analytics.

The second is to reduce the cost of the stages prior to the contact stage, by using the full range of channels available to them and automating these stages as far as possible.

The third is to ensure that the conversion rate from contact to close is as close to 100 per cent as possible.

NEW REALITY – REAL-TIME MULTI-CHANNEL CONTACT MANAGEMENT

The purpose of this section is to discuss how the need for real-time multi-channel 'conversations' that engage customers requires a change in thinking and organisation.

The prime purpose of customer relationship management and analytics is to optimise the organisation's contact capacity to personalise the customer experience and create maximum sustainable value.

Why 'real-time multi-channel' contact management?

Because, it's 'reality' – it is the world that your customers now live in (and so do you, if you choose). Consumers now expect immediate fulfilment. "I want it, and I want it now!"

Due to changing consumer attitudes, behaviours and technologies such as the Internet, broadband always on connections, 3G, mobile smartphones, email, SMS Text, chat, iTunes, YouTube, Facebook and Twitter, consumers live in a 'real-time' world, where conversations, news, information and services are always immediately available. Content now streams 24x7.

In a connected world it's no longer acceptable to take a week to follow up a quotation on the Internet; to take three months to prepare a direct marketing campaign or not to synchronise offers across channels so that the customer isn't offered the same product tomorrow that they rejected yesterday.

Never has 'right customer, right offer, right channel, right time' been so important. Many customers are connected 24x7 by mobile smartphone and there's evidence that many Gen Y customers' attitudes are different to Baby Boomers. As they're always connected they're more accepting of relevant, timely and personalised contact from organisations that they do business with during their leisure time.

First-generation contact management thinking was dominated by automation that resulted in centralised mass direct mail marketing with little differentiation developed around simple propensity models because customer data was often out of date or missing.

As customers were selected on propensity to buy, rather than their need, most campaigns failed to achieve more than 2 per cent response rates, as they were irrelevant, not timely nor personalised in the customer's eyes.

The end-to-end processes involved manual data extraction and modelling, offer letter and application form design, product pricing, advertising control, compliance and legal. In all, most direct mail campaigns had a 16-week lead-time.

As a result, customers could have already bought the product between the data being extracted and receiving a now, irrelevant, direct mail. It was not unusual for customers to receive up to four or five direct mail shots a month from their bank: for example, credit card; personal loan; home insurance and mortgages because the data was in silos and mined independently for different product managers with no filters or prioritisation across offers.

Customers could only respond to campaigns in one of two ways: return a completed paper application form to the branch or a central back-office unit for processing or visit the branch and ask to buy the product. Branches often did not know that a customer had been mailed and so the conversation was often an embarrassing one. Application forms were rarely personalised, that is pre-completed with known information, to help the customer. Personalisation was non-existent as all customers received the same offer.

It is not surprising that customers regarded the bank's attempts as 'junk mail' and frequently asked the bank to stop mailing them.

Second-generation contact management thinking resulted in fragmentation of the customer experience as new channels came on stream and marketed independently.

Firstly, the call centre offered the opportunity to outbound call customers using automated call technology that offered productivity gains and the ability to contact customers after branch opening hours at home. However, calling customers at home with unsolicited offers, often whilst they were having dinner or relaxing was not popular and customers asked banks to turn off this channel.

Email was seen as a replacement for direct mail as it offered a lower unit cost, however, it suffered from security issues as 'phishing' concerns prevented many customers from clicking on the link embedded in the email. Because 'spam' emails many customers have become immune to email messages that are not immediately relevant and personalised.

And finally, Internet banking offered the opportunity to revolutionise the customer experience, but fell short. Offers conflicted with off-line channels – they were either different or not synchronised. Straight through processing of products offered on-line was limited, even for existing customers, forcing them to the branch to complete the sale.

Because there were now four channels: branch, direct mail, Telephone banking and Internet banking, this increased the pressure on customers. Often, campaigns were uncoordinated, with conflicting campaigns on Internet banking and the branch, for instance.

In response to customers 'switching-off' all marketing because of poorly coordinated contact, banks adopted 'contact preferences' that allowed customers to specify which channels and at which time they permitted the bank to contact them with marketing contact.

In some instances banks had separate 'direct' marketing teams who managed Internet banking and email campaigns. This led to a disconnected multi-channel contact management and sales process, with the customer frequently required to download application forms and process them through the branch or centralised unit. Initially, little STP existed as branch processes were adopted and not designed for the channel.

Third-generation 'intelligent' thinking recognises that the customer demands three things: relevance, timeliness and personalisation. In a world where the customer is bombarded daily with advertising, most of it irrelevant, your message has to be relevant to get the customer to look at it once, never mind buy the product.

It also has to be timely, that is, you make it at a time that coincides with a customer need. This sounds complex, if not impossible, unless you are able to detect 'events' that connect need to a solution or develop an understanding of your customer's future needs and respond at the appropriate time. We call this 'sense and respond contact management'.

Finally, customers demand a more personalised service. This means not only making the offer in the most relevant or stated preferred channel, but also providing the customer with the right information to meet their needs.

What does it take to achieve third-generation thinking?

It involves building an organisational and delivery model that is fit for the new world.

Real-time multi-channel contact management is a process by which all customer contact, irrespective of proposition, segment, product, channel or media is created using a single engineered process, with the objectives of improving the customer experience; optimising channel capacity and delivering sustainable value.

What is the 'real-time multi-channel' process?

Real-time multi-channel customer management must accelerate the entire end-to-end production, distribution and fulfilment process.

- Production – streamline the process for all marketing activity to eight steps consisting of pre-constructed 'components' that cuts down production time, can be replicated on several campaigns simultaneously and avoids re-work;
- Distribution – streamline how offers are made available across multiple channels at the same time and co-ordinated to make the next best offer to the customer – the one that is most relevant, timely and personalised;

- Fulfilment – once the customer has received and accepted the offer, how it is actively presented in the channel of the customer's choice for follow-up, sale and fulfilment. Fulfilment tracking – customer and bank should track to the point where the product is being used. A visible, streamlined process;
- Requires effective straight through processing to speed up the process, from the customer point of view, reduce customer input, especially of known information and avoid unnecessary processes that do not add value.

Re-engineering the multi-channel contact management process

All existing channel and product marketing must be re-engineered. Principles include:

- Multi-channel contact management requires a dedicated and coordinated team formed from the key functional stakeholders: marketing analysis; segment managers; product managers; marketing managers; finance; advertising control; legal; compliance and channel distribution. Key members of this team are given responsibility and accountability for delivering and managing all contact management. The RACI model that we described in chapter 17 is used to ensure that responsibilities and accountabilities are clearly understood and approval is only sought from persons with actual accountability and responsibility;
- Process tracking technology is used to ensure that the 'components' are in place for assembly, quality assurance and approval at the right time and completed in a timely manner by the right people;
- A series of milestones, approve the 'contact/event/offer', with relevant parties being responsible, accountable, consulted or simply informed. Milestones require approval by responsible and accountable parties only;
- To improve efficiency and end-to-end processing time and costs, all contact and offers must only be processed once;
- The principle of re-usable 'components' will ensure that new or revised 'contact/events/offers' can be assembled quickly and cost-effectively;
- Multi-channel will require single data mining, for all relevant customer attributes, and not mined separately for Internet banking, call centre and branch;
- Wherever possible the 'contact/event/offer' message will be standardised for customer experience consistency. For example, a SMS Text message will be 140 characters long, the same message should be re-used on branch/call centre CRM system, Mobile banking, Internet banking and on ATM if appropriate. The objective is to provide a message that is quickly understood and actioned. Proximity alerts for loyalty.

Chapter 23 – New metrics for a new reality

If you can not measure it, you can not improve it
Physicist Sir William Thompson, Lord Kelvin

EFFECTIVE CHANNEL PERFORMANCE

In this chapter, we summarise how banks might manage their channels more effectively.
For this purpose we will consider the following channels:

- Branch – CSR, teller, overall;
- Branch – Relationship Manager with portfolio;
- Branch – Financial Planning Manager;
- Call centre – CSR;
- Internet banking;
- Mobile banking;
- ATM;
- Social media.

BANK THINKING

First-generation thinking performance reporting focused on back-office efficiency and simple sales metrics, e.g. number of loans sold.

Second-generation thinking saw an increase in channels, all of which had separate metrics and reporting, making a holistic view of what was going on difficult and much of the reporting was inconsistent and contradictory.

Third-generation thinking needs to focus on metrics around the customer, such as customer value, and will look at how the customer interacts with all of your channels, for what purpose and with what outcome. It also requires banks to think about how they optimise their channels to best serve different segments or groups of customers, remembering that not all customers are the same.

"WHAT GETS MEASURED GETS DONE"

It's a fact that, unless you are focusing on the right metrics, you won't manage your channel performance – or the customer experience.

Unfortunately, because many banks manage their channels as separate silos (with sometimes conflicting ambitions – 'cock-up not conspiracy') they find it difficult to understand the full picture. This hides inefficiencies in their processes and propositions.

It's a generalisation, but reporting for the branch (CSR, teller and RM/FPM) will tend to focus on that channel and the information will be biased towards that channel. It won't report where the leads came from, and where they were ultimately fulfilled. Likewise, a call centre report often won't identify where the leads originated from and where they ended up.

It becomes difficult to see which channels are enablers (or barriers) to the customer experience and the sales process. It is impossible to see the pinch points that slow things down.

Sometimes the way you measure can hide real insight. Take employees handling customer sales lead follow-up. Many CRM systems simply allow employees to 'click' to say that the lead was 'actioned' without any further information.

Regardless of the source of the lead, every contact with a customer should result in the bank learning something: that the product is relevant and the sales process continues; that it is relevant, but the timing is wrong, and that the bank can contact again when the customer says so; that it is not relevant because (customer already has product with competitor, product is uncompetitive, customer doesn't want the bank to market to them). Every contact is an opportunity to deepen the relationship by demonstrating that you listened and actioned what your customer told you.

However, if employees simply click 'actioned' the bank loses the opportunity to get it right next time (whether it's not contacting the customer again about the product, even though they meet the propensity model).

Banks fail to learn whether a product meets customers' needs and should be modified or withdrawn. Or whether the product is right, but the marketing channel is wrong (a call from a CSR in a call centre may not be the right channel when following up a personal pension offer, but might be right for a credit card one. A specialist FPM, in a branch or call centre might be the best resource).

In considering how you want to measure your multi-channel performance, you have to start with the customer and not products or channels. Perhaps it should be called 'effective customer performance' as you will look at how the customer interacts with all of your channels, for what purpose and with what outcome.

MULTI-CHANNEL ACTIVITY METRICS

The following is meant as a guide and is not extensive.

The objective is to understand the source and journey of leads and sales.

Volume or time	Branch employee	Branch RM	Branch FPM	ATM/Self-service	Telephone banking	Internet banking	Mobile banking	Direct mail	Email	In-bound mail/email
Transaction – pay-in	✓	✓	✓	✓						
Transaction – withdrawal	✓	✓	✓	✓						
Transaction – transfer	✓	✓	✓	✓						
Transaction – bill pay	✓	✓	✓	✓						
Information update	✓	✓	✓	✓	✓	✓	✓			✓
Needs fact find completed	✓	✓	✓		✓	✓				
Product enquiry inbound	✓	✓	✓		✓	✓	✓			✓
Contact opportunity loaded	✓	✓	✓	✓	✓	✓	✓	✓	✓	✓
Initial contact made	✓	✓	✓	✓	✓	✓	✓			
Follow-up contact made	✓	✓	✓	✓	✓					
Quote provided	✓	✓	✓	✓	✓	✓	✓			
Appointment held	✓	✓	✓		✓	✓	✓			
Sale agreed in principle	✓	✓	✓	✓	✓	✓	✓			
Sale completed	✓	✓	✓	✓	✓	✓	✓			
End-to-end sales in channel	✓	✓	✓	✓	✓	✓	✓			
Multi-channel sales/channel	✓	✓	✓	✓	✓	✓	✓	✓	✓	✓
Contact terminated	✓	✓	✓	✓	✓	✓	✓			

Source: © Intelligence Delivered (Asia) Limited 2011

End-to-end sales in channel charts the number of sales completed in that channel.

Multi-channel sales/channel charts the number of sales commenced in one channel (contact made), followed up (quote provided/appointment held) in the same or another channel and completed (sale completed) in another channel.

Contact terminated charts where and at which stage the contact was terminated. This allows the organisation to understand where the sales process is breaking down.

THE SALES FUNNEL – THE INCONVENIENT TRUTH

Most banks' sales funnels are extremely inefficient, due to factors ranging from a lack of understanding of customer needs and preferences, poor lead generation and qualification, disconnected channels, passive rather than active management of the process and poor employee motivation.

We have observed this many times in practice, and despite what appears to be evident in the metrics available to management, it is often difficult to acknowledge and therefore take the steps necessary to actively manage their sales funnel and a positive customer experience. We call this 'The Inconvenient Truth'.

Figure 19 – The Inconvenient Truth

"The Inconvenient Truth"

7 opportunities
3 appointments
2 proposals (kyc)
1 sale

14%

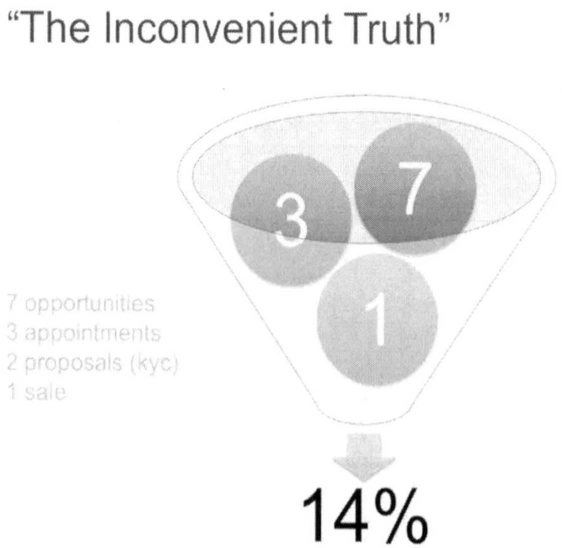

Most banks end up being 'leads rich, sales poor' as a result.

The growth of channels rarely co-incided with a growth in consolidated meaningful management information. It was usual for channels to produce their own management information that often contradicted other channels.

MANAGING THE SALES FUNNEL

Success in sales is made up of four components, all of which drive success or failure:

- Target
- Sales process
- Offer
- Motivation

Too often companies only focus on two of these, the offer and the target. This leaves the frontline to explain away poor sales by saying the offer is not competitive (typically price) or the target group is wrong. In most organisations this 'binary' argument fails to address the main reasons opportunities don't turn into sales.

Target – most banks have more potential leads than they could ever handle, but a sales process that can only handle a certain volume. Poor targeting causes focus on low value leads and customers to the detriment of more valuable customers and leads.

Banks have to make decisions about how they will match opportunities to capabilities. Most banks have six segments of customers, but the resources to effectively manage three or four.

Banks need to establish a customer management strategy, based upon prioritisation, value, potential and capability to deliver. For example, if a bank can't handle Wealth Management service don't stimulate demand, it will only end up disappointing customers who will go elsewhere to satisfy their need.

Sales process – this determines how many leads/customers can be processed to a conclusion.

Different sales processes evolved during second-generation thinking and often the channels failed to co-ordinate, resulting in multiple sales processes that failed to connect when the customer switched channels. This resulted in customer frustration and lost sales.

Even though banks have implemented Internet banking many sales processes are branch-centric, forcing the customer to visit the branch to complete the sale for simple products such as savings, credit cards, personal instalment loans and general insurance. Very often it is simply to complete the documentation. This creates a bottleneck, especially if the branch is meant to focus on higher value wealth management advice and sales. Banks should invest in straight-through-processing (STP) that allows the customer to complete the sales online and reduce paperwork and other purely administrative tasks.

Changing attitudes and expectations of electronic channels as customers learn to buy non-financial products will spill over to banking. Expect pure Internet banking sales to grow as the process gets better (STP) and customers become more comfortable with the process.

The sales process is dynamic. By that we mean there isn't a single one, each customer will approach the research, decision and sale differently, depending upon their need, attitude to technology, experience and a number of other factors. Forcing customers down a rigid process rarely works as many will default to human channels when you don't want them to.

The bank should map out several potential journeys as it follows there's not one – and no customer behaves the way most are currently designed.

The sales processes should be reviewed against actual channel data to ensure that they are designed to reflect customer behaviour (or is this self-defining?). Do customers behave the way that the process was designed? Or are they behaving in a way that is different and you are risking the customer experience?

Offer – in order to achieve the highest levels of satisfaction and sales the offer should be relevant, timely and personalised. Offers should be based upon known customer needs gathered through conversations or triggered by events detected in the bank's data or externally.

Motivation – we have split motivation into two sections: the employee role and incentivisation.

The employee's role

Key to motivation is the employee; how they are managed and recognised; trained; what their future looks like; together with how they are rewarded for doing their job. Some of this final point is covered by incentivisation.

Most people come to work wanting and able to do a good job, but unfortunately, the organisation can inadvertently place barriers in their way.

It may be the way that new technology is being implemented, the technology tools to help them do their job (CRM, Blackberries, laptops etc), or lack of training opportunities to help them to perform better.

It may be unnecessary administrative tasks, that we call 'time bandits', that divert employees from doing their job.

One of the most important factors is an employee's relationship with their boss. If their boss is not doing their job, then most employees will suffer a drain on their motivation.

Recognition is important; it does not always have to be backed by reward, but peer-group recognition for doing a good job re-inforces motivation.

Employees require clear and honest communications, from and with their management, in order to build engagement with the organisation.

Employee sales activity reporting offers significant benefits and challenges. It should provide employees with the information to self-motivate themselves, for example status of pipeline and completed sales figures against targets, peer-group analysis and the ability to plan their short-term activity to improve performance. The information should also be available to supervisors to identify individuals who require coaching and training to help them achieve their potential.

By removing the barriers to an employee doing their job, including the 'time bandits', ineffective technology or processes and poor management techniques will improve motivation to 'do the right thing'. Rewarding them for this is incentivisation.

Incentivisation

It's common for economists to state that 'people respond to incentives', and whilst we believe that this is true we'd offer some cautionary advice when implementing employee incentive schemes. Over the last few years employee incentivisation has come in for a lot of criticism as it has been linked to mis-selling, particularly where a significant proportion of an employee's take-home pay is determined by on-target sales quotas being met and exceeded.

- Many employee incentive schemes focus on the final outcome, rewarding the seller, and ignoring the contribution other channels and employees made to the sale.
- Many schemes focus purely on achieving sales quotas that achieve short-term business and employee objectives, but have a far greater detrimental impact on longer-term customer satisfaction.
- Some employees (and even business units) will quickly 'game' the system to maximise their personal benefit through a number of divisive means, including: not actioning leads originated in another channel, but creating new leads that they action (to maximise personal incentive); 'churning' customers within a period; actioning lower priority easy leads rather than more complex customer-generated leads. As you can see, this activity will normally have a negative impact on the customer as it disrupts the experience/journey.
- The distinction between 'sales' and 'paperwork' is often ignored, with branches, who simply get customers to sign the agreement, being credited with the sale, rather than the channel, such as the call centre, that actually 'sold' the product.

We'd offer these comments:

- Do not incentivise employees purely for sales. Incentivise them for 'demonstrating the right behaviour' that encompasses service, customer satisfaction and compliance. This means putting in place cultural changes as well remuneration changes. Make sure that employees understand how the scheme works, what customer-centric behaviour is expected of them and what will happen if they transgress. As we highlighted earlier, the Which? Banking Manifesto actually calls for sales incentives to be banned and calls for a switch to rewarding employees for providing high-quality service linked to overall levels of customer satisfaction, complaint levels and regulatory compliance (senior executives only).
- Track all interactions across all channels to ensure that the channels are rewarded for their contribution and gaming is deterred. You will also understand how your customers really buy!
- Reward for contribution to the sale, not just the sale. If a CSR in a call centre initiates a lead following a conversation with a customer (that they cannot fulfil for regulatory reasons, e.g. personal pension) that is then sold by a specialist FPM in a branch, reward both parties.
- Reward relative to the amount of skill required to sell the product. In the above example, would you reward the CSR more than the FPM?
- Ensure that 'claw-back' and other mechanisms are in place to deter 'churning' and other gaming tactics. The bank must assess the likelihood of customers churning themselves –

which may indicate that the product was wrong for the customer in the first place.

- Keep a long tail to the reward payment – 60% when the product is 'sold' (see below), 20% year 2, 20% year 3. If the product is closed during that period – no reward (as the bank's income stream on which the reward is based terminates too!).
- An incentive scheme should include elements of the following: 'The right product, sold the right way, keep it sold.'
- Don't reward employees until the product is 'sold'. What does this really mean? When the customer says that they want the product? When they sign the paperwork? When the product is underwritten or approved? We've seen employees rewarded for sales that never happened (sometimes not entirely the employee's fault) – this might account for a 10%-15% overpayment!

We suggest it's sold when 'value is transferred from the customer to the bank' – only then should the employee be rewarded, particularly on 'big ticket' sales:

- The mortgage or loan is drawn down;
- The first premium on insurance or pension is collected;
- Investment account is transacted;
- Savings account is funded;
- The credit card first transaction.

We believe that this strategy also discourages 'sale and go', by ensuring that the salesperson (or channel) services the customer.

DO YOU KNOW WHAT YOUR MOST EXPENSIVE CHANNEL DOES WITH THEIR TIME?

Probably not.

Most banks have established a differentiated proposition for higher value customers, usually having a name that focuses on 'premium' service. Potential premium customers are invited to join the service that is usually free provided the customer maintains some sort of minimum 'total relationship balance' across accounts and products such as investments, insurance and mortgages.

The key service that the banks offer in return is to offer the customer a better service by being managed by a named relationship manager who will meet their needs. Other benefits may include separate telephone 'hotlines', separate counter-service and waiting areas (with refreshments) in branches and other benefits associated with the customers' perceived proposition lifestyle.

Premium relationship managers will typically have a portfolio of between 300 and 500 customers and may be supported by an assistant (or team), who may also support several other premium relationship managers.

So what do they do? Here's a sample description of the role:

"Key Responsibilities
- *Develop our customer business and establish long-term relationships by managing an assigned Premium clientele portfolio*

- *Manage the total wealth of your clients by matching our financial and investment product solutions to their needs."*

In short, an 'advisory and sales' role. So how does this work in practice?

The relationship manager's dilemma

We've found that 60% of a relationship manager's time is spent on non-sales activity: the breakdown is as follows: 40% sales and acquisition; 25% credit and monitoring; 35% service and other. It means that they can't manage the entire portfolio. Our observations from practice indicate that RMs face a dilemma as outlined in the following diagram:

Figure 20 – The RM's dilemma

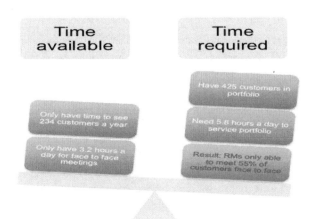

Research backs up our observations:

- Customers say that their RM is very important, but Finalta reported that only 50% of customers in a relationship manager's portfolio claimed to know who they were.
- 30% of customers in a relationship manager's portfolio do not meet the criteria. 20% of a relationship manager's portfolio never visits the branch.
- Most relationship managers rarely service all of their customers – typically they service between 54% and 75% of their portfolio.

What are they doing with their time? They've become 'fixers'. Fixing customers' day-to-day problems to retain their business.

Assuming credit sales are included in the sales and acquisition activity, most of the credit and monitoring activity is spent on processing and monitoring credit – should a RM be spending so much time on paperwork? The 35% 'service and other' is spent on two activities: service – retaining customers by fixing the bank's broken/disconnected processes, and internal meetings.

How can banks re-address the situation and help the RM focus on customers?

- Fix the day-to-day self-service processes across all channels, so that the RM doesn't need to intervene;
- Allow premium customers to complete sales online without having to divert to the RM to complete the sales (to get the reward – incentivise the RM for 'not getting in the customer's way');
- Straight-through-process credit applications, for what should be your best customers, to reduce RM paperwork;
- Get your credit department thinking about customers, not products. Rethink credit management for your most valuable customers – that focuses on the overall customer and not managing single product risk. This means using sophisticated credit assessment techniques, such as behavioural credit scoring, to automate 'pay/no pay' decisions for small short-term overdrafts at non-penalty rates (if they are your best customers there should be some current value to 'give away') and then contacting customers with the good news, not bad and listen to what they say (and act on it too!);
- Eliminate the barriers – this means changing the culture of RMs and their line managers; how they work; how they are rewarded; by integrating channels and making processes easier for the customer to complete themselves.

MULTI-CHANNEL OPTIMISATION

Introduction

Multi-channel optimisation refers to the automated management and presentation of 'sense and respond' relevant, timely and personalised best offers to customers by applying mathematical, segmentation or rules-based techniques.

The same process is applied across all channels to deliver a consistent and joined-up experience for the customer, supporting individual channels to progress an interaction or sale across multiple channels of the customer's choice. The results from previous interactions are used to predict the next best offer or step in the process to be presented to the customer.

It includes not only which offer to present or interaction to follow up, on which channel for each customer, but also how and where the message is placed on channels such as Internet banking.

There are three steps to multi-channel optimisation:

1. **Channel strategy** – details the channels you will offer to different segments of customers. For example, you may only wish to offer relationship managers to higher value customers and this will determine which customers are selected for relationship managers' portfolios, but also how offers are made to these customers. For example, can only RMs respond to customer needs and make offers, or can Internet banking and Telephone banking if the customer is deliberately using those channels? The result of the strategy is also a 'target operating model' that outlines how each channel will operate to service existing customers and new customers and how the channels will join up to provide a superior customer

experience. It also outlines the operating costs, revenue and other benefits from each channel.

2. **Channel integration** – this takes the 'target operating model' and identifies the data required to deliver the desired multi-channel customer experience. This includes not only the data itself, but also how the data will be managed. One crucial point to consider is how to enable integration and therefore optimisation (where value is created) without having to build an 'all singing, all dancing' solution – that may take years. The objective is to enable a degree of integration quickly to deliver optimisation that benefits customers.

3. **Channel optimisation** – this provides the capability to 'sense and respond' to customers and make relevant, timely and personalised offers in real-time across all channels.

Consumers want personal service from their bank but the marketing department has interpreted this as a dedicated relationship manager. However, this is unsustainable for economic and practical reasons. In a multi-channel bank customers want personal service in terms of people and systems knowing you and responding appropriately and this may involve a dedicated 'use case' manager rather than an RM for complex interactions like buying a home.

CUSTOMER VALUE

One of the critical features of the new world is not about who has the most customers or sells the most of a particular product, or has the most customers using the latest in-vogue channel. It is about who understands where sustainable customer value is created. Banks that fail to understand this, will fail.

There are a number of different measures of customer value: historic value; current value; future value and lifetime value.

Historic value is relatively easy to determine. It is the difference between revenue generated and servicing costs in the past.

Similarly, **current value** is the difference between revenue being generated now and current servicing costs, and is often calculated on a twelve-month rolling basis. The current value for each product is calculated monthly and combined into a customer-level score. It does not have to agree totally with the bank's profit and loss account, but its quality must be sufficient to be actionable – it must be possible to use this information as a basis for taking action.

It can be argued that including penalty charges (e.g. excess overdraft fees, returned cheque fees) should be avoided as the bank may find that its highest value customers may also be its most risky, which may not be a sensible business model in the long term. Penalty rate interest should be included as it reflects the cost for using the bank's capital.

Future value requires banks to make an assessment of customers' future revenue and servicing costs and buying behaviour. Future value is often calculated using a medium-term (3 to 5 year) view of the customer value projection. A longer-term view may be taken for customer segments such as students. Future value is only a prediction and the bank must remember that they must actively develop the customer relationship to achieve the future value – it rarely happens on its own.

Future value will usually be similar to or higher than current value. This indicates that the bank needs to decide upon a retention or customer development strategy with that customer.

However, there may be situations where future value is estimated to be significantly lower than current value. This may be because a large loan or mortgage is due to be repaid during the calculation period (stopping a significant proportion of revenue flow). This would be a clear indication to the bank that they need actively to develop the customer relationship to replace the lost income (maybe another loan or investing the spare cash, depending upon the customer's needs).

'Propensity to buy' modelling plays an important part in calculating future value to project what products a customer might buy if the bank successfully develops the relationship, and nominal values can be assigned to these products to calculate an overall future value. Propensity is discussed in more detail in chapter 19.

Lifetime value

The customer's lifetime value is the value of the customer over the whole life of the relationship. Or is it?

Lifetime value – 1

One view is that lifetime value is current value and future value over a period of three to five years. This assumes that historic value is fully amortised and should be ignored. The rationale for this is that the customer should receive a level of service and a customer experience appropriate to the customer's value at the time. All three of these will change over the customer's time with the bank and there is no reason why a higher level of service should be provided because the customer was valuable in the past.

As an analogy, no bank would every attempt to calculate a 'lifetime credit score' for a customer. Most demographic-based or behavioural-based credit scoring models calculate a score based upon the likelihood of a customer defaulting in the next six months.

The argument for disregarding historic value is that it can result in banks making decisions based on the past rather than the future. The resources available to banks to retain and develop their most valuable customers are finite, and they must concentrate these on what they can influence – that is current value (retention) and future value (growth). If they do not do this, the risk is that either they'll fail to retain and grow their best customers or their sustainable income will drain away as their earnings from previously profitable customers decline.

The argument for disregarding long-term projections of customer value is that they are unpredictable and purely academic. Life, as we know, is uncertain. And so is customer value.

Lifetime value – 2

The other view is that lifetime value is the total of historic, current and future value. If this approach is used, the calculation takes a long-term view of future value. This rewards customers for the long-term value that they have created.

The argument for including historic value is that this rewards loyalty. Using historic value as a measure of loyalty reflects the shift from tenure to value that we described in the previous section. Rewarding loyalty, in turn, may benefit the bank through the loyalty ladder.[clxxvi]

The idea of the loyalty ladder is that organizations wishing to take a relationship approach to dealing with their customers should attempt to migrate them through five stages: prospect, customer, client, supporter, advocate.[clxxvii] Advocates, the highest level, are customers who actively help to promote the bank. This fits with third-generation thinking and the rise of the social media as a means of peer-to-peer recommendation.

It is possible that any decline in current or future value may be the result of some form of transfer, for example an inter-generational transfer of resources from parents to children. If the result of this is that the parents receive less favourable treatment, will this encourage them to recommend the bank to their children?

Lifetime value – conclusion

We will avoid taking a dogmatic position on this, not least because we are not in full agreement as to which is the best approach! Whichever approach is adopted, any measure of value created must be capable of practical application. This is usually to allow the bank to provide different customer treatments and types of customer experiences depending on value.

Customer value in practice

We have said that any measure of customer value must be actionable. How can this be achieved in practice?

Intelligence Delivered (Asia) take the view that using customer value in practice is a simple matter of following two rules:

Rule #1 – identify and retain your most valuable customers
Rule #2 – find more like them…

Yes. They contend that it really is that simple.

Let us consider air travel. The customer experience is entirely based on current value.

Everyone gets on the same jet and gets the same basic service. The service is this: the captain to talk soothingly to the passengers before take-off, to take-off and land safely, and not to hit anything bigger than a pigeon on the way. That's it. That's the basic service that everyone gets. But, the people on that aircraft can pay very different prices for this.

Some people pay more to get on first (having had a nice free drink or six in the lounge), sit at the front in nicer seats, get better food and get some nice exclusive toiletries, fluffy socks, soft earplugs and eyeshades. The majority of people choose to pay less and sit at the back in less comfortable seats, use plastic cutlery and hope against all the odds that they'll get upgraded next time. Some people hedge their bets and pay a bit more to sit nearer to the front (usually between the two main emergency exits – that's a hint!), with bigger seats (more legroom and a seat that reclines without concussing the person behind), nicer food (but still with plastic cutlery), the same fluffy socks, earplugs and eyeshades and not-so-exclusive toiletries. However, for the duration of the flight they do exactly the same job.

The airline is exchanging current value (what passengers paid for their tickets) for the customer experience that they get on THAT flight (they are the acknowledged world champions at this sport). Yes, they give passengers all sorts of extra air miles and points towards a higher status (and different coloured bag tag), but these are incentives to keep their customers hooked. The airline is continuously assessing customer value – they are 'Platinum/Gold/Silver', nice precious-metal-sounding names to recognise their status.

And the baggage handlers treat all luggage exactly the same way. It's the basest of metals: 'Iron'.

Banks increasingly use customer value as a strategic tool to differentiate the customer experience and the channels that are offered to the customer. Customers with higher current value may be allocated designated or personal relationship managers or priority call centres. Customers with moderate current value, but with potential higher value may be offered supported self-service channels, for example virtual relationship managers. Low current value customers, however, may be restricted to less personalised channels. All customers receive a banking service in line with their value – but the customer experience is better for some people than for others.

One difference between banks and airlines is that banks are able to project a reasonable estimate of customer future value, and to offer an experience that encourages loyalty and creates continued sustainable value. Banks have significantly more demographic, transactional and behavioural data available than most other retail organizations.

Banks often use a combination of current and future value for marketing campaigns, lead prioritisation or customer service recovery processes. Banks usually display value information on their front-office CRM system screens to help employees make customer service decisions. However, it is in a coded form (such as Gold/Silver/Bronze) that the employee understands and never as the actual amount. This not only makes it easier for employees to understand (imagine trying to decide how much more service £231.56 gets compared to £225.42), but avoids embarrassment if the customer asks for some of it back!

It is not unusual for customers to see their own information on front-office computer screens, so employees should be prepared to offer a straightforward explanation of the information to the customer. Using a categorisation such as Gold/Silver/Bronze can help customers to understand how they might achieve a higher level of service.

The following diagram outlines how a bank might use its customer value model to differentiate the customer's channel experience and develop their relationship with them.

Figure 21 – Using the customer value model

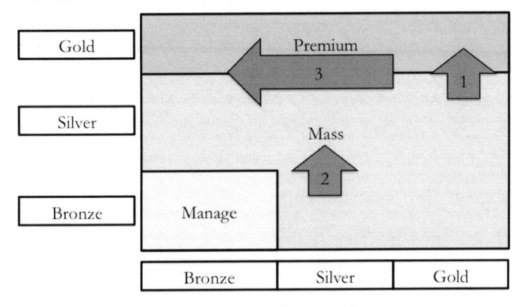

Having determined individual customer current and future value scores, the bank should ensure that the right customers are receiving the best service by offering (or promoting) them to their premium service and channels. This may include a named, dedicated relationship manager at their branch, special fast-track queues in branches, premium call centre numbers (that are answered onshore or by human representatives). The object, and benefit, for the bank is to ensure that these most valuable customers are, first of all, retained, and then that their value is increased by the relationship manager pro-actively helping the customer grow their wealth and realise their future value to the bank. These will typically be the 'Gold/Gold' customers.

Arrow 1 on figure 21 shows what happens to 'Silver/Gold' customers. These are customers who are currently moderately valuable but whose demographic profile and propensity to buy shows that they may potentially be more valuable in the future. These customers may be receiving a service experience that is largely undifferentiated from the mass of lower value customers. Firstly, it is crucial to retain them and, secondly, the bank must embark on a managed strategy to realise their potentially higher value.

One way of achieving this may be by automatically redirecting the customer to a human operator if the customer is calling the call centre via the bank's automated (Interactive Voice Response – IVR) Telephone banking service. The human operator will help the customer resolve their query and then may use the opportunity to offer products and services that are prompted through the bank's Customer Relationship Management (CRM) system.

Arrow 2 shows what happens to customers in the mass market who are 'Silver/Silver'.

What should the bank do with them? First of all – retain them! They are moderately valuable now and will remain so for the foreseeable future (the next 3 to 5 years). So how might the bank approach them? The first thing might be to check to ensure that what is known about them is actually correct. Has the bank correctly identified and linked their products into a single view? Are there many duplicate customers in this segment (it's the mass segment)? Might the bank be in danger of losing the relationship because it can't recognise the customer's value?

The big challenge is what to do with the 'Gold/Silver' or 'Gold/Bronze' customers – arrow 3 on figure 21. Who might they be? Why might their value be falling? How might the bank manage them in the future?

It would be a mistake to ignore the signals. It is important to establish exactly why the future customer value is predicted to fall, which requires further analysis by the bank. Particular attention should be paid to the customer's demographic data and whether the drop in value is due to average balances falling on certain types of products.

One reason why future customer value might be predicted to fall is that customers are running down balances prior to leaving the bank. If this is the case, can the bank retain them? Or is there another explanation?

There are a number of possibilities. Older customers may be retired and living off their assets, including savings and investments. Younger customers, especially couples or females, may have become economically inactive because they've just had a child. This will show up as a fall in their monthly credit turnover over a 3 to 6 month period, as they run down assets such as savings.

Instead of ignoring these customers (and hoping that they will become more valuable somehow) the bank should be proactive and contact the customer to see if it can help – 'be on their side'. Conducting a financial review with the customer will allow the bank to identify new opportunities to continue to develop the relationship – by first retaining the customer. Banks must never forget that these people are currently some of their most valuable customers.

SEGMENTATION

Introduction

Customer segmentation is not a new concept in banking, but few banks have successfully translated the theory into practice. Many segmentation models were developed before computers had access to the vast amounts of data they have available now and were based upon preconceived ideas about society, customer characteristics and their needs.

'Mad men' segmentation

Traditional life-stage segmentation seeks to give banks insight into their customers and to leverage their knowledge to offer the right products to the right customers at the right time. It created a number of categories with typical customer characteristics and potential product needs. Simple demographics, such as age, income, marital status and number of children were assessed to decide which single segment to put the customer in. It often required gathering information from face-to-face interviews and 'Know Your Customer' data collation, and rarely reached 100% of customers, meaning that it was rarely 100% accurate.

A typical example might look like this:

Lifestage	Characteristics	Products
Teenagers/students	Initiate banking relations	Current and savings accounts
Single adults	Enter college, workforce	Credit and debit cards, auto loans
Childless couples	Marriage	Joint account, ISA, investments
Young families	Birth of a child	Mortgage, loans, insurance, education plans
Established families	School age children	Home equity loans, education plan, insurance
Empty nesters	College bound children	Investments, education loans, second mortgages
Mature adults	Retirement	Investments, estate planning, plan distribution

It assumes a linear pattern to life, based around the 'nuclear family', that progresses from one stage to the next in an orderly fashion.

However, we know that life's not like that.

The past 30 to 40 years have seen significant socio-demographic upheaval that has invalidated simple 'nuclear family' based models such as the one above. In 2011, one in five young people aged between 16 and 24 are 'neets' (not in education, employment or training), 20% of UK households are single parent, usually headed by a woman; the number of single adults living alone aged between 35 years and 64 years has risen significantly and a new class of mid-lifer adults is also rising quickly – a 'sandwich generation' who are caring for grown-up single children or 'kidults' (25% of men and 13% of women aged 25 years to 29 years still lived with parents in 2009) and as well as supporting parents who are in their eighties or nineties. In the 1960's the average age of a first time buyer in the UK was 23, now it is 35.

Other socio-demographic changes meant that many customers found themselves going through lifestages twice. For example, as a result of the rising divorce rate it was not unusual for customers to repeat the 'young families' stage, having completed the 'established families' or 'empty nesters' stage. Obviously the customer's characteristics and needs might be radically different, and banks might have difficulty making relevant offers.

Organisations have found it increasingly difficult to translate traditional life-stage models into meaningful and actionable activity. Apart from missing new and statistically relevant lifestages, the model also attempts to force customers into preconceived ideas of how customers will behave and what they need. As a result, many customers will reject offers on the basis that they are simply not relevant to them.

Finally, considerable effort is required to complete a lifestage modelling exercise and banks rarely updated it on a regular basis, meaning that its insight soon became outdated.

Gravitational segmentation

Gravitational segmentation takes a more dynamic approach and effectively allows the customers to segment themselves using a much wider data set than traditional lifestage modelling.

Gravitational segmentation involves allowing analytics to build 'gravitational' data models with no preconceived input from humans (especially marketers!). You define a number of dimensions and let the computer cluster customers. Then you add humans to create the 'customer personas' from the data clusters.

Depending upon your dimensions, the resulting 'customer personas' will allow you to target customers more effectively with relevant, timely and personalised contact.

A customer could be in a traditional lifestage segment for as little as two years (childless couple to young family) or as much as 10 to 15 years (empty nesters to mature adults). But, unless you are able to track lifestage changes your marketing will use old assumptions and fail to be relevant or timely.

Gravitational segmentation personas are based on common customer behaviours, activity and attitudes, irrespective of fixed markers such as age and income (age is used, but it is not a dominant factor as it is in traditional segmentation). How customers use existing products is a pointer to the next potential product but also how other customers without the product represent latent potential demand.

One cluster of customers, we'll call them 'Safe Savers', based upon how they use the bank's simple savings products and who show little or no evidence of investing outside the organisation (through transactional activity). Irrespective of their age, income or status anyone in employment in the UK should be making the most of tax efficient savings products, such as Cash ISAs that also retain the safety and flexibility of simple savings products. Understanding why 'Safe Savers' behave in a particular way may offer insight into their need, particularly if it is saving for a deposit on a home, which is more usual, these days. In the past, buying a house meant liquidating the deposit – and any tax advantages that any Cash ISAs provided. However, banks may be able to lend more, with the Cash ISA as collateral offset against the additional borrowing and allow the customer to continue to maximize their tax allowance. It also helps the bank's deposit ratio as the cash remains as a deposit and is not paid to the seller.

Because it is based upon how customers are behaving or have behaved in the past, gravitational segmentation also offers more insight into potential demand during the next financial year. During the annual planning process, after taking into account predicted economic conditions, analytics will predict demand for each product group for the year ahead and predict the channels where offers should be made (entry) and where they will be sold (exit).

This enables distribution to determine channel capacity for the entry and exit points and for downstream fulfillment. At this point marketing and distribution can identify spare capacity and plan to downsize or stimulate demand using marketing campaigns.

CHANNEL PERFORMANCE

How do banks know whether their distribution strategy is correct? How do they assess whether their investment in channels is earning a satisfactory return? The only way to achieve this is by measuring the performance of their channels.

There are two types of analysis: quantitative and qualitative.

Quantitative analysis measures easily quantifiable factors such as transaction volumes, sales, expenses etc. Performance is usually measured on a quantitative basis.

Qualitative analysis measures factors that cannot easily be reduced to numbers. These often relate to *why* and *how* customers make decisions and take actions.

Measures such as customer satisfaction and factors such as customer behaviour can be reduced to numbers for quantitative analysis. However, it is difficult to interpret the results without further qualitative analysis. Techniques such as focus groups can be used for this.

Internet banking

Collecting quantitative information for Internet banking, like other virtual channels, is straightforward. All of the customer's actions are recorded and can be analysed to determine exactly what the customer did, when, and how long it took.

The Internet also has tools for monitoring access to websites, so banks can record the number of people looking at the website. It can also track the number of people clicking on links.

Qualitative information is more difficult to obtain. It is possible to ask people to take part in surveys, but response rates are not very high.

Branch banking

Collecting quantitative information for branch banking is much more difficult. The branch performs a number of roles and it is not always easy to separate these – completing a transaction at the counter and gathering information, for example.

Counter transactions are recorded, but the speed of the transaction is affected by other factors such as the number of people waiting. Therefore average transaction times might not be very meaningful.

Useful information is recorded on the customer contact history. But most customers will not have any useful information to record, which makes it difficult to account for the time used to try to obtain it.

Customer interviews are easier to measure. The time that the meeting takes and the outcome are recorded (this information is also used in calculating the conversion rate, which is discussed further in the next chapter).

Another source of information is time and motion study or operations research. This uses an observer to record and time branch activities. This allows the bank to develop a set of standard times, that activities should take, and to look for differences between these and the actual times.

Qualitative information is easier to obtain, as customers are more likely to respond to a direct question from a member of staff than an anonymous survey form appearing on an Internet browser. However, techniques such as focus groups must be used to get any depth of information.

Another source of information is the mystery shopper. Mystery shoppers act in the same way as customers and assess how well their transactions are performed.

Telephone banking

Quantitative information for telephone banking systems can be collected through: the telephone banking system (transactions completed), the Automated Call Distributor (ACD – for inbound call centres), and the Powerdialler or predictive dialler (for outbound call centres).

Supervisors can listen in on calls to obtain qualitative information about how well the agent is dealing with the customer. Calls are recorded and computer software can be used to analyse the calls, to identify the use of courtesy words (such as 'please' and 'thank you'). Both of these were discussed in chapter 8.

It is possible to call customers back after the call to obtain qualitative information.

Mobile banking

Mobile banking operates in much the same way as Internet banking and similar quantitative information can be collected. Mobile banking is not a suitable channel for the collection of qualitative information.

COSTING

This is not an accounting text and it will not attempt to go into any detail on costing. However, there are some general principles.

Banks should be able to identify all of the costs associated with a channel. For example, the costs associated with the telephone banking call centre include the cost of the buildings, equipment, communications links and agents, as well as the Head Office costs for the telephone banking service.

Banks can use this information to calculate their transaction costs by channel. 'Kita Bank', a pseudonym for a large North American bank, developed a methodology for calculating the profitability and contribution of each of its channels and outlets.[clxxviii]

This involved building a database of transactions by outlet, and combining this with income and cost data. Their analysis took account of 'soft' benefits, such as the contribution to brand equity and customer satisfaction, as well as the 'hard' cash factors.

Producing an analysis at this level allowed the bank to fine tune its distribution strategy, for example by adding or removing functions from individual outlets.

The magnitude of the analysis should be emphasised. Transfer pricing often has an element of subjectivity and the bank made a number of judgement calls, for example allocating the spread between loans and deposits to the account-holding branch, that could be challenged. However, it resulted in measurable efficiency improvements and at the end of the study the bank had improved its position relative to its competitors.

NETWORK EFFECTS

The value of a channel may be greater than the revenue it produces. This is because of what are sometimes called network effects or complementary assets.

We have already discussed the idea that customers have a preference for certain channels, and that some customers (who we have called traditional customers or b customers) have a preference for the branch.

These customers will only choose a bank that has branches. Therefore the value of the branch to the bank is not only the revenue that it generates but also the additional customer recruitment for which it is responsible.

Branches produce other network effects. What is the value of information collected at the branch, for example? The branch plays host to self-service and virtual channels – what is the value of this role?

These effects are very difficult to quantify and attempts to quantify them carry the risk of double counting. However, it is important for managers to appreciate that these effects do exist and that channels and outlets should not be assessed purely on a cost vs. revenue basis.

BENCHMARKING

How do you know whether you are really out-performing your competitors or whether you are just benefiting from benign market conditions?

Benchmarking is the process of comparing your business performance metrics to those of your industry (you and your competitors) to identify opportunities to improve your performance. It is increasingly used as a strategic tool to help banks understand their market position, their customers and how they use their channels and core products.

How often have you heard people say, "all banks are the same"? Well, in many respects they are; most retail banks operate in a broadly similar way and provide services to customers through similar channels.

As a result, banks' executive management continually strive to differentiate themselves from their competitors and to gain a financial advantage. To do this they have traditionally used customer research to understand customer activity and behaviour and to find answers to questions posed by their CEO such as:

- "Who is best at attracting premium customers and on what channel?"

- "How effective are my sales and service teams?"
- "Who is eating my lunch?" (A common term used by the CEO to ask who's taking your business!)

To do this they use quantitative and qualitative techniques to gather data from their own customer base and from some of their competitors' customers. Techniques used to gather the data include mailing questionnaires, on-line or telephone surveys and face-to-face focus groups. To provide bank and customer anonymity in the process and to avoid any possible distortion of results banks use specialist market research agencies to conduct the research.

But these traditional techniques are increasingly flawed:

- Most customers don't respond – most surveys have response rates between 15 and 25 per cent and do not guarantee that the views expressed are representative of the 80 per cent who did not respond;
- 'Intent' not 'action' – the customer does not always do what they say they will do. It is human nature and can distort results;
- Lost in translation – sample sizes and weightings (to ensure like-for-like analysis) can distort results as there is no way to survey the entire market.

Financial services is a dynamic marketplace that has seen an increase in new entrants and channels in the last few years, with CEOs now judged on their performance quarterly, if not monthly. Unfortunately, these techniques take many months to set up, mail questionnaires, gather and analyse the data to produce the information needed to run the business. Frequently, the information is out of date before it's delivered and only confirms what happened. It has been said that it is like trying to steer a supertanker – using the rear-view mirror only, whilst wearing blinkers!

There are other reasons that these methods don't deliver the intelligence that a bank's executive management needs:

- Surveying the entire market on a regular basis is impractical and beyond the financial means (and capabilities) of most banks;
- Customers who respond to surveys often do so for reasons that distort results and can cause banks to misinterpret customer attitude or behaviour;
- Attempts to incentivise response rates usually lead to misleading results as many people only do so to get the monetary incentive and are not too bothered about the results. Also, this is an extremely expensive way of getting a response;
- Like direct mail, customer fatigue is causing responses to survey questionnaires to fall steadily. Customers, quite rightly, have also become more cynical about being asked their views when they usually see no change (improvement) or benefit for them;
- Concerns about Internet security and receipt of 'junk mail' or 'spam' can reduce the effectiveness of online or email-based surveys;
- The cost of regular comprehensive surveys can be prohibitive, especially if they are

conducted by mailed questionnaires or face-to-face groups;

- Finally, the bank is forced into a series of compromises: how many people to survey? What segments and/or channels? And at what frequency to survey their customers without alienating them? These compromises can render the data meaningless rather than delivering any form of intelligence.

Benchmarking solution

Benchmarking offers a practical solution to many of the challenges.

It uses the most reliable data there is – the bank's!

A financial services benchmark is where a major proportion of the industry agrees to provide desensitised statistical data to an independent third-party to collate, analyse and distribute the benchmark results amongst the member banks.

It is important to recognise that banks will not give each other strategically important data and that a trusted and experienced third-party benchmarking company is used to collate, normalise, analyse and distribute the benchmark results.

Most markets around the world have more than twenty banks operating (some have as many as five hundred or more local credit unions!) and it would appear potentially daunting to try and gain acceptance of a benchmark in those circumstances. However, four or five banks typically dominate 80 per cent of the market share and this means that an initial benchmark can be established without recruiting everyone. The question is: is 80 per cent sufficient to understand the market?

As the intelligence delivered by the benchmark is only available to subscribing banks it soon becomes apparent to non-members that it is crucial to their market position or survival to join. In some ways, they can gain more than their larger competitors, as they often don't have the same level of resources to devote to performance management, yet gain all of the advantages from the benchmark.

The economics of benchmarking are also favourable; the annual cost of a quarterly benchmark is estimated to cost less than two product or channel customer research questionnaires.

By gathering internal data from banks a comprehensive picture of the market can be built quickly and accurately. Most of the data is readily available and is used on a day-to-day basis by banks and so is usually reliable. However, there can be differences in definitions.

One of the key tasks of the benchmarking company is to 'normalise' the data from their clients. Many banks have different definitions for the same data element – we have seen several definitions of a 'sale'. Is it when the customer says they want the product? When the new product is opened? When, in the case of credit or insurance, it is approved or underwritten? Or is it when the product is activated by the customer (e.g. drawn down, funded or transacted)? There is often a 10 to 15 per cent gap between the product being 'sold' and the product being activated. The clue is it is 'sold' when value is transferred from the customer to the bank.

The benchmark is based on reality – it is a true picture of market share of new customers and segments; customer channel penetration and usage; sales channel effectiveness and other key metrics such as retention.

Because the data is readily available it can be collated, analysed and the intelligence acted upon within a shorter time than traditional methods. Many benchmarks are six-monthly or quarterly, but where the metrics are very dynamic a few can be monthly.

The frequency of the benchmark is determined to allow banks to be able to assimilate the data, formulate and implement performance improvement initiatives and record the results internally ahead of the next quarter's benchmark.

Benchmarking copes with complexity of multi-channel interactions as the underlying data can track the various channels where a sale was started, handled and completed. This helps banks determine which parts of their sales process are adding value and which parts are destroying the customer experience when compared to leading practice.

Each bank receives a confidential personalised report highlighting their position, performance and a SWOT analysis. Only subscriber banks see the data, and even then they only see their position or ranking – all other competitors are anonymous.

The benchmark data cannot be distributed to or bought by non-subscribers, and banks will normally restrict internal distribution given the potential sensitivity of their position in the marketplace.

To interpret the results the benchmarking company will provide one-to-one review sessions with executive management to help them understand the results and advise on leading practice.

By gaining a deep understanding of the market the benchmarking company is able to provide relevant, timely and accurate advice and help their clients improve and monitor their performance. Of course, the benchmarking company will not divulge any information regarding its clients to competitors.

There are usually restrictions on how individual banks may use the collective data for Public Relations (PR) or marketing purposes. Any data used is usually highly desensitised to avoid any banks being identified. Benchmark banks will rarely be divulged.

Benchmark data

Typically benchmarking data will include the following types of data:

- Numbers of active customers in defined segments;
- Number of products held per customer;
- Transactions by type by channel;
- Numbers of service and sales employees.

The number of data points will depend on the scope of the benchmark and the detailed data points will usually be protected by a non-disclosure agreement between the benchmark company and the subscriber banks.

Benchmark metrics

The following are common benchmark metrics:

- Actual market share of key segments e.g. affluent customers;
- Percentage of customers registered to use and actually using particular channels during the period;
- Sales and referrals per adviser registered during period;
- Percentage of sales started in a channel that are completed by that channel.

The specific metrics will depend on the scope of the benchmark and their proprietary nature will usually be protected by a non-disclosure agreement between the benchmark company and the subscriber banks.

Benchmark report

Although significant amounts of data is gathered, processed and analysed, benchmark reports are designed to deliver the intelligence that the reader needs to understand their market position and take action as required.

Because the benchmark is conducted on a regular basis, quarterly for example, trending can be used to help the reader understand the impact of performance initiatives, such as introducing a new proposition or channel.

Whilst performance metrics are agreed between all subscribers in advance, a client can ask for additional analysis of the data if a particular metric causes concern – sometimes called a 'deep dive'. Of course, the information will be provided in an anonymous format with only the client's own data identified.

Benchmarking is flexible and is not 'all or nothing'. For instance, if you have not launched a mobile banking proposition or cannot provide it at this moment in time you will not be able to provide any data and so will not see the results of others (this prevents banks deliberately withholding specific data to see the market position). You will, of course, see all of the results for the data you do provide.

The benchmarking process

The benchmarking company will develop a proposal with the leading banks in the market and define a common set of agreed objectives and rules (these include scope and frequency of reporting), usually in the form of a formal document and contract.

The banks and benchmarking company then work together to define and agree all aspects of the data, common definitions and the metrics to be measured and reported.

Once data definitions are agreed the benchmarking company will audit members to ensure that the data is available and of the agreed quality.

Benchmarking has another significant advantage over market research. As one of the objectives is to produce trended information, historic data (say, for the previous four quarters) can be extracted from the banks' business intelligence systems to populate the benchmark database and make the current quarter's data more relevant and productive.

Test data will be supplied to prove the collation and production process and to finally verify data quality. Once the processes and data have been proven the benchmark report will be produced and distributed.

The benefits of benchmarking

Benchmarking has been likened to 'performance information for the real-world', in the sense that that's where the data comes from.

Because benchmarking data is comprehensive, reliable, relevant and timely it is now used by many bank executive committees to measure and monitor their performance in today's dynamic marketplace.

In a world where people say they are increasingly short of time, benchmarking delivers the intelligence banks need without interrupting or disturbing their customer in any way.

When banks start benchmarking they often receive a severe 'reality check' that overturns established or pre-conceived beliefs about their business, performance and future prospects.

- They may discover that their profile of affluent customers is out of line with the market and instead of being an 'affluent bank', they are catering for the 'mass market'.
- Or, as new low cost channels are deployed, they may discover that their customers are migrating at a slower pace than their competitors, and as a result they will not reduce their transaction costs as a result – only incur more channel costs.

The following are examples of where benchmarking has provided insight that would not have been evident from traditional methods:

- One bank accelerated the implementation of its mobile banking proposition as it saw competitors gaining acceptance (penetration and usage) from customers. The mobile banking team were able to use relevant, accurate industry data to prove to their executive management that this new channel was being rapidly adopted, that they were currently at a competitive disadvantage and that significant cost savings could be achieved;
- Another bank reviewed and changed its sales adviser recruitment criteria, training program and incentive scheme after it discovered that they were below the sales adviser effectiveness industry average;
- A leading bank implemented a new on-boarding process (the process for developing its relationship with new customers during the first '90 day honeymoon' period) after it discovered that at the end of this period it was failing to achieve the cross-sales ratios compared to competitors that had a defined, measured and monitored process.

It is not a case of 'either/or' where traditional research and benchmarking are concerned.

Whilst benchmarking can be very effective at understanding the entire marketplace dynamics, your competitors, and your customers' actions, it cannot determine a customer's attitude towards your brand, propositions and channels.

Some banks are now using benchmarking and traditional customer research in tandem. Benchmarking provides a rapid, but broad, view of the market and performance and traditional research is used to explore in more detail key issues that benchmarking uncovers. This offers a cost-effective use of resources for many banks and opens them up to leading practices in their own market or in similar markets overseas. For example, European bankers may be interested in understanding how Asian bankers deliver services to affluent customers.

Chapter 24 – The new reality

PATTERNS FROM HISTORY

History has demonstrated that a technology, product or channel's S-curve isn't infinite. They decay and are prone to being replaced by new products and technology or new channels. For example, Internet banking has supplanted the branch for most day-to-day transactions.

In an article: 'Predictions for Civilian Space Flight Based on Patterns from History, Journal of the British Interplanetary Society November/December 2010'[clxix] Marc G. Mills outlined how any successful technology S-curve is surpassed by a subsequent different technology in what he called 'cycles of innovation and obsolescence'.

The pattern reflects what is happening in banking: new entrants are making modest investments in new technology, such as contactless payments, and individually are making minor advancements, that will collectively lead to a breakthrough when the technology is proved viable. This is the stage where we are at present with multiple and competing options searching for the best and most accepted technology solution. Once this point is reached the dominant technology is mature and will become widely established. However, it will reach a 'point of diminishing returns' where it will be replaced by a new alternative, with its own S-curve – such as mobile contactless payments.

Figure 22 – Technology cycles of innovation and obsolescence

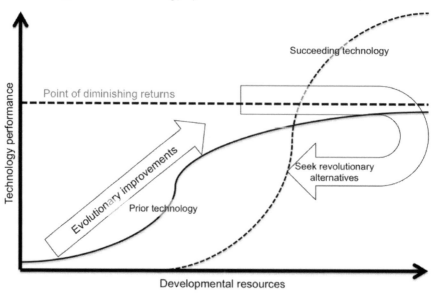

Source: Adapted from: Predictions for Civilian Space Flight Based on Patterns from History, Marc G. Mills, Journal of the British Interplanetary Society November/December 2010.

As Mills states: "History has shown that simply improving existing technology is not sufficient to sustain competitive advantage. For example, jet aircraft did not result from mastering piston-propelled aircraft. Transistors were not invented by mastering vacuum tubes. Photocopiers did not result from mastering carbon paper. The recurring theme is that entirely different operating principles were pursued to surpass the limits of prior technology and thus sustain competitive advantage. The recurring lesson is that it is time to look for revolutionary approaches when the existing methods are approaching the point of diminishing returns."

Mills also stated that there were four stages to the process.

1. **Resistance to change** – incumbent organisations find it difficult to consider alternatives when their familiar approaches are at the point of diminishing returns.

2. **Change agents** – considering that mature incumbent organisations can lose sight of what is happening in the market, revolutionary advances often come from outside the establishment. A classic example is how the Wright Brothers (who were bicycle mechanics) succeeded in heavier-than-air manned flight well in advance of the government-funded establishment of the Smithsonian Institute.

3. **Pride before the fall** – this is where incumbents finally notice that things are changing, but fail to adapt. Instead they try to recapture their prior position by repeating what was successful before, without success. Their competitors are launching genuinely new products based upon contemporary opportunities. It is only then that they realise that things have changed.

4. **After the inevitable** – this is where transition occurs. With new entrants vying for market dominance the incumbent is faced with two options: reinvent themselves by abandoning their old priorities in favour of new ones consistent with the changes that occurred around them. This may be branching out into new markets or using new technology. There are some advantages in having an established infrastructure, such as distribution chains, but what they do must actually be new – tailored for contemporary needs and better than the competition, not just a re-hash. Alternatively, the incumbent attempts to sustain their current customer base and proposition, but reducing their activities to fit within their reduced market share and finding a niche position.

As history has a habit of repeating itself, the new dominant organisations will someday mature and face new changes and they too will have difficulty in recognising and adapting to the next wave of change.

So what does this have to do with multi-channel banking?

One could argue that there have been few disruptive new entrants in the past 30 years; however, there are some pointers that this may change soon:

- Mobile banking will disrupt the traditional IVR-fronted call centre. Call centres reached their point of diminishing return in 2012, when Mobile banking starts to reach a critical mass (10% and rising) and will replace the day-to-day transactions (balance or transaction enquiry, inter-account transfers and bill payment).

- Mobile banking will also disrupt the ATM and branch's traditional day-to-day transaction and service role (balance or transaction enquiry, inter-account transfers and bill payment).
- It will also disrupt the ATM/self-service role by enabling P2P payments to reduce the number of 'birthday' cheques, splitting lunch payments and other incidental irregular payments.
- Although many banks have transitioned to electronic account statements, it's still not what many consumers want: they want to manage their money better, and Mobile banking with a PFM app does just that; add Mobile payments transactions and you've got a better picture of what you spend than you ever had with your bank.
- Mobile Payments, available with or without Mobile banking, may disrupt ATMs' cash dispensing and deposit role by reducing the frequency of visits to an ATM to stock up on cash and pay surplus cash into a bank account. The tipping point will be the highly anticipated NFC-enabled iPhone 5 and new NFC android powered smartphone that integrate NFC technology and an e-wallet – for example Google Wallet. Preceding that NFC-enabled credit cards will start the process, NFC-enabled mobile wallets will finish it off.
- Mobile banking will also disrupt Internet banking, as consumers will probably use Mobile banking on an iPad rather than log into Internet banking whilst watching TV or having a coffee at Starbucks. Actually, it is the iPad that disrupts the PC, but it follows that consumers will select the best application for the device and well-designed Mobile banking apps are designed for touch-screen casual use.

Implications for banks

We believe that the full impact of disruptive Mobile banking and payments technology will start to impact from 2012 when they start to gain pre-critical mass. Banks should re-evaluate their call centre strategy to consider how they may transition from a 'transaction' centre to an 'interaction' centre to support Internet banking and Mobile banking. How will the call centre manage customers who are not driving change?

Mobile payments will start to move the UK to a 'less cash' society ('cash less' is someway off) and we anticipate that ATM cash and non-cash transactions will drop because Mobile banking and payments will replace the need to go somewhere physical to get pocket cash. Debit cards and credit cards, but particularly debit cards will replace higher value cash transactions, and Mobile banking P2P transactions will replace them.

Banks need to get on the bandwagon. As not only will they be viewed negatively by customers, but new entrants will take some of their payments income.

New entrants, such as Simple and MovenBank are building their business model around Mobile banking and Mobile payments as the smartphone are, literally, capable of doing everything that a branch and ATM could do 30 years ago. And that includes sales!

CAPITAL IS NOT FREE AND IS SCARCE

During the continued financial crisis capital in most banks is in short supply and many banks are battling for their very survival. Their strategy has been to implement drastic cuts to their investment budgets and range from undifferentiated 30 per cent reductions throughout all activities to complete investment stoppages.

However, there is another dilemma for banks wishing to transform their businesses to meet changing customer demands and behaviours. In a crisis, fresh capital is usually invested in those areas where it was found in the past; the bottom-up process of capital allocation will direct capital into the hands of the mature units.

The restriction on capital will force some changes in strategy: banks will have to decide whether it is better to risk being a 'laggard' and lose customers or be a 'pioneer' and risk capital at a time when it is in short supply. Few banks will be able to pursue more than one major strategy.

BANKS HAVE NO RIGHT TO SURVIVE

Banks have enjoyed a privileged position in society that is now under threat from a number of different sources. Their standing has been impacted by the financial crisis when many received support from their central banker or government. Taxpayers have borne the brunt of the support and many are looking for a change in the way banks work and serve the people who fund them (customers/taxpayers). Some banks have been criticised for their bonus policies in the midst of government bailouts and the financial crisis. Add the mis-selling scandals (Lehman Bros Mini bonds, PPI) and it's clear to see how public opinion has turned against many banks.

In this environment it is difficult to be a traditional bank. Your revenue sources are under attack from a variety of new nimble competitors, who don't want to be a bank, but want a slice of your revenue by providing banking. Scarce capital makes it difficult for many banks to radically transform their business model (legacy systems, networks etc.) to compete with the new competitors, who are exploiting new banking S-curves.

New entrants will position themselves as alternatives to traditional banks and will gain media and consumer support if their business model and practices are seen to be more consumer focused. They will avoid the regulatory problems (and costs) that banks got themselves into by positioning themselves as intermediaries backed by FSA or FDIC regulated product providers. And to be honest, when starting with a clean sheet and new accessible technology, it will not be difficult.

Many new competitors are creating business models that avoid undue regulation allowing them to 'provide banking, without being a bank'. They focus on areas of consumer dissatisfaction and exploit banks' inability to react quickly. In some cases, their reason for entering the market and capturing market share will be to be bought out by an established player.

MOST BANKS WILL BE OVERWHELMED BY CHANNEL PROLIFERATION AND COSTS

The first- and second-generation rationale for banks creating new channels was cost drive and was to move lower value customers and transactions into lower cost channels and to automate back-office processes.

However, as we have discussed, this was not always entirely successful. The bank almost always drove the rationale for new channels and the customer wasn't always a willing participant. As a result, the customer resisted or exploited the change and it often had the reverse effect – the higher value customers that the bank wanted to use the branch abandoned it for more convenient and effective internet banking; lower value customers still used the branch in preference to other channels. In some cases there was an exponential increase in traffic across all channels and little opportunity to discontinue channels.

As a result banks face a growing problem of maintaining capacity on all channels at an optimal level and there is little evidence that banks will be allowed (by government or consumers) to significantly reduce the size of their largest channel, the branch network, to compensate for growth in other channels.

Capital scarcity means that large-scale branch network transformations (from transaction to interaction-based branches) will be slowed, whilst costs continue to climb.

Maintaining capacity in multiple channels isn't sustainable, and some banks will be overwhelmed by the costs of maintaining unused capacity.

REGULATION AND CONSUMERISM IS HERE TO STAY

As a result of the financial crisis and mis-selling scandals (Lehman Bros Mini bonds, PPI) regulators are increasing oversight and implementing new procedures that make it less attractive for banks to continue to offer the wide range of investment and insurance propositions that they once did.

The implications are: that banks' business model and revenue streams will be disrupted by new regulatory regimes at a time when revenues are recovering, but costs are rising. Scarce capital will be directed to regulatory projects in priority. You need to keep your banking licence to operate; some banks may completely review their multi-proposition offerings to focus on different segments, providing a full service to some, limited to others.

Consumers' attitudes have changed; during the financial crisis many customers lost faith in banks and became more self-directed decision makers using new technology such as the Internet to access price comparison sites (price comparison and peer-to-peer recommendation) and social media (peer-to-peer recommendation and pressure groups) to support their decision making.

The implications here are less serious than the regulatory changes. In the face of rising consumerism banks need to shift their focus to be customer-driven, rather than simply profit-driven. This is third-generation thinking.

The end of the 'permissive era'

Banks are facing yet another game changing event. The 'permissive era' of marketing is ending and banks will have to change their behaviour. Consumers are in control once more.

With customers' data freely available, organisations perceiving that it belonged to them (and rarely asking customers' permission to use it) and rules that meant it was the customer's responsibility to opt-out, the 'permissive era' of marketing grew rapidly during the past few decades. The corresponding growth of the Internet fuelled massive amounts of new data on customers (particularly click stream data collected and tracked), often without them understanding what was being collected, how it was being used and how they could gain control of it.

Regulation such as the Data Protection Acts (1984 and 1998) Privacy and Electronic Communications Regulations (PECR) (2003 and 2011) and the Electoral Roll opt-out (2003 and 2011) has gradually caught up with the 'permissive era'. It is anticipated that the proposed European Data Protection Directive (due for publication in 2012) will strengthen individuals' rights so that the collection and use of personal data is limited to the minimum necessary, there is greater transparency concerning how, why, by whom and how long their data is collected and used. In effect, consumers will be required to 'opt-in' to businesses using their data, for example for marketing and have the 'right to be forgotten' when the data is no longer needed.

This may change forever the balance of power and will require banks to prove to customers and regulators that using their customers' personal data is of value to the customer. They can only do this by becoming more relevant, timely and personalised to customers and demonstrating to regulators that that they are doing the right thing.

We're now entering the era of 'permitted marketing'.

BANKS WILL BE DISINTERMEDIATED

For the reasons discussed at the start of this chapter the market will change due to new technology and entrants. If banks don't remain relevant to their customers, they will lose them. Combined with falling barriers to entry and innovative business models new competitors will disintermediate banks from their core business such as current accounts, payments, lending and investments by providing customers with a superior customer experience.

CUSTOMERS DESIRE A NEW COVENANT

We have discussed some of this above. Customers are in control and know it. They are demanding that banks do business on their terms and have the power to make it happen. Switching suppliers will become easier, the Internet provides the comparison tools to select a new provider and government is implementing new regulations to make it easier and quicker for consumers to switch current accounts (the product least easy to switch).

The post-crisis customer wants a bank that they can trust; is transparent in all of its dealings with them; that provides value for money and provides convenient easy-to-use access to their money and to expertise when they need it.

SENSE AND RESPOND IS THE ONLY WAY

Customers have moved from the industrial age of 'make and sell' to the information age of 'sense and respond'. Banks that do not make the move are doomed. Banks that 'make and sell' to customers who want a 'sense and respond' relationship are doomed to failure and disintermediation by new competitors who get what customers want.

As we embrace third-generation thinking for survival we have to realise we that have to earn our relevance!

"Banking is necessary, banks are not." – Dick Kovacevic, Wells Fargo CEO

Index

M

M25 effect, 3, 117
Make and sell, 141, 146-151, 239
Marketing, 1, 12-13, 17, 19-20, 54-56, 61-63, 65, 68-69, 90-92, 97, 114, 125, 127, 134-136, 140-144, 146-147, 149-153, 170, 173, 178, 180, 187-193, 198-208, 217, 220, 224-225, 230, 238-239
Marks and Spencer, 98, 101
Martini banking, 15, 31, 47
MasterCard, 31, 95, 113, 183-185
Metrics, 173-174, 207, 209-210, 227, 230-231
Mobile banking, 24, 32, 44, 82-84, 86-87, 89, 109-110, 114, 126-127, 130, 139, 141, 144, 155-156, 158-159, 165, 168-169, 172, 175-176, 178, 181-182, 190, 193, 206-207, 226
Mobile customers, 27, 82, 85
Mobile payments, 110, 155, 158-159, 175, 178, 181-183, 185, 190, 236, 253
Mobile wallet, 110, 169, 185-186, 236
Morrison's, 98-101
MovenBank, 110, 181, 236
M-Pesa, 88
Multi-channel, 13-15, 23-24, 39, 43, 49-51, 111, 119, 122, 125, 127-128, 136-138, 144, 149-156, 166, 180, 187-192, 196, 203, 205-10, 216-217, 230, 235
Multi-channel strategy, 24, 127, 144, 155, 187-189, 192

N

NatWest, 55-57, 98-99, 113
Near Field Communications (NFC), 169, 184-186, 236
Network effects, 227
NFC. See Near Field Communications (NFC),

O

Obopay, 88
Octopus, 87

Offshoring, 41, 137
Orange, 185
Outsourcing, 98, 137

P

P2P. See Social Lending,
PayPal, 6, 87-88, 129, 185
Personal financial management (PFM), 66, 109-110, 175, 236
Personalisation, 23, 130, 151, 204-205
PFM. See Personal financial management (PFM),
Price comparison services, 106-108, 134
Project Verde, 10

R

Relationship manager, 131, 144, 158, 164-166, 170-173, 196, 207, 214-216, 220-221
Relevance, 54, 62, 201-202
Return on investment, 54, 62, 201-202
Royal Bank of Scotland, 68, 98, 100

S

Sainsbury's, 98-102
Sales funnel, 202-203, 210-211
S-curve, 12, 116, 120, 161, 234, 237
Second-generation thinking, 4,7-8, 57, 127, 142-3, 156, 174, 179, 188, 191-196, 207, 211
Security First Network Bank (SFNB), 5, 14, 113
Self-directed, 21-23, 134, 141-143, 147, 164-165, 170-171, 238
Sense and respond, 141, 144, 147-152, 205, 216-217, 239
Short Message Service (SMS), 77, 83-87, 90, 150, 156, 174-177, 193, 203, 206
Social lending, 106-109
Social media, 127, 130, 134-138, 141, 155-157, 166-167, 178-181, 207, 219, 238
Standard Chartered, 166

Supermarket banking, 66, 98-105

T

Technology Acceptance Model, 29
Telcos, 83, 88, 106-107, 139
Telemarketing, 74
Telephone banking, 74-89, 110-112, 123-
127, 130-131, 141, 151, 158-159, 172-178,
209, 216, 221, 226
Teller, 1, 34, 64-65, 93-95, 112, 123, 158-160,
166
Tesco, 98-105
The new reality, 158, 234
Third-generation thinking, 178-179, 187-
191, 195-196, 205-207, 219, 238, 240
Twitter, 54-62

V

Validator, 21, 143, 164-165
Virtual worlds, 55
Visa, 183-185

W

Walmart, 104
Web 2.0, 6, 12-13, 54, 156
Web chat, 15, 48-49, 74, 77, 130

Y

Yodlee, 109-110, 175
YouTube, 54-62, 89, 150, 166, 178, 180, 203

References and works cited

[i] Batiz-Lazo, B., 2009 Emergence and evolution of ATM networks in the UK, 1967-2000. Business History, 51(2): p1-27 is a useful source

[ii] Salmen, S.M. and Muir, A., 2003. Electronic customer care: The innovative path to e-loyalty. Journal of Financial Services Marketing, Dec 2003, Vol. 8 Issue 2, p133-14

[iii] For example: Internet Banking: Emigrant migrates across the nation. Bank Technology News, Vol. 18, Issue 3

[iv] Costanzo, L.A., Keasey, K. and Short, H., 2003. A strategic approach to the study of innovation in the financial services industry: The case of telephone banking. Journal of Marketing Management, Apr 2003, Vol. 19 Issue 3/4, p259-281

[v] Blake, R. and Mouton, J., 1970. Change by design not by default, SAM Advanced Management Journal (00360805), 35, 2, p29

[vi] ABA Banking Journal, 2001. What we have here is channel evolution. ABA Banking Journal, Sep 2001 Supplement, Vol. 93, p14

[vii] Kaplan, A.M. and Haenlein, M., 2010. Users of the world, unite! The challenges and opportunities of Social Media. Business Horizons, 53 (1): p59–68

[viii] Hammer, M.M., 1990. Re-engineering work: Don't automate, obliterate. Harvard Business Review, July/August, p104–112

[ix] Hammer, M.M. and Champy, J.A., 1993. Reengineering the Corporation: A manifesto for Business Revolution, Harper Business Books, New York, 1993

[x] Fawcett, P. and Flower, G., 2000. Managing information in financial services. Canterbury: Financial World Publishing

[xi] Fawcett, P. and Flower, G., 2005. Customer Information Management. Canterbury: Institute of Financial Services p198

[xii] Fawcett, P. and Flower, G., 2005. Customer Information Management. Canterbury: Institute of Financial Services p198

[xiii] Porter, M.E., 1979. How Competitive Forces Shape Strategy. Harvard Business Review, March/April 1979

[xiv] Independent Commission on Banking, 12 September 2011

[xv] Independent Commission on Banking, 12 September 2011

[xvi] Miles, R.E. and Snow, C.C., 1986. Organizations: New concepts for new forms. California Management Review, Spring 86, Vol. 28 Issue 3, p62-73

[xvii] Lieberman, M.B. and Montgomery, D.B., 1988. First-mover advantages. Strategic Management Journal, 9, p41-42.

[xviii] Peppers, D., Rogers, M. and Dorf, R., 1999. The one to one fieldbook: the complete toolkit for implementing a 1to1 marketing program. New York, NY: Doubleday

xix   Original source http://www.share.uni-koeln.de/ quoted in http://www.teachus.eu/basics/?Doing_wp_cron last accessed 28 May 2012

xx   Research by Wells Fargo and Bank of America, cited in Sciglimpaglia, D. and Ely, D., 2006. Customer account relationships and e-retail banking usage. Journal of Financial Services Marketing, May 2006, Vol. 10 Issue 4, p109-122

xxi   Last accessed 18th May 2011

xxii   Shostack, C.L., 1977. Breaking Free from Product Marketing. Journal of Marketing, 41 (2), p73-80 and Lovelock, C.J., 1981. Why Marketing Needs to be Different in Services. In Marketing of Services, Donnelly J.H. and George W.R., eds., Chicago: American Marketing Association, p5-9.

xxiii   Zeitgeist, Wikipedia definition http://en.wikipedia.org/wiki/Zeitgeist last accessed 28 May 2012

xxiv   Strauss Howe Generational Theory, Wikipedia http://en.wikipedia.org/wiki/Strauss-Howe_generational_theory last accessed 28 May 2012

xxv   Prensky, M., Digital Natives, Digital Immigrants. From On the Horizon, MCB University Press, Vol. 9, No 5, October 2001.

xxvi   http://work.lifegoesstrong.com/article/new-poll-reveals-future-financial-worries-many-us last accessed 28 May 2012

xxvii   http://en.wikipedia.org/wiki/Generation_X last accessed 28 May 2012

xviii   Coughlin, J. F., and D'Ambrosio, L. A., 2009. Seven myths of financial planning and baby boomer retirement, Journal of Financial Services Marketing, Vol. 14, 1, p823-91

xxix   Accenture, Customer 2012, Time for a new contract between banks and their customers?

xxx   Accenture Press Release 30 May 2011, Banks' relationships with customers under growing pressure in UK and Ireland http://newsroom.accenture.com/article_display.cfm?article_id=5216 last accessed 28 May 2012

xxxi   http://www.accenture.com/fr-fr/Documents/PDF/C2012-One-Pager-071610a-v3.pdf last accessed 28 May 2012

xxxii   The Future of Banking Commission, The Future of Banking report 13 June 2011, http://bankingcommission.s3.amazonaws.com/wp-content/uploads/2011/01/Which-Issues-Paper-Resonse.pdf last accessed 28 May 2012

xxxiii   A new era of customer expectation. Global consumer banking survey 2011. Ernst & Young http://www.ey.com/Publication/vwLUAssets/A_new_era_of_customer_expectation:_global_consumer_banking_survey/$FILE/A%20new%20era%20of%20customer%20expectation_global%20consumer%20banking%20survey.pdf last accessed 28 May 2012

xxxiv   Banking for consumers, The Which? Banking Manifesto http://www.which.co.uk/campaigns/personal-finance/about-the-banking-and-credit-campaign/the-which-banking-manifesto/

xxxv   Fawcett, P. and Flower, G., 2005. Customer information management. Canterbury: Financial World Publishing

xxxvi   Customer Priorities: what customers really want, Institute of Customer Service, Customer First Newsletter, Issue 9, April 2007 http://www.customerfirst.org/newsletter/issue9/article4.html

last accessed 28 May 2012

xxxvii Byers, R.E. and Lederer, P.J., 2001. Retail Bank Services Strategy: A Model of Traditional, Electronic, and Mixed Distribution Choices. Journal of Management Information Systems, Fall 2001, Vol. 18 Issue 2, p133-156

xxxviii Davis, F.D., 1989. Perceived usefulness, perceived ease of use, and user acceptance of information technology. MIS Quarterly, 13(3): p319–340

xxxix Collan, M. and Tetard, F., 2007. Lazy User Theory of Solution Selection. In Proceedings of the CELDA 2007 Conference, p273–278, Algarve, Portugal, 7–9 December 2007

xl Vandermerwe, S., 1993. Achieving Deep Customer Focus. MIT Sloan Management Review, Spring 2004, Vol. 45 Issue 3, p26-34

xli Forester, T., 1992. Megatrends or Megamistakes?: What ever happened to the Information Society (part 1). EFFector Online, Issue 4.01, December 17 1992, p6 available at http://w2.eff.org/effector/effect04.01 last accessed 28 May 2012

xlii Taken from http://en.wikipedia.org/wiki/Savings_and_Loan_Crisis last accessed 28 May 2012

xliii http://www.interbrand.com/en/best-global-brands/best-global-brands-2008/best-global-brands- 2010.aspx last retrieved 28 May 2012

xliv http://www.guardian.co.uk/media/organgrinder/2009/apr/06/pollack-colin-rebrand-consignia last accessed 28 May 2012

xlv Xue, M., Hitt, L.M. and Harker, P.T., 2007. Customer Efficiency, Channel Usage, and Firm Performance in Retail Banking. Manufacturing & Service Operations Management, Fall 2007, Vol. 9 Issue 4, p535-558

xlvi See, for example, the literature survey in Mavri, M. & Ioannou, G., 2006. Consumers' perspectives on online banking services. International Journal of Consumer Studies, Nov 2006, Vol. 30, Issue 6, p552-560

xlvii HSBC internal presentation 1999

xlviii McCartan-Quinn, D., Durkin, M., and O'Donnell, A., 2004. Exploring the application of IVR: Lessons from retail banking. Service Industries Journal, May 2004, Vol. 24 Issue 3, p150-168

xlix Holmsen, C.A., Palter, R.N., Simon, P.R. and Weberg, P.K., 1998. Retail Banking: Managing competition among your own channels. McKinsey Quarterly, 1998, Issue 1, p82-92

l Stuart-Menteth, H., Wilson, H. and Baker, S., 2006. Escaping the channel silo: Researching the new consumer. International Journal of Market Research, 2006, Vol. 48, Issue 4, p415-437

li Li F., 2001. The Internet and the Deconstruction of the Integrated Banking Model. British Journal of Management, Dec 2001, Vol. 12, Issue 4, p307-322

lii From the cartoon by Peter Steiner that appeared on page 61 of the July 5, 1993 issue of The New Yorker, (Vol.69 (LXIX) no. 20)

liii Sunikka, A. and Bragge, J., 2009. Promotional messages in multichannel banking: Attractive or annoying? Journal of Financial Services Marketing, Dec 2009, Vol. 14, Issue 3, p245-263

liv EFMA/Atos Worldline survey reported in the EFMA report The expanding role of e-channels in CRM May 2011

lv   EFMA/Atos Worldline survey reported in the EFMA report The expanding role of e-channels in CRM May 2011

lvi   Catalan, R.T., 2004. Banking Channel Management – Global Trends and Strategies. Boston: Massachusetts Institute of Technology p64-65

lvii   Kaplan, A. M. and Haenlein, M., 2010. "Users of the world, unite! The challenges and opportunities of Social Media". Business Horizons, 53 (1): 59–68.

lviii   Tancer, B., 2008. Click: What millions of people are doing online and why it matters. New York: Hyperion cited in the Huffington Post 17th September 2008 available at http://www.huffingtonpost.com/2008/09/17/study-social-networking-s_n_127122.html last retrieved 28 May 2012

lix   Robinson, K., 2007. Another world, another business. The Banker, Vol 57, No. 979, p178-180

lx   EFMA report Social media at the starting blocks November 2010 reported in EFMA report Retail financial services: Strategic insights and best practices April 2011

lxi   EFMA report Social media at the starting blocks November 2010 reported in EFMA report Retail financial services: Strategic insights and best practices April 2011

lxii   Available at http://www.youtube.com/watch?v=jGC1mCS4OVo last retrieved 28 May 2012

lxiii   Ann Minch triumphs in credit card fight 21st September 2009 available at http://www.huffingtonpost.com/2009/09/21/ann-minch-triumphs-in-cre_n_293423.html last accessed 28 May 2012

lxiv   Fabulis: Citibank Shuts Down 'Objectionable' Gay Website's Bank Account 25th February 2010 available at http://www.huffingtonpost.com/2010/02/25/fabulis-citibank-shuts-do_n_476753.html last accessed 28 May 2012

lxv   Available at http://www.banking4tomorrow.com/2010/07/the-5-stages-of-social-media-grief/ last retrieved 28 May 2012

lxvi   MacLeod, D., 2007. Students celebrate Facebook triumph over HSBC. Education Guardian, Guardian.co.uk Thursday 30 August 2007. Can be found at http://www.guardian.co.uk/education/2007/aug/30/highereducation.studentfinance last accessed 28 May 2012

lxvii   Available at http://www.facebook.com/group.php?gid=2371122959 last accessed 28 May 2012

lxviii   Fawcett, P. and Flower, G., 2005. Customer information management. Canterbury: Financial World Publishing, p28-31

lxix   Fair Debt Collection Practices Act and Social Networks http://socialmediabanking.blogspot.com/ last accessed 28 May 2012

lxx   Available at http://www.theaustralian.com.au/news/nation/bank-threatens-staff-with-sack-over-social-media-comments/story-e6frg6nf-1226000454432 last accessed 28 May 2012

lxxi   EFMA report Social media at the starting blocks November 2010 reported in EFMA report Retail financial services: Strategic insights and best practices April 2011 p19

lxxii   Source: UK Payments Administration http://www.ukpayments.org.uk/resources_publications/key_facts_and_figures/cheques_and_bankers'_drafts_facts_and_figures/ last accessed 28 May 2012

lxxiii   Stein, G., 2010. Fewer, leaner and more engaging. ABA Banking Journal, Aug 2010, Vol. 102 Issue 8, p26-32

lxxiv   Royal Bank of Scotland breaks vow not to close last branch in town 26th June 2011 available at http://www.thisismoney.co.uk/money/article-2008120/Royal-Bank-Scotland-breaks-vow-close-branch-town.html last accessed 28 May 2012

lxxv   The last branch in town: Drive for profit is leaving huge swathes of Britain without access to a local bank 13th April 2011 available at http://www.thisismoney.co.uk/money/article-1376239/The-branch-town-Banks-drive-profit-leaving-huge-swathes-Britain-access-local-bank.html last accessed 28 May 2012

lxxvi   Pole, K., 2006. Retail Management in Financial Services. Canterbury: ifs School of Finance

lxxvii   A good day to bury bad news? HSBC cuts hundreds of posts from branches 1st July 2011 available at http://www.independent.co.uk/news/business/news/a-good-day-to-bury-bad-news-hsbc-cuts-hundreds-of-posts-from-branches-2305161.html last accessed 28 May 2012

lxxviii   Mendonca, L. & Nakache, P., 1996. Branch banking is not a dinosaur. The McKinsey Quarterly, 1996, Issue 1, p136-146

lxxix   Kungl, D., 2005. In-store branches: The trend grows stronger. ABA Banking Journal, Jan 2005, Vol. 97 Issue 1, p10

lxxx   McCartan-Quinn, D., Durkin, M., and O'Donnell, A., 2004. Exploring the application of IVR: Lessons from retail banking. Service Industries Journal, May 2004, Vol. 24 Issue 3, p150-168

lxxxi   http://www.flexibility.co.uk/cases/future-travel.htm last accessed 28 May 2012

lxxxii   Santander brings call centres back to UK 8th July 2011 available at http://www.bbc.co.uk/news/business-14073889 last accessed 28 May 2012

lxxxiii   New Call Telecom Mumbai call centre moves to Burnley 5th July 2011 available at http://www.bbc.co.uk/news/uk-england-lancashire-14025904 last accessed 28 May 2012

lxxxiv   Source BBC News web site http://www.bbc.co.uk/news/10569081 last accessed 28 May 2012

lxxxv   Fiserv/Syniverse Technologies research paper, 2009. Mobile channel addresses offline consumers' needs for frequent transactions while reducing bank channel costs

lxxxvi   Syniverse mobile banking survey result cited in Fiserv/Syniverse Technologies research paper Mobile channel addresses offline consumers' needs for frequent transactions while reducing bank channel costs, 2009

lxxxvii   Vyas, C., 2009. From niche play to mainstream delivery channel: U.S. mobile banking forecast 2008-2013. Tower Group, May 2009, cited in Fiserv/Syniverse Technologies research paper Mobile channel addresses offline consumers' needs for frequent transactions while reducing bank channel costs, 2009

lxxxviii   Fiserv/Syniverse Technologies research paper, 2009. Mobile channel addresses offline consumers' needs for frequent transactions while reducing bank channel costs

lxxxix   Chibber, A., 2010. Visa Contactless Card Use in Hong Kong. American Banker, October 2010, Vol.175, No.152, p7

xc   http://www.nfctimes.com/project/uk-orange-and-barclaycard-announce-plans-launch-nfc-rollout last accessed 28 May 2012

xci   http://www.nfctimes.com/news/survey-says-most-consumers-are-not-waiting-mobile-wallets last accessed 28 May 2012

xcii   Shining a light on m-payments. Electronic Payments International, Jul 2010, Issue 277, p1

xciii   http://www.thinkmoney.com/banking/news/bump-allows-users-to-transfer-money-between-bank-accounts-0-4433.htm last accessed 28 May 2012

xciv   https://www.thepaypalblog.com/2010/08/paypal-launches-mobile-app-for-android/ last accessed 28 May 2012

xcv   http://www.zdnet.com/blog/apple/new-paypal-mobile-feature-photograph-a-check-and-deposit-it-updated/8342 last accessed 28 May 2012

xcvi   http://en.wikipedia.org/wiki/M-Pesa last accessed 28 May 2012

xcvii   Mas, I., and Kumar, K., 2008. Banking on Mobiles: Why, How, for Whom? Available at http://www.cgap.org/p/site/c/template.rc/1.9.4400/ last accessed 28 May 2012

xcviii   http://en.wikipedia.org/wiki/Obopay last accessed 28 May 2012

xcix   http://conversations.nokia.com/2010/02/15/nokia-money-pilot-begins-in-india-video, last accessed 28 May 2012

c   Heydt-Benjamin, T.S., Bailey, D.V., Fu, K., Juels, A. and O'Hare, T., 2009. Vulnerabilities in first-generation RFID-enabled credit cards. Economic Perspectives, 2009 1st Quarter, Vol. 33 Issue 1, p50-59

ci   US m-banking uptake stalls over security fears – Javelin, 22nd July 2011 available at http://www.finextra.com/news/fullstory.aspx?newsitemid=22795 last accessed 28 May 2012

cii   American Express Extended Payment Option – see: https://www212.americanexpress.com/dsmlive/dsm/loc/us/en/extendedpaymentoption.co?vgnextoid=795ef79645aa3110VgnVCM100000defaad94RCRD&cc=D&inav=MYCA_OPEN-Extend_Payment_Option last accessed 28 May 2012

ciii   http://www.paymentscouncil.org.uk/media_centre/press_releases/-/page/1575/ last accessed 28 May 2012

civ   http://www.bbc.co.uk/news/business-11070217 last accessed 28 May 2012

cv   Welch, P. and Worthington, S., 2008. Retail therapy: Are Financial Services a core competence got retailers? Australian Centre for Retail Studies, Monash University, p2

cvi   Welch, P. and Worthington, S., 2008. Retail therapy: Are Financial Services a core competence got retailers? Australian Centre for Retail Studies, Monash University, p3

cvii   Knight, E., 2009. The Use of Price Comparison Sites in the UK General Insurance Market. Consumer Intelligence, p8-9

cviii   Knight, E. 2009. The Use of Price Comparison Sites in the UK General Insurance Market. Consumer Intelligence, p10

cix   Laffey, D., and Gandy, A., 2009. Comparison websites in UK retail financial services. Journal of Financial Services Marketing, 14 (2), p173-186

cx   http://www.aviva.com/media/news/4382/ last accessed 28 May 2012

cxi   Pope, D.G. and Syndor, J.R. 2011. What's in a Picture? Evidence of Discrimination from Prosper.com. The Journal of Human Resources, 46 (1), p53-92

cxii Research by Celent, quoted in the September 20, 2009 issue of The Washington Post. Available at http://www.washingtonpost.com/wp-dyn/content/article/2009/09/19/AR2009091900124.html last accessed 28 May 2012

cxiii Pope, D.G., and Syndor, J.R. 2011. What's in a Picture? Evidence of Discrimination from Prosper.com. The Journal of Human Resources, 46 (1), p53-92

cxiv Press release 10th May 2011 available at http://uk.zopa.com/ApplicationResources/press/2011/Banks%20continue%20to%20treat%20 customers%20with%20contempt.pdf last accessed 28 May 2012

cxv http://lanzen.net/?p=828 last accessed 28 May 2012

cxvi http://www.finextra.com/news/fullstory.aspx?newsitemid=18049 last accessed 28 May 2012

cxvii See Online banking is about to undergo a generational shift, says Yodlee CEO for more details – available at http://m.ibtimes.com/online-banking-is-about-to-undergo-a-generational-shift-says-yodlee-ceo-169704.html last accessed 28 May 2012

cxviii Fiserv/Syniverse Technologies research paper, 2009. Mobile channel addresses offline consumers' needs for frequest transactions while reducing bank channel costs

cxix McCartan-Quinn, D., Durkin, M. and O'Donnell, A., 2004. Exploring the application of IVR: Lessons from retail banking. Service Industries Journal, May 2004, Vol. 24 ,Issue 3, p150-168

cxx http://www.mondex.org/mondexuk.html last accessed 28 May 2012

cxxi Ofcom Communications Market Report 2010 available at http://stakeholders.ofcom.org.uk/market-data-research/market-data/communications-market-reports/cmr10/ last accessed 28 May 2012

cxxii Ofcom Communications Market Report 2011 available at http://stakeholders.ofcom.org.uk/binaries/research/cmr/cmr11/UK_CMR_2011_FINAL.pdf last accessed 28 May 2012

cxxiii Costanzo, L.A., Keasey, K. and Short, H, 2003. A strategic approach to the study of innovation in the financial services industry: The case of telephone banking. Journal of Marketing Management, Apr 2003, Vol. 19, Issue 3/4, p259-281

cxxiv What's love got to do with it? GfK Financial. March 2010 cited in the Tenemos case study on Metro Bank available at https://www.metrobankonline.co.uk/Global/CS_MetroBank_Final_Web.pdf last accessed 28 May 2012

cxxv Lieberman, M. B. and Montgomery, D. B. 1988. First-mover advantages. Strategic Management Journal, 9.

cxxvi Lowe, A. and Kuusisto, J., 1999. The institutional stature of the retail bank: the neglected asset? International Journal of Bank Marketing, Vol. 17 Iss: 4, p.171–182

cxxvii Taken from the EFMA report Retail financial services: Strategic insights and best practices April 2011

cxxviii Rogers, E. M., 1962. Diffusion of Innovations. Glencoe: Free Press and Rogers, E. M. (1983). Diffusion of Innovations. New York, Free Press

cxxix As proposed by Diniz, E., 2000. Evolução da uso da web pelos bancos. RAC, Vol. 4, No. 2,

Maio/Ago 2000, p29-50 and the Tower Group Inc., 2000. An Internet bank primer.

[cxxx] John Kirkbright is Chairman of the Efma Retail Bank Advisory Council and this opinion is expressed in Retail financial services: Strategic insights and best practices April 2011 p7

[cxxxi] http://en.wikipedia.org/wiki/Database last accessed 28 May 2012

[cxxxii] Fawcett, P. and Flower, G., 2005. Customer information management. Canterbury: Financial World Publishing, p356

[cxxxiii] Payne, A., 2006. Handbook of CRM: Achieving Excellence in Customer Management. Oxford; Burlington, MA: Elsevier, p185

[cxxxiv] Holmsen, C. A., Palter, R. N., Simon, P. R. and Weberg, P. K., 1998. 'Retail Banking: Managing Competition among your own channels', McKinsey Quarterly, 00475394, Issue 1, p82–92

[cxxxv] DeYoung, R. 2001. The financial performance of pure play Internet banks. Economic Perspectives. Federal Reserve Bank of Chicago. (1 Part 4): p20-75

[cxxxvi] M.E. Porter, 2001. Strategy and the Internet, Harvard Business Review. 79(3), p62-78

[cxxxvii] Payne, A., 2006. Handbook of CRM: Achieving Excellence in Customer Management. Oxford: Burlington, MA: Elsevier, p192-193

[cxxxviii] Payne, A., 2006. Handbook of CRM: Achieving Excellence in Customer Management. Oxford: Burlington, MA: Elsevier, p213

[cxxxix] Katuri, S. and Lam, M., 2007. Switching customers from branches to Internet: A credit union's journey. Journal of Financial Services Marketing, Feb 2007, Vol. 11, Issue 3, p229-248

[cxl] Holmsen, C.A., Palter, R.N., Simon, P.R. and Weberg, P.K., 1998. Retail banking: Managing competition among your own channels. McKinsey Quarterly, Issue 1, p82

[cxli] Holmsen, C.A., Palter, R.N., Simon, P.R. and Weberg, P.K., 1998. Retail banking: Managing competition among your own channels. McKinsey Quarterly, Issue 1, p82-92

[cxlii] Council on Financial Competition research 2007.

[cxliii] Gertz, D. and Baptista, J., 1995. Grow to be great: Breaking the downsizing cycle. Free Press

[cxliv] http://www.merriam-webster.com/dictionary/relevance

[cxlv] Fawcett, P. & Flower, G., 2005. Customer information management. Canterbury: Financial World Publishing

[cxlvi] Business Dictionary.com, http://www.businessdictionary.com/definition/discontinuous-change.html last accesses 28 May 2012

[cxlvii] Haeckel, S. H., 2003. Leading on demand businesses – Executive as Architects, IBM Systems Journal, Vol 42, No 3

[cxlviii] Haeckel, S. H., 2010. The post-industrial manager, Marketing Management, Fall 2010

[cxlix] The way we Pay 2010, The UK's Payments Revolution, Payments Council.

[cl] BAI Banking Strategies Transform the Branch Model – Before It's Too Late http://www.bai.org/bankingstrategies/distribution-channels/branches/transform-the-branch-model—-before-its-too-late last accessed 28 May 2012

[cli] Asian Banker Research, White Paper 2010 Successful Branch Transformations: Achieving needs-based sales and service-oriented delivery

clii In 2011 Capital One showed the following chart to their investors to gain approval to buy ING Direct US business.

cliii 28th Annual Abstract from the British Bankers Association http://www.bba.org.uk/media/article/bba-publishes-annual-banking-industry-statistics last accessed 28 May 2012

cliv There is a future for the bank branches. Deloitte and Vlerick Leuven Gent Management School, February 2009

clv The evolution of branch banking. Steve O'Neill, head of branch marketing at HSBC, talks with Finextra about how the branch still has a place in the future of retail banking http://www.youtube.com/watch?v=9BiNtdQyg0U last accessed 28 May 2012

clvi RFID chips spell end to branch lines for high-value customers, The Financial Brand.com, 21 February 2011, http://thefinancialbrand.com/17053/standard-chartered-rfid-tags-for-premium-customers/ last accessed 28 May 2012

clvii RFID chips spell end to branch lines for high-value customers, The Financial Brand.com, 21 February 2011, http://thefinancialbrand.com/17053/standard-chartered-rfid-tags-for-premium-customers/ last accessed 28 May 2012

clviii http://www.facebook.com/dbs?sk=info last accessed 28 May 2012

clix Dupaco's social media contest puts game leaders on billboards 25 August 2011, http://www.dupaco.com/page.php?page=701 last accessed 28 May 2012

clx Transforming mass market advisor time-spend Finalta Viewpoint, June 2011

clxi BAI, Banking Strategies, Distribution Channels, Call Center, Contact Centers: Overcoming the 'Three Rs': http://www.bai.org/bankingstrategies/print.aspx?id=C9463F7C-CCCC-4A4E-9E69-626D2E509FEB last accessed 28 May 2012

clxii Bank Innovation Monitor, Online Banking, Q32011 Survey

clxiii Future Foundation/Monetise Emerging Trends in Mobile Banking 2011, http://www.futurefoundation.net/page/view/Monitise last accessed 28 May 2012

clxiv Fawcett, P. and Flower, G., 2005. Customer information management. Canterbury: Financial World Publishing

clxv Contactless Cards http://www.contactless.info/UpdateOnUkRollout.asp last accessed 28 May 2012

clxvi UK Consumers take first steps towards "less cash" society http://www.visaeurope.com/en/newsroom/news/articles/2011/steps_towards_less_cash.aspx last accessed 28 May 2012

clxvii Payments Council, Review of the contactless and prepaid card markets, Summary of findings and actions May 2010

clxviii Orange and Barclaycard transform buying on Britain's high-streets with the launch of the UK's first contactless mobile payments service http://newsroom.orange.co.uk/2011/05/20/orange-and-barclaycard-transform-buying-on-britain-s-high-streets-with-the-launch-of-the-uk-s-first-contactless-mobile-payments-service/ last accessed 28 May 2012

clxiv EFMA/Finalta Multi-channel Sales Productivity Report 2009 clxv   EFMA/Finalta Multi-channel Sales Productivity Report 2009

clxvi   EFMA/Finalta Multi-channel Sales Productivity Report 2009

clxvii   Frawley, W., Piatetsky-Shapiro, G. and Matheus, C., 1992. Knowledge Discovery in Databases: An Overview. AI Magazine, Fall 1992, p213-228

clxviii   Fawcett, P. and Flower, G., 2000. Managing information in financial services. Canterbury: Financial World Publishing p274

clxix   Peppers, D., Rogers, M. and Dorf, R., 1999. The one to one fieldbook: the complete toolkit for implementing a 1to1 marketing program. New York, NY: Doubleday

clxx   http://en.wikipedia.org/wiki/Analytics accessed 28 May 2012

clxxi   Pole, K., 2006. Retail Management in Financial Services. Canterbury: ifs School of Finance

clxxii   Christopher, Payne and Ballantyne, 1991. Relationship Marketing: Bringing Quality, Customer Service and Marketing Together. Oxford: Butterworth Heinemann

clxiii   Council on Financial Competition, 2002. Many channels, one customer: Integrating distribution resources into customer strategy.

clxix   Mills, M.G.Predictions for Civilian Space Flight Based on Patterns from History, Journal of the British Interplanetary Society November/December 2010